the alps approach

accelerated learning in primary schools

**Brain-based methods for accelerating
motivation and achievement**

ALISTAIR SMITH
&
NICOLA CALL

This is what learning is.
You suddenly understand something you've
understood all your life, but in a new way.

Doris Lessing, *The Four Gated City*

Published by Network Educational Press Ltd
PO Box 635
Stafford
ST16 1BF

First published 1999
Revised 2000
Reprinted 2002, 2003

ISBN 1 855 39 056 6   Paperback
ISBN 1 855 39 066 3   Hardback

Managing Editor: Janice Baiton
Design: Neil Hawkins – NEP
Illustrations: Oliver Caviglioli & Pamela Pierce

Printed in Great Britain by MPG Books Ltd, Bodmin, Cornwall

Contents

Part Three: The learning journey

Part Four: Resources

Foreword

The *Accelerated Learning Series* attempts to pull together new and innovative thinking about learning. The titles in the series offer contemporary solutions to old problems. The series is held together by the accelerated learning model which, in turn, is underwritten by an informed theoretical understanding.

The term 'accelerated learning' can be misleading. The method is not for a specific group of learners, or for a given age range, or for a category of perceived ability. The method is not about doing the same things faster. It is not about fast-tracking or about hothousing. It is a considered, generic approach to learning based on research drawn from disparate disciplines and tested with different age-groups and different ability levels in very different circumstances. As such, it can be adapted and applied to very different challenges.

The books in the *Accelerated Learning Series* build from the accelerated learning cycle. The cycle starts by attending to the physical, environmental and social factors in learning. It proposes the worth of a positive and supportive learning environment. It then deliberately attempts to connect to, and build upon, prior knowledge and understanding while presenting an overview of the learning challenge to come. Participants set positive outcomes and define targets towards reaching those outcomes. Information is then presented in visual, auditory and kinesthetic modes and is reinforced through different forms of intelligent response. Frequent, structured opportunities to demonstrate understanding and to rehearse for recall are the concluding feature of the cycle. *The ALPS Approach* sits within the accelerated learning cycle and provides strategies for teachers who work with younger learners.

The ALPS Approach starts by inviting us to journey to an 'ideal' school. By visiting the ideal where the ALPS methods are in place and both children and teachers benefit from their application, we can begin to make purposeful comparisons. Subsequently, and throughout the book, the means of continuing the successful journey are provided in full. Inevitably, you will make comparisons with your own departure point.

School began, for me, one morning in a draughty Scottish classroom in the 1960s. It came as a shock. The teacher's name was Miss Carr. She wore home-knit twinsets, with tartan skirts and brogues. She drove a green Austin A40. She wrote things I couldn't read on an enormous blackboard. She smelt of chalk and lavender. On my first day she belted me with a 21-inch leather belt for being out of my seat during milk time. I had made an over-enthusiastic and premature bid to become milk-straw monitor. It was to be my first lesson in turn taking. My mother carried me back to school that afternoon kicking and screaming. My learning journey had begun.

You removed your wellies by the door and put on plimsolls. Gordon, my friend, got to be wellie monitor and put them in pairs in a row. We were jealous of Gordon. We wrote with pieces of chalk on slates: 'tib, bob, cat, dog'. We shouted out the times tables. You stood in the bucket by the door if you got your sums wrong. Sometimes we had to take turns by the bucket. At first when you got the sum wrong the teacher said 'bucket' and you'd trudge over to the corner. The class let out a collective sigh of relief, and a few brave ones pointed and sniggered. Eventually, she'd just look and nod in its direction and off you'd go. John Rutherford had a path worn out between his seat and the bucket by the end of Primary Three. You sat in rows and at desks with cast iron frames, in the order of success or failure in the last spelling test. It was years before I got away from the back. When we did geography she'd point with a big stick at the map of the world curling above the radiator. You'd copy from the atlas on tracing paper and name the countries in pink. She'd remind you of all the great Scots missionaries who'd travelled abroad and, who knows, maybe you could go to that pink place one day and be a missionary too?

On days when it rained we did gym inside. Pirates! Richard Philip dislocated his shoulder on the wallbars and hung there, crying. Marian Chalmers said he looked like Jesus. Then the headteacher and the janitor arrived and lifted him down. Once a week, we did gym to the radio. Morag Mackay struggled: she had a calliper. For the rest of us, there was great energy and mirth as we quickly changed from being a tree – arms out, standing still, head flopped and 'just get your tongue back in Alistair Smith' – to being the wind, on your toes, swishing around, cheeks fully puffed. Free expression at the end gave a chance to pretend you'd scored the winner in extra time. Once a month, fingernail and nit check from the nurse. Then some time later, a new teacher. A man! Mr McDougall. Soon to be known as 'beat the belt McDougall'. You got three goes to get the answer right and if you didn't, then you got belted. No more free expression. When a new school was being built, we spent a year nearby in a temporary one. It was even older. We had to get a double-decker bus there and back. One day the milk crates fell off the back of the bus and the bottles rolled down the hill onto the high street. We screamed in delight and shouted for the milk monitors to be sacked! Our new school had outside toilets and a playing field with frogs. Mr McDougall didn't come with us. The word 'breakdown' was whispered across the breakfast table. And then, before you knew it, it was over. Our primary school years were no more. A new journey was about to begin.

My learning journey began like this in the 1960s and it continues. Each of our learning journeys is as unique as the adults we have become, or the children we were. Such 'journeying' is no different in its varied demands and points of significance for the children of today. Schools, schooling and the professional understanding of educators is better now than it has ever been. We want it to be even better. Throughout *The ALPS Approach*, Nicola Call and I have elected to extend the metaphor of a difficult but fulfilling journey. It is our view that schools have come a long way since our formative years, but the world the children will now inherit has come further. We need, therefore, to continue to be open to new possibilities and new understandings without throwing out the best of the old. We hope *The ALPS Approach* provides you with this balance.

Alistair Smith
Accelerated Learning Series General Editor
June 2000

How to use this book

Organization and structure of the book

This book is organized in a way to accelerate your learning. The structure is simple and deliberate. We organized the book to model the practices that we espouse.

The organizing metaphor for the book is that of a journey. In this case a journey with the learners in your class into the ALPS. ALPS stands for 'Accelerated Learning in Primary Schools'. The book is about the ALPS method™ and how to do it.

We begin the book by pre-processing your understanding. This is an attempt to engage your curiosity and secure your interest via the Big Picture, or overview. We do this in two ways: now through a description of how the book is organized in words and images, and later with a description of a typical day which, hopefully, you are just about to read.

The book has an Introduction and four Parts. The Introduction has six chapters; Part One has four; Part Two has five; Part Three has six; Part Four, which is about resources, has nine.

In the Introduction we describe a typical day in the ALPS. We visit some classes in a school and observe what is going on there. This helps the global or holistic learners among you – those who benefit from large chunk learning. The ALPS method™ is then explained in a step-by-step fashion for analytical learners – those who like to work in smaller chunks and do so progressively. We examine the seven-stage cycle of the ALPS model and explain its origins.

The ALPS method™ derives, in part, from brain research, and so we begin to connect theory with practice by considering what is happening in the brains of four children in the class. We call this 'a meeting of minds' because we would like you to 'meet' their minds!

Next we provide an explanation of the new three 'Rs'. We argue the case for going beyond the training of discrete skills and explain why the three Rs of resilience, resourcefulness and responsibility matter for the children of the millennium. Brain research is linked with the new three Rs via the ALPS method™.

Dip into the Introduction. Read any or all of these short contextualizing introductions and use the ideas in each as you wish.

Each Part is previewed with both a memory map and a synopsis and then reviewed through summary questions. Part One concerns itself with creating a positive and purposeful starting point for learning. Part Two is about the building and maintaining of positive classroom strategies for learning. Part Three is about the mechanics of learning – what to do and when. Part Four contains many of the resources you will need to take your interest further.

Throughout this book we refer to pupils as 'he' or 'she', and we tend to refer to the teacher as 'she'. This is for simplification.

Where to begin

Here are some guidelines that you may wish to follow to help get the most out of the book. They are based on speed-reading principles and can also be adapted for the classroom.

- Ask yourself at the outset, in what ways will you use the methods described in this book? Have an outcome in mind before you begin to read then,

- future-base – by the end of reading this book what will the successful achievement of that outcome begin to be like? Describe it to yourself then,

- relax – short breaks provide space for assimilation –

- now get the overview: survey the book first – flick through the pages to get a 'feel' for its content and layout – do this quickly and simply scan for visual information and as you do so you will begin to notice certain keywords; look at all parts including the index and appendices

- relax again before 'speed-reading' the book – move through a page at a time taking in the visual information from all the page, soften the focus of your eyes so that all information is available, spend about a second or two on each page

- formulate questions for those sections you wish to use before returning to those sections and scanning down the centre of the page, dip into the text for more focused reading, finding cues that will begin to answer your questions

- relax again and return to the outcome you originally had in mind, before,

- beginning to rapid read those areas of the text that the cues have alerted you to, read for meaning and comprehension at this stage.

Preview and review

To get the best out of a book like ours, a positive and purposeful state of mind where you, as the reader and recipient of the ideas, are receptive and open is essential. Part of our strategy for helping you to get the most out of the book is to use preview–review.

Preview–review means that each part is preceded by a synopsis in words and in pictures and concluded with a set of summary review questions.

The summary review questions provided can also be used for stimulus material for staff development activities.

In classroom lessons we recommend using preview–review or (p–r) as a regular feature of the teaching method. We describe this in detail in Part Three.

Please enjoy what is offered here and begin to use the methods as soon as you wish.

the alps approach – Accelerated Learning in Primary Schools

Acknowledgements

The ALPS Approach – Accelerated Learning in Primary Schools – is the result of a genuine collaboration between Alistair Smith and Nicola Call.

Alistair

I would like to thank the many hundreds of primary school colleagues who have shared their thoughts and ideas during, before and after staff development events around the country. Oliver Caviglioli wrote the essay on his son, Pascal. Ian Harris did the research for and wrote the literacy scheme comparison and helped Oliver with the memory maps. Howard Kennedy provided the headteacher's perspective. The original inspiration for the three Rs comes from Guy Claxton and his book *Hare Brain Tortoise Mind* to whom recognition is due. Kirsty kept the phone calls at bay to allow me to get on with it. Ani kept me motivated.

Nicola

I would like to express my thanks to Heather Anderson, Vicky Desmond, Kate Barnes and Siobhan Burrows, and the many teachers who shared ideas from their classrooms. Beverley Clarke provided a sounding board and contributed for the past few years to my growing understanding of child psychology. In general, thanks to the headteachers, colleagues and other professionals who worked so tirelessly to raise standards of expectation in the schools in and around London where I worked. I will never lose sight, however, of the fact that my greatest teachers were the children who shared my personal journey into the foothills of the ALPS. My husband, Josef, contributed with his All-American brand of absolute confidence in my ability to write this book. Thank you.

The methods described in this book have been successfully used in hundreds of schools throughout the United Kingdom.

Introduction

Extending the horizons of possibility

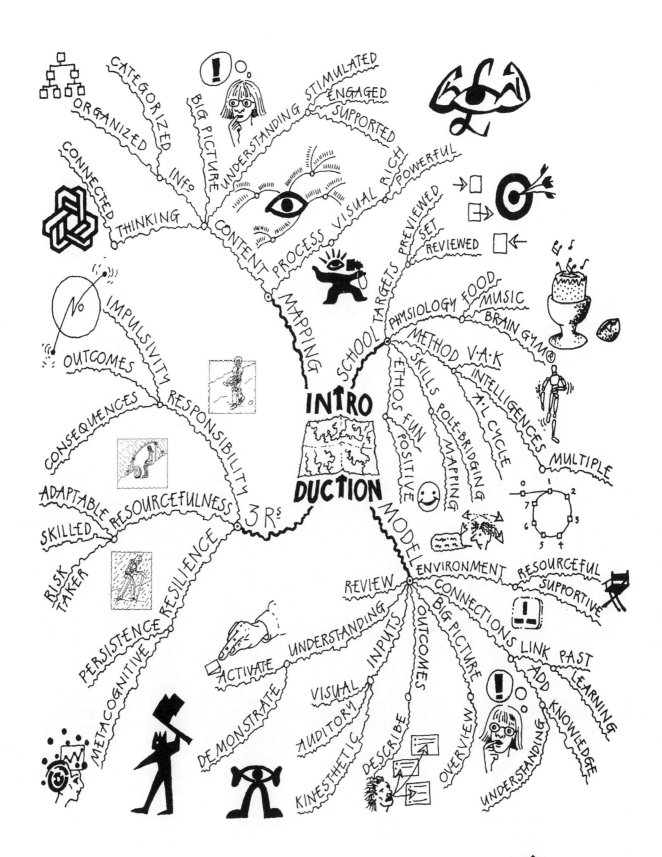

Preview of Introduction

Extending the horizons of possibility

In the Introduction you will:

experience a preliminary visit to a typical ALPS school so that you know what sort of journey lies ahead for you.

find a step-by-step route descriptor of the accelerated learning cycle and the ALPS method™.

meet four 10 year olds and find out some of the things that are happening in each of their brains during the course of a classroom lesson.

be reminded of the nine principles derived from research into the way the brain 'learns' and upon which the ALPS method™ is based.

be introduced to the new three Rs – resourcefulness, resilience and responsibility – with a little about why they are the key learning attributes.

find out about maps and mapping and why they are important for your journey through the ALPS.

the alps approach – Accelerated Learning in Primary Schools

Extending the horizons of possibility

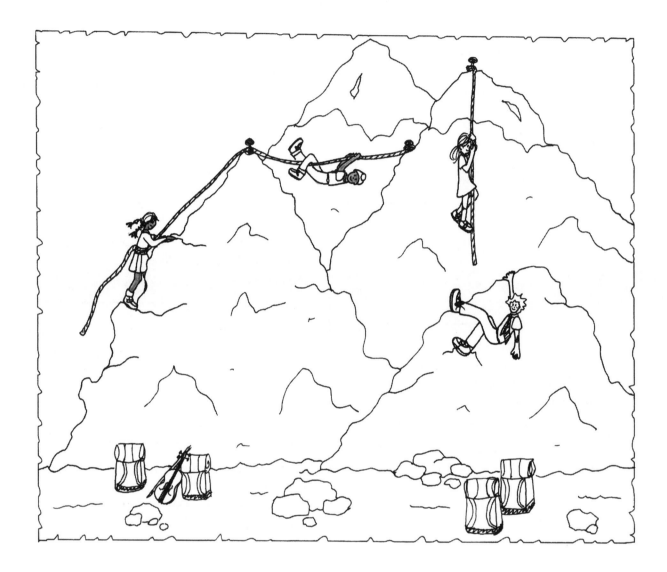

the alps approach – Accelerated Learning in Primary Schools

❶ A visit to the ALPS: what's it all about?

" In the past teachers have just told us stuff and we do it. Now the work is harder, but the learning is easier. If your teacher uses accelerated learning, you do harder work but you find it easier! "

Laura, age 10

" Teachers who use accelerated learning seem more intelligent. You listen to them and think: 'That's how I want to be!' "

Andrew, age 10

IT IS MONDAY MORNING, AND THE CHILDREN are coming into school. We are going into the Nursery class. Fruit is placed in a colourful bowl ready for morning snacks. This is a well-settled, lively group of children with an energetic teacher, so her chosen music for the morning reflects the mood of the class. Parents tap their feet to the Gipsy Kings' *Greatest Hits* as they bring their children into the classroom. Next door the more sedate Reception Class are entering to the strains of Debussy's *Clair de lune*: a different mood for a different situation. The Nursery children join in with the music, wiggling their hips as they look with their parents at the weekly planner on the board. Copies of the planner are taken home by the parents and referred to during the week. These very young children are being given the Big Picture as they look at today's To Do list. Top of the list for today is to build a sandcastle for each of the Three Bears. On Friday they will be taking their own bears for a Teddy Bears' Picnic, but there is a lot of learning to be done before then.

Boffin of the week is

Mehreen Ajaz

Congratulations!

A few doors down the corridor, a Year 2 teacher is welcoming her class. As each child enters, he is given eye contact and welcomed using his name. If anyone is missed because the teacher is drawn into conversation or otherwise distracted, his name is used soon afterwards. Small details of children's lives are recalled and mentioned. The teacher remembers that James's grandparents were visiting his family that weekend and asks if he had a good time. She takes care to listen to his response. She has marked some comprehension tasks at the weekend and is ready to reward Rahul. She recognizes his achievement: 'Rahul, you worked hard in comprehension on Friday.' This is followed up with the affirmation: 'You are always so conscientious about reading the text thoroughly.' She then praises him: 'Well done, thank you for such a good piece of work, I really enjoyed marking it!'

the alps approach – Accelerated Learning in Primary Schools

In Year 6, children are already opening their task books. They have reminded themselves of the items on today's To Do list, which they wrote on Friday afternoon. There is a series of tasks written on the board for them to complete after they have handed in their homework. All tasks are linked to work done the previous week. Revision and recall is invited, along with some more advanced thinking:

π Write the square root of these numbers: 25, 144, 4, 49, 196, 64.

π Use your calculator to work out five different square numbers.

π Make a hypothesis for a 'cubed root'.

This is setting the scene for today's maths lesson, when the class are going to investigate patterns in squared and cubed numbers. The children have no difficulty with this lesson – because they wrote their To Do lists with the teacher on Friday, they knew that cubed roots were coming up in maths. Each table has at least one child who has worked on this topic with a parent or sibling over the weekend. Even at this early hour, there is a buzz and a feeling of achievement and success in the classroom. Collaboration is encouraged. The classroom assistant is working with an individual pupil on this task, helping to guide the way but allowing him to think, to experiment with the numbers and a calculator, and to feel the success. Later his work will be differentiated further, but now he is being challenged on a par with his peers.

Next door in Year 5, a group of children are busy putting work on the special board designated for additional research or work done at home. One girl has printed some information about bacteria on her computer at home, while a group of three boys have written fifty opening phrases for exciting stories. The other members of the class are busy working on their tasks from

the alps approach – Accelerated Learning in Primary Schools

the list on the board. The teacher starts to call the register. 'Good morning, creative Alma,' she says, and creative Alma looks up to answer, 'Good morning, imaginative Miss Morris.' Two children are busy on the computer typing new desk labels from a list of adjectives drawn up by Miss Morris.

We walk along the corridor and see two Reception class children taking the register to the office. On their way they are looking up at the ceiling, counting the number of letter 'n's they see up there. They almost collide with the pair from Year 1, who are looking for the words 'breakfast', 'tea' and 'dinner'.

> Hayley
> has mastered
> apostrophes!!
> Hooray!

In Year 4 they have begun their spelling test. Several children shut their eyes and trace letters in the air as they recall the spellings. After the test has finished, the teacher begins marking while the class work on their tasks from the board. Once the tests are marked, a child takes the results to the headteacher. It is soon time for assembly, and the classes begin to line up.

In Reception class the children are busy with their Brain Gym® as they line up. In Year 1 they are counting in twos as they form a queue, while in Year 4 children are tracing today's three spellings in the air as they stand in line. On the way to assembly, Nursery and Reception children all look for the letter 'n' on the ceiling and point to each one, saying 'nnnnnnn' as they go. Once in the hall, there is plenty to look at and listen to. Mozart's Concerto for Flute and Harp is playing serenely in the background, while the first words from this week's spelling list are up on the wall in bold print. Some children write the words on their palms with their finger, while others trace them in the air. Many have their eyes shut. Others read the proverbs on the wall and look at the cartoons depicting each meaning. At the end of assembly there is the sound of applause as the 100 per cent pupils receive recognition and praise.

Back in most classrooms, literacy sessions are beginning. We go into Year 3, where children are listening intently to the Big Picture and watching the teacher write the lesson targets on the board. When she has finished her explanation, a child tells her: 'I'm on an amber light.' She repeats the explanation until every child is 'on a green light'. A piece of work from the previous week is then given out along with individual target cards. The children read the teacher's comments. Some begin to write, while others go to seek dictionaries or thesauruses. A few go to the teacher to discuss their work. Within a few minutes everyone understands their individual targets in addition to the lesson target. It is time to begin the first block of work.

> Let's celebrate!
> We all completed all our tasks in time on Monday.
> We're the greatest!

By the time we reach Year 4, they are ready for their first brain break. They are developing playscripts from fairytales and have mind mapped their initial ideas. The teacher leads them in an arm activation activity for two minutes before they resume work. Children will take a brain break every ten or twelve minutes throughout the session, often coinciding with beginning a new part of the task. Before any child shows his work to the teacher, he checks off that he has followed all the Task Rules displayed in the classroom.

19

Back in Year 2, the first half of the literacy session is drawing to a close. This class completes half the session before breaktime and half afterwards. All the children demonstrate 'good listening' before going out to play. On the Nursery playground children are building sandcastles and measuring teddy bears, while some of the Reception children are playing at being aeroplanes that fly fast and make the sound 'nnnnnnn'. The playground is full of activity and games. Simple equipment for physical and imaginative play is supplied. There is plenty for everyone, and the teacher on duty suggests, directs and organizes games for those who do not play independently. She participates and communicates with the children, recognizing and praising good social skills.

> **Fantastic homework from Dawn this week. Thank you!**

As the children line up to go back inside, already some are practising their songs for remembering new vocabulary, their Brain Gym® for new spellings, or their counting in twos, threes or fives. Marching is great fun for five year olds as they chant: 'Two – Four – Six – Eight!' Back inside, we visit Year 1, who are sitting on the mat ready for their snack. The children recap on the rules for 'good sitting' before the fruit and drinks are handed out. They then move on to maths. Counting in fives, they go to their maths desks and stick their blue nametags on the desks as they sit down. The maths lesson begins with connecting the learning to what was covered last week, and the outcome is described.

Meanwhile, in Reception class, everyone can remember the words 'horizontal' and 'vertical' in addition to 'short' and 'tall' from last week. Few of the children need to remind themselves by looking at the posters on the wall. 'Mrs Burrows, that door is vertical, isn't it?' chirps one little chap. 'Yes, but the washing line is horizontal' says another, and so the conversation goes on. When the groups sit at desks to begin tasks, one girl tells the others on her table: 'I'm going to get ten out of ten today.' 'Let's all be 100 per cent pupils!' suggests another. They concentrate well for five or six minutes, then it is time for the teacher to refocus them. Affirmations and reminders of targets are used whenever there is likely to be a drop in concentration. Brain Gym® is used to break lessons into short chunks.

This is us coming into class in the afternoon

Up in Year 5 kinesthetic learning is helping with the concept of division and multiplication by hundreds and thousands. Children jump decimal places back and forth, following the arrows

the alps approach – Accelerated Learning in Primary Schools

above the board. There is a lot of laughter, but also some serious thinking. 'If you don't think, you could go the wrong way and crash into somebody!' warns the teacher. By lunchtime, everyone can bounce correctly, and they bounce towards the door to line up. A round of applause celebrates the group's success.

At lunchtime, several of the older children work indoors on the computers. They sign in and out as they come and go. In the library, a group of children are reading. Many others have chosen to read outside, as it is a warm day, and the benches are full of children absorbed in books. Others choose to play out on the tarmac, while some engage in conversation with the lunchtime supervisors. Several Year 6 children are revising, using folders to make notes and share ideas. Many others are writing in exercise books. Blake, who is in Year 2, is halfway through writing his first novel.

> Three cheers for Leigh and Gemma for their art work this week.

As children file into class after lunch, they are greeted in the classrooms with music that will set the mood for the afternoon. Some teachers have found that uplifting music breaks bad moods following disagreements on the football pitch, while other classes respond at this time of day to relaxing classical music. Many children are thirsty and pour out glasses of water. Year 6 opt to put on a relaxation tape. They shut their eyes and listen to the words as they relax their bodies from the toes up to the top of their skulls. The teacher then quietly calls the register, greeting everyone by name, just as she did this morning. She gives three children new desk labels.

During the afternoon, Year 6 work in the hall. It is a science lesson, and they are incorporating last week's work in PHSE on tobacco into this lesson. This is the class where we meet Amrit, Nisha, Annie and Eddie. We will meet these four children again throughout this book. Some children wave lengths of blue crêpe paper while six with red masks march by, joined by three with blue masks. They are joined by three other girls wearing brown masks, and all twelve begin to chant 'NICOTINE! NICOTINE! NICOTINE!' as they march. The teacher suddenly joins the six who are nutrients, clutching a huge A and a beer glass. She works

> Superbrains are hard at work in this classroom!

her way through the intestines until she is taken by a blood cell to the liver. The liver dies a terrible death, and the class breaks into a round of applause. The children go back to class to mind map what they have learned.

We move on to Year 3, who are getting changed for PE. While they change, they are singing the Henry VIII rap that they composed last week. They can all remember the names and fates of the wives in sequence. No dead time in this classroom! Down the corridor, the Reception children are in the hall finishing their PE lesson by playing the ABC game. Today's new letter in the game is 'n'. Everyone can recognize it, although some are faster than others at reaching it! On the way back to class, they sing their 'Letter n song', which is on its fifth rendition before most of the children are changed back into their school clothes.

It is the end of the day and most classes have begun to review their day. Celebrations are going on in all classrooms. Superbrains are collecting certificates in Year 2, the Year 4 Brainbox is choosing a toy from the Brain Box, three children from the Nursery are receiving stickers in the headteacher's office, and the sound of applause is coming from one of the top classrooms. A good-humoured chant of 'Boff, Boff, Boff' is accompanying the Year 6 Boffin of the Day as he shakes hands with everyone in the class. Spelling certificates are given out, homework folders are collected, and several children take pencil cases from their teacher. Books are signed out from the library.

On every board in the school is tomorrow's To Do list. Colours are used to highlight important facts to recall, and suggestions are written up about research that could be done in advance at home. The older children make notes in their diaries, while in some classes notes are posted up in the windows to give parents information. In Reception and Year 1, parents come into the classroom to look at the To Do list with their children. As children leave, it is noticeable that everyone is clutching something. Maybe it is a certificate, or maybe a Target Terminator Card. Some have posters, while others have mind maps or revision notes. Every child has at least one book. Many children have signed out equipment: in Year 5 many have signed out protractors, while in Year 4 several children have borrowed calculators.

> The Super Boffins in Mental Arithmetic today were Daniel Jones and Nikki Roberts

The bell goes and many children leave. Yet for others this is not the end of the school day. Homework Club is available in some classes. Children settle in rooms where teachers carry on with their normal after-school duties – marking, tidying and drawing up lesson plans. There is an atmosphere of calm. Everyone has a job to do, and everyone does it. A group of Year 4 children have stayed back to work on the computers. High Achievers Groups are meeting with the headteacher in her office. They are investigating parallelograms. There is a lot of giggling, as the children spread out on the floor in parallel lines.

By four o'clock every child has gone home. We follow one of the teachers into the staffroom. The office staff have ensured that the room is tidy and that refreshments are available. The headteacher comes in and congratulates the staff on the high number of 100 per cent pupils that day. There is a buzz in here too! Every comment about every child is positive. Words like 'amazing', 'superb', 'fabulous' and 'remarkable' come to our ears.

We realize that these are ordinary teachers, like us. They tell us that they started out like us, good teachers, but now they feel that they are great teachers. The results of their work in the ALPS are also amazing to them – they are discovering greater possibilities every day. They have the same difficulties as us, we hear snippets of discussions about attendance and behaviour, but the language that is used is entirely positive as solutions are found.

> Congratulations to Jayne and Debbie for their outstanding history project

In the chapters which follow, we will find out how the schools who provided the composite profile just described were so successful and share with you all the methods used to achieve their success.

② The ALPS model explained

ALPS STANDS FOR 'ACCELERATED LEARNING IN PRIMARY SCHOOLS'. It is a structured approach to organizing learning based on well-proven methods. It derives from the models described in the books *Accelerated Learning in the Classroom* (1995) and *Accelerated Learning in Practice* (1998) by Alistair Smith.

The intention behind these and the present book, as well as the hundreds of training programmes that have supported them, is to provide a structured approach to organizing classroom learning that draws upon new knowledge about learning. This book, like the others in the series, makes reference to the most recent published research on the brain and learning. It also draws on widely differing but not unrelated disciplines such as the psychology of motivation, memory research, Neuro-Linguistic Programming, transactional analysis and studies of human intelligence. Coming nearer to home it derives some authority from the experience of many hundreds of classroom practitioners who have made the original ideas work and then gone on to improve them.

The ALPS approach starts by building and maintaining a positive and supportive learning environment. It was the Elton Report on Discipline in Schools that observed that 'teachers who exist through a diet of rare praise, frequent criticism and an emphasis of sanction over reward

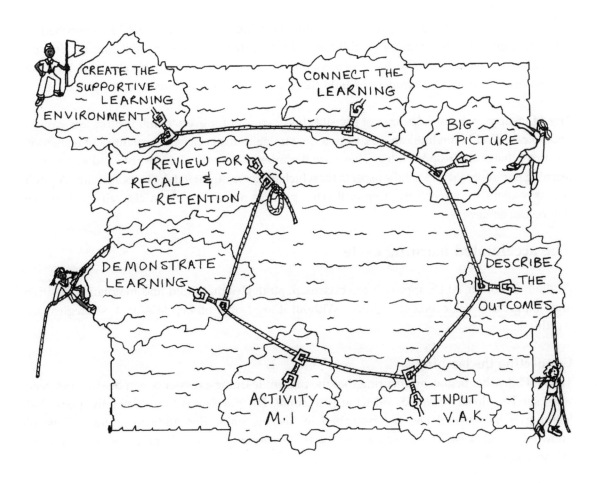

23

are rewarded in turn with more, not less, misbehaviour' (Elton, 1989). In the ALPS classroom children are safe from intimidation or put-down. They can take risks. The emphasis is on what they can do – not on what they cannot. The teacher actively encourages a 'can-do' attitude.

Creating a positive and supportive learning environment

The teacher needs to create a positive and supportive learning environment, externally and internally. External aspects would include some areas of experience over which you have little or no direct control; internal aspects are those attitudes of mind and habits of thought that you can directly influence. In both aspects you have to operate within your remit. For example, you may not be able to impact on levels of poverty within the community from which your school draws. It may be that you can have little or no influence on the consistency of care provided for pupils outside of school hours. You may be unable to directly influence for the better the pattern of relationships within the pupil's family. These things are not, perhaps, your responsibility. You operate within your remit, but you should do so positively, without allowing all the other impacting variables to be an excuse for inaction. ALPS teachers work to improve the things that they can improve, realizing that they cannot improve everything.

The external aspects of a positive and supportive learning environment are those interventions that can be made in and around the classroom to create the best conditions for learning. These interventions involve structuring opportunities for positive learning interactions between pupils, and between pupils and other influencers. This requires an appreciation of task design and of balancing the learning diet within the constraints provided.

The internal aspect of a positive and supportive learning environment could be described as 'providing invisible body armour for children'. This is to do with children's self-esteem. How do they perceive themselves? Do these perceptions liberate or limit their life chances? To what extent are the perceptions hardened? Might they be susceptible to influence and change?

The ALPS approach provides a set of invisible body armour for every child. It turns low-can-do and no-can-do children into can-dos. Classroom strategies foster personal qualities of resilience, resourcefulness and responsibility. These are the internal aspects of a positive and supportive learning environment and are the aspects for which teachers ought to take responsibility. A pupil who is resilient, resourceful and responsible has positive self-esteem and a disposition to believe that he can achieve.

The accelerated learning cycle

At the heart of the ALPS approach are classroom strategies that build and maintain a positive and supportive achievement culture. Without these, any other classroom strategies are worthless.

Connecting the learning

The ALPS teacher begins by ensuring that the present learning experience can be sited between what she has already covered and what is to come. The purpose is to reinforce the point that learning is incremental and not packaged in discrete units. She adds to a store of useful knowledge and skills. Effective connecting activities are pupil-centred and involve a high level of participation.

Giving the Big Picture

At the beginning of any learning experience the ALPS teacher helps children to orientate by providing an overview. She says what the class is going to do and how they are going to do it. She helps the pupils to see how today's learning will be organized and begins to challenge their understanding. She gives a summary of what is to come and provides an initial exposure to key ideas and key terminology.

In each lesson give the Big Picture by:

◆ describing what is to be done and how the class will do it – be explicit.

◆ embedding open-ended questions to engage curiosity and challenge understanding.

◆ identifying the key terminology and reinforcing it visually.

Describing the outcomes

At a more specific level the ALPS teacher helps pupils think in terms of their own learning outcomes. She asks questions such as 'What are you going to be better at today?' and 'By the end of the lesson how will someone else know that you had learned the topic really well?' This is an opportunity for target-setting. In Part Two the process of target-setting in the ALPS is discussed. Target-setting is firstly about a mindset, so the ALPS teacher encourages pupils to think in terms of achieving a successful outcome. She teaches them to be able to describe that outcome, in detail, to themselves and later to others. The outcomes can then be written and thus become part of a target-setting approach.

Providing input

The input of information should be, wherever possible, multisensory. This engages different types of processing pathways in the brain. The ALPS teacher provides experiences that exploit visual, auditory and kinesthetic learning preferences.

Activating understanding

The ALPS approach borrows from Howard Gardner's multiple intelligence model. The ALPS teacher uses this model to design reinforcing activities. Gardner identifies eight different types of intelligence and suggests that each person has a different balance or share of these propensities. By structuring school and classroom learning activities across the different intelligences, the teacher provides a structure for building variety and challenge into the day.

Demonstrating understanding

The ALPS teacher provides frequent opportunities to show understanding and to test that understanding. The use of pole-bridging – murmuring your thoughts aloud – and mapping techniques are both central elements at this stage.

Reviewing for recall

Planned review sessions occur during and at the conclusion of learning experiences in the ALPS. Regular review lifts the level of simple recall and makes each subsequent lesson more effective.

Throughout the ALPS approach the teacher endeavours to develop content and process engagement. By the end of the ALPS experience the child should be confident and skilled in the use of the new three 'Rs': responsibility, resourcefulness and resilience, which are lifelong learning entitlements implicit in the ALPS approach.

❸ The children who journey with you

A meeting of minds

> It's just phenomenal how experience determines how our brains get put together. If you fail to learn the proper fundamentals at an early age, then you are in big trouble. You can't suddenly start to learn when you haven't laid down the basic brain wiring.

Martha Pierson, Baylor College of Medicine, Houston (quoted in Kotulak, 1996)

> The impact of a stimulating or boring environment is widespread throughout the regions of the brain involved in learning and remembering.

Marian Diamond, 1998

IT IS MID-AFTERNOON. YOU ARE A TEACHER IN A PRIMARY CLASSROOM. You teach 10 year olds. There are thirty in front of you. You have just been to the hall to model the distribution of oxygen in the bloodstream. Now they are all individually engaged in learning. As you look on you become aware that within the room there are, apart from your own, thirty brains, each suspended in fluid and floating at distances of between four foot (Kevin) and five foot four (Karen) above the ground. The brains are interacting with each other, with their own thoughts, with the science equipment and, you hope, with the experience you have just shared with them.

What is happening in those heads? If you could find out, would it help your teaching? Maybe finding out would lead to profound insights, radical changes, disbelief, or possibly despair?

If your headteacher could stretch the budget to provide portable scanning equipment that would allow you instantly and without any extra effort to probe each child's brain, how might that change your teaching? By using a Smith and Call Ultimate Scanner – or SACUS for short – you can identify the chemical and electrical changes in each of these thirty brains at the precise point your brilliant teaching hits home. Thrill to the sight of synaptic connections being formed with your well-considered questioning technique! Gasp in wonder as you watch your thesis about the beginnings of Greek civilization become hard-wired in long-term memory!

Unlikely? Perhaps, but a great deal more about the brain and learning is known now than at any other period in history.

So with the advantage of the SACUS, what might be going on in those brains? Let us consider the neural history of four children in our class. We will call them Amrit, Nisha, Annie and Eddie.

Amrit's brain

> Long thought to be a clean slate to which information could be added at any time, the brain is now seen as a super sponge that is most absorbent from birth to about the age of twelve.

Ronald Kotulak, 1996

Amrit is 10 years old. Like the others in this class, he was born with all his brain cells or neurons in place. Given good health, a child is born with all the brain cells that he or she needs. There are about 100 billion of them and they started to communicate with each other while Amrit was still in the womb. This has been important for his abilities as a learner. His brain thrived on the early stimulation of a normal caring environment, and trillions of connections between neurons were established in that period. These connections were reinforced as he played and responded to the world around him and grew older, so that by now, most of the connective superhighways that he will need for the rest of his life are permanently in place.

Amrit

In the early years it is a case of 'use it or lose it'. Deprived of such a stimulating environment, a child's brain suffers. From the earliest age, exposure to positive interactions with a parent or other caregiver will begin to establish the neural circuitry in the brain for a child to succeed. Children who are rarely touched or experience the physical contact of a parent or other caregiver (Schanberg, quoted in Kotulak, 1996) are physically smaller than others who get this contact. Researchers at Baylor College of Medicine suggest that there can be as much as 20 to 30 per cent less neural density in such children (Newsweek, 1997). This means a permanent impairment on the capacity to store and manipulate new information. At the University of Chicago, Peter Huttenlocher led a research team who counted the connections between brain cells. They found an amazing rate of connectivity at sensitive periods in a child's development.

> If you want to significantly influence a child's ability to think and to acquire knowledge, the early childhood years are very critical.

Peter Huttenlocher, Professor of Neurobiology, University of Chicago, 1984

In a sample from a 28-week-old foetus, Huttenlocher and his team found 124 million connections between the cells. A similar sized sample in a new-born had 253 million synaptic connections. A sample from an eight-month-old showed a massive increase to 572 million. At the fastest rate, connections were being built at the incredible speed of 3 billion a second, eventually reaching a total of about 1,000 trillion connections in the whole brain. After that point, the connections begin a gradual decline. By about age 10 or so, half the connections have died off, leaving about 500 trillion, a number that remains fairly constant through most of life (Huttenlocher, quoted in Kotulak, 1996).

Each of these connections has to be instructed. Each electrical and chemical connection is prompted by a stimulus. The stimulus comes when the child interacts with his environment. An impoverished environment leads to fewer connections.

Amrit was lucky. Not only did he benefit from interacting with adults, but they also talked to him and with him. From the earliest age, the language centres in the left hemisphere of his cortex were developing. His mother does not know it, but when she sang to him before and after he was born she was activating the connections between neurons used for language. She was helping develop pathways used in pitch discrimination and later in identifying patterns of sound in the phonemic stage of reading. These connections for language processing are not yet fully laid down and they will not be until he is about twelve, in two years' time. However, Amrit's brain is running out of time to be really good at another language. If his parents want him to become fluent in a second or third language, they should be teaching him now.

In today's lesson, Amrit is working with a classroom assistant. She is helping him to manipulate a soldering iron, and he is talking himself through each action and trying to use the proper names for things: 'The soldering iron melts the soldier ... no, solder – it's solder, not soldier, it sounds the same though, a bit ... The flux helps the solder flow along the wires to make a good connection. A good connection mustn't be bumpy, it is smooth, sort of ... solder, it's solder. That's the word, funny that it sounds like soldier!' His teacher has told him to talk aloud like this. His teacher says that this is a good learning trick because it means that you use different parts of your brain and so put down even more connections. What is actually happening is that different clusters of neurons are firing in a partly random and partly rehearsed way.

As Amrit struggles to find the right word to describe aloud what he is doing, the neural assemblies associated with language functions – identifying, structuring and articulating patterns of sounds – are connecting with other sites. These include regions associated with different sorts of memory and centres for voluntary control, planning and co-ordination of movement. This would be problematic if there was impairment in the connectivity between the visual cortex and the language centres in the left hemisphere of his brain, or with the cells whose role it is to tell the visual cortex about rapid changes or movement. With these circumstances, Amrit might have been susceptible to what has become known as dyslexia. Fortunately for Amrit, he does not have such problems, and the activity of describing aloud what he is doing is relatively easy and enjoyable for him.

Amrit is so preoccupied with the task that he does not pay much attention to Nisha, who is working nearby.

Nisha's brain

Each connection has to be instructed.

Professor Colin Blakemore, University of Oxford, 1998

Nisha's neural history differs in some ways from Amrit's. She is a girl. As a girl, she may experience an early advantage with language acquisition. At twenty weeks after conception, Nisha could hear *in utero*. Most of us could. Within an hour of her birth, she preferred her mother's voice and would turn in response to it. By the time she was three to four months old, she was taking in most language, and at 18 months old her brain experienced an explosive improvement in the capacity to recognize and emulate patterns of sound. Humans are wired for language and Nisha's parents realized that she had this wiring at a very early age! If Nisha had not been exposed to speech by her eighth birthday, then she would have lost the ability to speak forever (Blakemore, 1998).

In research done in Alaska and Kansas, scientists found that exposure to language varied dramatically according to home circumstances. Children from some of the welfare families in the longitudinal survey experienced up to 13 million fewer words of cumulative language experience by the age of four. The researchers claimed that exposure to language and particularly to positive structured interactions with a parent or caregiver could be correlated to IQ scores (Kotulak, 1996). The more the children were exposed to talk and talked with, the higher their performance in IQ tests. A headline in the *Daily Express* from October 1998 proclaimed 'How to Boost your Child's IQ'. The answer – apparently – is: talk to him!

Nisha

The language centres in Nisha's brain are more widely diffused than Amrit's. When she is asked to listen to words she uses both left and right hemispheres. There is electrical and chemical activity in both. She not only hears the words, but also registers an emotional response. The isolation and recognition of the patterns of sound largely takes place in her left hemisphere; registration of an emotional response occurs in the right. She is better equipped to pick up subtle nuances of language. When she is a mother, she will be able to 'read' the mood of her adolescent children with an accuracy that will amaze her husband, who will usually wait for a door to slam shut before realizing that his teenaged daughter has a problem.

The *corpus callosum* is a structure found deep within the brain that acts as a highly powered relay station to conduct signals from one side of the brain to the other. Nisha's *corpus callosum* is thicker and has more neuronal density than Amrit's. Nisha's brain is thus better structured for internal communication. She is more adept, at this stage, at manipulating language. By the time he is 50, Amrit's *corpus calosum* will have shrunk by as much as 20 per cent (Kotulak, 1996). Nisha's will not shrink. She is more intuitive. She is a better communicator under stress. She is a girl.

As a one-day-old baby, she also preferred to look at faces rather than other visual stimuli and within a few days began to recognize and favour her mother's face. If Nisha had not utilized her eyesight within the first twenty-six weeks of life, then the capacity to do so would have been lost forever. Within the sensitive period, subtle differences in the visual data being filtered in from the external world and attended to by her brain developed Nisha's capacity to discern shape, depth, colour and contrast. There are specific sensitive periods for things such as binocular vision, vertical and horizontal line, slope and depth of line.

Nisha was blessed with eidetic memory, which is like a photographic memory, up to the age of four: she could remember with startling accuracy the appearance of objects. As an adult, she will have a propensity for learning through visual cues. She will remember the 'look' of words spelled on the page and the layout and spatial organization of images. She will remember faces and will be good at mentally rehearsing and imagining scenarios.

In later life Nisha will be an artist. In a joint research project conducted by Oxford and Stanford Universities,[1] it was shown that the brains of artists work differently to those of other people. The visual cortex is the region that is responsible for taking in and processing visual information. The scientists found that artists tended to use the visual cortex less than non-artists. Artists, such as Nisha, use the front of the brain more. This area is associated with forward planning, complex thinking, meanings and making emotional responses.

Despite struggling with her science and maths SAT tests, Nisha has an extraordinary brain. We all have! By the end of Nisha's lifespan, her brain will have formed a total of 10^{16} connections. Every second of her life, her brain is making as many as 10 million connections. She is a phenomenal learning organism!

Annie's brain

> Our profession has paid little attention to emotion. And yet, our emotional system drives our attentional system, which drives learning and memory.

Robert Sylwester, 1998

At the back of the class is Annie. Our neural development is a complex interplay between nature and nurture. Some call this 'emergentism'. At successive stages of development, different genes have turned on and interacted with everyday experience to create Annie's personality. Her genes have made a brain that is capable of re-designing itself and has done so during what are known as sensitive periods. She was most vulnerable at six to twelve weeks after gestation. During this time insults to the embryo – arising from her mother smoking, taking drugs, drinking alcohol to excess, becoming seriously ill or exposed to radiation – could have affected the migration of cells at a time

Annie

the alps approach – Accelerated Learning in Primary Schools

when a quarter of a million new cells were being created every minute! Thankfully this did not occur and her capacity to learn has not been inhibited.

Annie is an exuberant child. Her teacher finds it difficult sometimes to express this on Annie's reports. Words such as 'lively', 'enthusiastic' and 'eager to please' spring to mind, along with 'needs to learn to concentrate for longer periods'. Annie is struggling this morning to focus on the work set for her. After about ten minutes she begins to stray from the workstation.[2] She had a broken night's sleep[3] and she rushed her breakfast. Physiologically, she is not in the best state for learning. Her energy levels are low. She is anxious about getting the work wrong and fears being shown up in front of the class. Her anxieties lead to a pattern of downshifting in her brain.

Under stress, Annie's brain shifts into another gear. The hypothalamus and adrenal glands flood the system with survival chemicals: adrenaline, cortisol and vasopressin. This cocktail results in a mental slowdown and leads to responses that are antagonistic to meaningful long-term learning: her capacity to index long-term memory is inhibited; her choices become conformist and she looks for ready answers; her capacity to discern meanings and generate new meanings is minimized. This is not good.

Unexpressed emotions can inhibit many functions, including learning.

Candice Pert, 1997

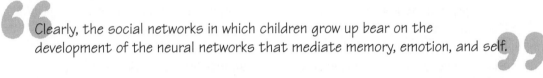

Clearly, the social networks in which children grow up bear on the development of the neural networks that mediate memory, emotion, and self.

Mary Carlson, PhD, Associate Professor of Neuroscience in Psychiatry, Harvard Medical School, 1998

Sometimes you will ask Annie a question and get a blank look or a quick, ill-judged answer. Her brain needs processing time to make synaptic connections and it needs feedback for those connections to be strengthened. Association rather than repetition or rote rehearsal drives her memory. When she is given regular reflection time and opportunities to explain or account for her understanding, she performs best. When in Reception Class, she responded enthusiastically to a question about the route to the park with: 'I've got a dog!' The class laughed, and Annie cried. She is not good in quick-fire question-and-answer sessions, and neither is her brain. A good maxim would be 'the younger the child, the longer the processing time in response to questions or certain sorts of challenges'.

Annie's energy levels are at their lowest twelve hours on from the mid-point of her previous evening's sleep. She went to bed at 9pm and got up at 7am. It is now 2pm. She is at her lowest. Her amine level is at its lowest. Amines are attentional chemicals present in the body that also help run the brain. They are stimulants, like amphetamine, and are at their lowest twelve hours on from the mid-point of the previous evening's sleep. What is more, Annie is dehydrated and full of additives and colourings from her lunchbox. Some light exercise – a brain break – might release some epinephrine and dopamine into her brain and shake her torpor, making her more receptive for learning. But no. The supply teacher in the class today believes in 'maximizing the time on task'. The teacher has not realized that short, brisk activity increases energy levels and that children tune in and out on a natural cycle of highs and lows over a period of 90 to 110 minutes. A better model for Annie would be to focus on the task for about twelve minutes, then on a diffusion activity for about two or three minutes, then back on the task and so on.

Annie will not remember a great deal of the cognitive learning from this afternoon's science lesson. The teacher favours lots of rote learning. Rote learning can be accomplished under a good deal of threat, but pattern discrimination and the more subtle choices suffer severe inhibition. Similarly inhibited are the use of oral language and any form of symbol manipulation. In Annie's brain, the amygdala and hippocampus are situated near to each other within an area known as the limbic system. In situations of anxiety or of high emotional arousal, the amygdala – involved in emotional responses – becomes more active. The hippocampus – involved in long-term memory – becomes less so. She will remember how she felt, but not what her teacher hoped she would learn. Her brain has helped code the emotional response and associated it with that sort of classroom learning activity. When another, similar activity comes along, then so will Annie's coded emotional responses. In next week's lesson, she will not recall the fact that pure water boils at 212°F at sea level, but she will recall the feelings of anxiety about pronouncing the word 'thermometer' in front of the class.

Eddie's brain

 Complex learning is enhanced by challenge and inhibited by threat. We want to deeply engage learners with their purposes, values and interests. Thinking and feeling are connected because our patterning is emotional. That means we need to help learners create a felt meaning, a sense of relationship with a subject, in addition to an intellectual understanding.

Geoffrey Caine, 1998

Eddie is in the corner of the class. Or at least that is where he was when you last looked! He is a very active child. Eddie's parents are convinced he has something called Attention Deficit Disorder (ADD). They read about it in a magazine and are concerned that he may have the symptoms. Certainly he has difficulty focusing his attention on one activity at a time and, what is more, seems actively to seek novelty. Eddie has difficulty waiting his turn and does not follow instructions.

As Eddie's teacher, you know that the symptoms of Attention Deficit Hyperactivity Disorder (ADHD) include two things: inattention and a combination of hyperactive and impulsive behaviours. All the children in your class are active and certainly more distractible and impulsive than adults. The question for you as you think about Eddie is: 'Does he display these symptoms significantly more than his peers do?' You know him well and you are of the view that he is easily distracted and needs a high level of arousal but not to the extent where it may require specific interventions. There is a

Eddie

32

child like Eddie in every class, and you've seen much worse, although that's not what you said when you retrieved him from the corridor for the third time this morning!

However, you have met with many parents who are concerned that their child has ADHD. In your opinion, the symptoms usually are due to other factors, such as poor role modelling, unsuitable diet, emotional factors, or a desperate need for attention. If you had a pound for every child who displayed the symptoms, you would be a millionaire by now! You often find that a positive discipline system can 'cure' the supposed ADHD child. The children that you worry about are the rare few that do not seem to respond to your discipline strategies.

True ADHD is not, as has long been assumed, a disorder of attention, but is a developmental failure in the brain circuitry that underlies inhibition and self-control (Barkley, 1998). Scientific research is showing that children with ADHD cannot inhibit impulsive motor response to sensory input. They are less capable of preparing motor responses in anticipation of events. They are insensitive to feedback about errors made in those responses. Their ability to plan, adapt and learn is overwhelmed by an immediate emotional response. The younger the children the less likely they are able to be aware of time or to give priority to future events over immediate wants. The behaviour patterns that arise usually do so between the ages of three and five. Boys are at least three times as likely as girls to be diagnosed as having ADHD.

As a boy, it is more likely that Eddie's brain will have a proportionately larger right hemisphere in the cortex than most of the girls in his class. This may contribute to a more marked ability in tasks that involve manipulating objects through three dimensions or imagining the movement of those objects, or spatial reasoning. In Reception class Eddie was a champion with the Lego®, although he found it difficult to share the bricks with other children! Now he enjoys doing mental arithmetic in class, particularly when they have competitions and try to do sums from memory. Statistically, as a boy, he is more likely than the girls in the class to enrol in a remedial reading programme, to be left-handed and to be dyslexic. Yet when it comes to making models and 3D designs, Eddie is the best in the class. It is interesting to you that he can concentrate on these kinds of activities for a very long time!

❹ Nine 'brain-based' principles

THE ALPS APPROACH UTILIZES MUCH OF THE current published research about the brain and how it learns. The nine principles for brain-based learning outlined below were first published in *Accelerated Learning in Practice* (Smith, 1998; see also Diamond and Hopson, 1998). Of course, the term 'brain-based learning' may be subject to question as it is difficult to imagine much in the way of learning that is other than brain-based! However, we propose to stick with it for the sake of clarity.

The nine 'brain-based' principles on which the ALPS approach is founded are:

> **1   The brain develops best in environments** with high levels of sensory stimulation and sustained cognitive challenge. ALPS teachers create environments for learning with high levels of learning-related sensory stimulation.

2   **The optimal conditions for learning** will feature sustained levels of cognitive challenge alongside low threat. ALPS teachers make it safe to take risks and to experience and learn from those risks. They help the learners develop the lifelong learning quality of persistence.

3   **Higher order intellectual activity** may be diminished in environments that are emotionally or physiologically hostile or are perceived to be so by the learner. ALPS teachers pay attention to the emotional and physical readiness of the learner for learning.

4   **The brain thrives on immediacy of feedback and on choice.** The ALPS teacher knows that when learners engage in what is described as 'pole-bridging' – a method for internalizing feedback – improvements in reasoning powers are dramatic.

5   **There are recognized processing centres in the hemispheres of the brain.** ALPS teachers use this knowledge as authority for structured variety in classroom input. They also notice and exploit different attentional states.

6   **Each brain has a high degree of plasticity**, developing and integrating with experience in ways unique to itself. The ALPS teacher makes the assumption that there are different intelligences and that she can teach for the development of these.

7   **Learning takes place at a number of levels.** An ALPS teacher engages both conscious and unconscious processing through suggestive methods, variety in questioning strategies and personal goal-setting. She integrates learning challenges.

8   **Memory is a series of processes rather than locations.** ALPS teachers recognize that the processes to access meaningful long-term memory must be active, rather than passive; they ensure that activities are engaging, accessible and rich in context.

9   **Humans are 'hard-wired' for a language response.** They may also be hard-wired for a musical response. The ALPS teacher exploits this by maximizing purposeful language exchange and musical responsiveness.

We will meet each principle regularly throughout this book.

Each brain is unique. Each of our four children is unique. Each neural history reflects a complex interactive dance between inheritance and environment. Sadly, and all too often, children's learning diet does not reflect this complexity. On too many occasions they will be expected to do the same things, at the same time, to the same level of difficulty while being measured against the same criteria, in spite of the fact that the brain develops in spurts and plateaus, spurts and plateaus. At any one point in time the four children of similar chronological age will be at different levels of receptiveness for learning. If only schools and schooling could better match the way that the brain is constructed for learning, then maybe they would reach more pupils and tap their natural propensity towards learning. That is what this book is about.

⑤ The new three 'Rs'

THE ALPS METHOD™ TAKES THE FINDINGS FROM RESEARCH into the brain and learning, and attempts to deliver a twenty-first century version of the three 'Rs'. We are indebted to Guy Claxton and his book *Hare Brain Tortoise Mind* for the inspiration for the three Rs model.

If you have ever been alone on a bus or train late at night, when someone else gets on you may have begun to experience the limits of your own comfort zone. The comfort zone is experienced when this unknown newcomer comes and sits next to you! This little imperfect circle of personal space forms an invisible barrier between you and the source of your anxiety. Some learning situations are like this. In conditions of high uncertainty, people resort to conservative learning choices. They go to the tried, the trusted, the tested and the familiar. The more vulnerable they feel in the midst of uncertainty, the more quickly they retire to their comfort zone.

Genuine long-term learning does not take place in environments where there is a high degree of anxiety. Classrooms characterized by high uncertainty, ambiguous relationships and an emphasis on penalties are classrooms where underperformance is the norm. Our challenge as teachers is to create and sustain a learning environment where a child will take the risk of learning. Anxiety inhibits the child's willingness to take risks. The best learning environments combine high and sustained cognitive challenge with low stress. It is not sufficient for a learner to have the traditional skills associated with an intelligent response. He must be willing to take the risk of using them.

The ALPS method™ provides a structure within which the skills of intelligent response can be deployed. It provides safe spaces for using them. There are a variety of factors that determine whether learners use these 'thinking skills'.

The Harvard University 'Patterns of Thinking'[4] Project looked at the attitudes, values and habits of mind that determine whether learners use their thinking skills. Starting from the position that 'skills in themselves are not enough', the project looked at the composition of all the other personal 'dispositions' – tendencies towards a particular pattern of intellectual behaviour – that allow the skills to be deployed. Most assessments of critical and creative thinking test the thinking skills students possess, but do not provide information about the extent to which students are actually disposed to use them. An analogy might be testing a child's ability to make skilled swimming strokes, without considering whether or not the child is willing to get in the water.

The major emphasis of the Patterns of Thinking Project was the development of disposition-centred assessment techniques. These assessments look at three aspects of high-level thinking:

1   Students' sensitivity to appropriate occasions to think critically and creatively.
2   Students' inclination to think critically and creatively.
3   Students' ability to think critically and creatively, independently of their dispositions.

The seven dispositions for good thinking are:[5]

1   The disposition to be broad and adventurous. The tendency to be open-minded, to explore alternative views; alertness to narrow thinking; the ability to generate multiple options.

2   The disposition towards wondering, problem finding and investigating. The tendency to wonder, probe, find problems; a zest for inquiry, alertness for anomalies and puzzles; the ability to formulate questions and investigate carefully.

3   The disposition to build explanations and understandings. A desire to explore the parts and purposes of things and to seek connections and explanations; a tendency towards the active use of knowledge; an ability to build complex conceptualizations.

4   The disposition to make plans and be strategic. The drive to set goals, to make and execute plans, to envision outcomes; alertness to lack of direction; the ability to formulate goals and plans.

5   The disposition to be intellectually careful. The urge for precision, organization, thoroughness; alertness to possible error or inaccuracy; the ability to process information precisely.

6   The disposition to seek and evaluate reasons. The tendency to question, to demand justification; alertness to the need for evidence; the ability to weigh and assess reasons.

7   The disposition to be metacognitive. The tendency to be aware of and monitor the flow of one's own thinking; alertness to complex thinking situations; the ability to exercise control of mental processes and to be reflective.

A key feature of accelerated learning and the ALPS model is the deliberate creation and maintenance of a positive and supportive learning environment where children are disposed to operate with intelligence. It produces opportunities for every child to demonstrate what we are calling the new three Rs. These lifelong learning attributes are the new three Rs of responsibility, resourcefulness and resilience.

WHAT IS RESPONSIBILITY? In the context of the ALPS model, responsibility is the recognition that actions have consequences, and the ability and willingness to consider fully those consequences before an action is taken. For example, Eddie does not demonstrate responsibility when he knocks over the paint pots in his rush to grab his favourite paintbrush from Annie! Managing impulsivity, delaying immediate gratification and thinking in terms of success outcomes are characteristics of the responsible learner. So too is the ability to empathize and to see things from multiple perspectives. Responsibility is also about locating one's own actions within a larger scheme of things. In fact,

Responsibility

Annie did not have Eddie's paintbrush. His brush was in the sink, where he had left it the previous day.

WHAT IS RESOURCEFULNESS? In the context of the ALPS model, to be resourceful is to be able to adapt to different learning challenges. This is about having the tools of a good learner and the skills with which to deploy those tools. A child who is never involved in positive decisions about her own learning will not have the attribute of resourcefulness. If, for whatever reason, a child develops a presupposition that learning is a passive activity, then the ability to make autonomous decisions about applying skills and utilizing learning tools will be significantly diminished. Annie has this tendency to believe that she is not in control of her own learning. She gazes helplessly at her painting. She is not surprised that the colours have run into one another because that is what happened last time. To be resourceful is also to be willing to take the risk of learning, which may involve revealing ignorance or making mistakes.

Resourcefulness

WHAT IS RESILIENCE? In the context of the ALPS model, resilience means being able to persist in the face of frustration or setbacks or when complexity is seemingly overwhelming. Metacognition, the ability to engage with and be curious about one's own thinking, is the sign

Resilience

of a resilient learner. The resilient learner has developed a range of coping strategies, and does not internalize or externalize blame. When Nisha's painting becomes too wet and the colours run into one another, she will not blame Eddie for switching brushes after he gave Annie's back to her. Neither will she blame herself for being 'useless at art'. She will learn that it is better to use the paper towel on the brush after each time that she dips it into the paint. Her next painting will be a success. The coping strategies of a resilient learner are bolstered by a positive self-image, which in turn emerges from high self-esteem. This allows the resilient learner to be able to place failure in context and to be able to see possibilities for learning within the experience. To a child with resilience 'there is no failure, only feedback'.

We believe that the ALPS method™ delivers the new three Rs and that the new three Rs epitomize the desirable attributes for success in the millennium. The outcome of ALPS is more than an ability to perform better within the formal curriculum. The new three Rs correlate with what the American author Daniel Goleman (1996) called 'emotional intelligence'. Emotional intelligence is considered by many to be the learning mantra for the millennium. In his book, *Emotional Intelligence: Why it can matter more than IQ*, Goleman described the significance of our underpinning emotions:

> In navigating our lives, it is our fears and envies, our rages and depressions, our worries and anxieties that steer us day to day. Even the most academically brilliant among us are vulnerable to being undone by unruly emotions. The price we pay for emotional illiteracy is in failed marriages and troubled families, in stunted social and work lives, in deteriorating physical health and mental anguish.

Daniel Goleman, 1996

Goleman has created worldwide interest in the phenomenon of emotional intelligence, arguing that teaching children the skills of emotional literacy is as important as teaching other forms of literacy and that EI is more important to lifelong learning than IQ.

Emotional intelligence encompasses the following five characteristics and abilities:

1 Self-awareness – knowing your emotions, recognizing feelings as they occur and discriminating between them.

2 Mood management – handling feelings so that your reactions are appropriate to the current situation.

3 Self-motivation – gathering up your feelings and directing yourself towards a goal, despite self-doubt, inertia and impulsiveness.

4 Empathy – recognizing feelings in others and tuning in to their verbal and non-verbal cues.

5 Managing relationships – handling interpersonal interaction, conflict resolution and negotiations.

Goleman cites evidence from the US National Center for Clinical Infant Programs that the most critical element for a student's success in school is an understanding of how to learn. In the ALPS classroom children learn, and learn how to learn. What Goleman describes as the characteristics of emotional intelligence we include in our new three Rs. We argue that they can be delivered via ALPS.

The ALPS model provides a powerful mechanism for developing lifelong learning skills and the personal dispositions to transfer those skills into the many different contexts in which they will be needed. In addition, the ALPS model fosters emotional intelligence via these new three Rs.

A key skill for both teaching and learning in the ALPS is memory mapping. In the next chapter we describe how memory mapping can help you on your journey.

⑥ Take a map on your journey

The memory maps used throughout this book summarize the key content. They are also an integral part of the ALPS method™. In this chapter we explain why visual reference systems are important, what mapping is, how it can develop thinking, how it works and how we use it throughout the book.

About visual processing

Our capacity to store and recall visual information is, we will argue, more powerful than our capacity to store and recall patterns of sound: pictures are easier to recall than words. So make your classroom environment visually rich! Learning posters in bright colours placed above eye level with easy-to-read information will help children to recall information from lessons. Laminate keywords used in language activities with visual cues on front and rear; desktop spelling lists and memory maps will access and exploit children's natural capacity for visual and spatial organization.

Up to about the age of four, a high percentage of children have what is known as eidetic memory, which is like a photographic memory. The *Oxford Companion to the Mind* describes the capacity of many young children to retain the rich pictorial quality of images. It says: 'shown a complex drawing for a few minutes, some children can subsequently report on many of its features, even seeming to re-examine it in detail when questioned about something not yet reported' (Gregory, 1987, p. 354). Children of a very young age are ready and willing to describe in elaborate detail the painting they have completed for you. To the child's narrative is added a whole imaginary world of people, places and events. They seem able to string visual references together to underpin the sequence of events in their story. They do so in ways that are natural and uninhibited. The next time you gaze at a wet blob of brownish green paint in the centre of a large piece of paper, listen carefully to the three year old's description of how Patty the cat is chasing the mouse, which ate his spaghetti (which he hates) and ran off down the hole to the den where the monsters live under the house. Just imagine what is happening in his brain.

Our capacity to internalize and manipulate visual images is a powerful one that some researchers have gone on to link to a stage in our evolutionary development. The ability to locate and move from a source of threat, or to map visually the position of traps, or to direct oneself back to a herd of migrating beasts would have helped our ancestors to survive. Perhaps sites within our brains were structured in ways to make this occur easily.

Nowadays the school experience of a child places a lot of emphasis from the outset on the written and the spoken. Perhaps our natural disposition towards organizing information in our heads through visual patterns and spatial relationships is undervalued. In arguing for the teaching and use of mapping techniques, we are arguing for the extension of the visual and spatial propensity that seems an inherent part of our neural architecture. All humans are mappers.

What is mapping?

What is happening in the brain when we map? Memories are not stored as discrete visual or aural units in a given area of the brain. Electro-chemical activity is patterned in response to stimuli from the external environment. Each precipitation activates connections between brain cells along pathways. The more varied the stimuli, the more varied the internal response, and the more pathways are established. Thus when learners pattern a series of connective possibilities, they establish a network of pathways. Accessing the same experience at a later date excites these pathways along with others, so that the assembly of complex connections is never quite the same.

In other words, the next time Eddie sees Annie with the paintbrush that looks so like his, he will not only recall that the last art lesson ended with tears, but also that his teacher showed him that there was some connection between wiping brushes and paintings getting too wet. He will also recall that the red paint mixed with the green when it was wet to make a brown that was useful for the trees in his picture. All this combines with innumerable other recollections, some distinct, some vague, and some minuscule, to create a unique map in Eddie's mind. Maps are pathways or organizations of connective possibilities similar to the neural pathways in the brain. Most researchers believe that 'all conscious and subconscious knowledge and behaviours are constructed as complex systems within the brain' (Restak, 1980).

Transferring the map in the mind to a map on paper requires the mapper to have an overview of a pattern of connective possibilities. It requires skills of categorization and an understanding of hierarchy. It challenges one's own understanding. Children cannot map without actively engaging their understanding. This is how one commentator described the connection between complex storage systems in the brain and our propensity for mapping:

> human knowledge is stored in clusters and organized within the brain into systems that people use to interpret familiar situations and to reason about new ones. When language – words and sentence structures – become part of the inter-weaving, the totality forms the basis for abstract thinking and problem-solving.

Ronald Kotulak, 1996

The mapping process thus becomes a very powerful tool for structuring and developing connective thinking. It also helps provide the Big Picture so that a learner's understanding is enhanced by the power of overview: the component parts are shown in relation to their overall purpose. The ALPS teacher shows her class how to map in a wide variety of contexts and makes it a fun, creative, productive activity. Very young children can learn to map. We have seen three and four year olds working as a group to produce wonderfully creative maps about their toys, their families or their favourite foods.

It is easy to teach children the principles of memory mapping from an early age. When you teach this skill it is important that you are clear with children that it is not an art test. Use props, artefacts, visual representations on shaped cards, and photographs to help demonstrate patterns of connection. Begin with something simple like the children's personal likes and dislikes, their families and friends, or categories of experience – such as games that they enjoy playing or holidays that they have enjoyed. Make it fun. Tell the class: 'We are going to show on just this one big piece of paper, the whole story of all the games that we like to play. We are going to show the equipment that we need, the places that we play, the grown ups who like to play with us, and the skills that we need to practise, all on one poster! When your mums or dads come to see it, they will see the whole story of how good you are at playing games!'

Start with easy-to-see keywords or pictures on small pieces of card so that they can be physically manoeuvred on a desk or tabletop. With 'games we enjoy playing' there are obvious categories: indoor or outdoor games; games you play on your own, games you play with friends; games that need equipment, games that need no equipment. Put up pictures or words on the map as children contribute. If you are working with young children, draw in the lines of connection, arrows and symbols for them. With older children, hand over coloured pens and let them do the work! As sub-categories start to emerge, children will begin to see connective relationships and ask questions of those relationships. Here are the principles of memory mapping:

- Practise from what is already well known and understood.
- Branch out and from the centre, spatially organizing as the map develops.
- Think of it like a tree with the more important items nearer to the trunk at the centre.
- Print the keywords – say them aloud as you go.
- Select and position significant pictures and images on your map.
- Emphasize the central topic by drawing around it.
- Emphasize related key topics by using bright primary colours.
- As the map builds up, survey the overall pattern of shapes and connections.

Encourage children to describe to themselves what they are doing as they do it. This is called pole-bridging. When they have completed their first attempt, ask them to describe each component and link within the map as they run their finger along it. Explain that a memory map is never really finished, that they will be able to add to it time and again as they learn more. For example, after you have taught them a new game in PE, they will be able to add it to the map under the category 'games that we can play on the playground' and maybe link it with an arrow to the category 'games that use bats and balls'. The possibilities are endless.

Read more about pole-bridging on page 209

Wow! Look at page 101 to learn about life maps

One of the most powerful uses of the mapping technique is to map individual and class aspirations – 'all about me!' These individual maps can be used as both a focus for goal-setting discussions and an assessment tool. Individual curriculum targets can be mapped. When the class life map for the year is displayed in a prominent place, you can use it as a reference point for any lesson. It immediately becomes a motivational tool and gives an overview of your plan for the lives of the children during their year with you as their teacher. By mindmapping your plan in consultation with your class, you give visual life to what otherwise would remain in your head and in the thirty little heads of the children in your class. All thirty-one of you then see and understand the itinerary for the journey ahead.

Pascal's story

The best justification for the mapping techniques exhibited throughout this book and for their use in schools comes from the experience of Oliver Caviglioli. Oliver is headteacher of a Special School in Chelmsford. His remarkable skills have been arrived at partly through his own fascination with thinking tools, and partly through his experience of helping his son, Pascal, develop his own methods of making sense of the world around him. Here is how Oliver describes Pascal's story.

> I have been using various ways of graphically mapping ideas and information for over twenty years and am a fervent advocate of this strategy. In addition to making personal notes from lectures or reading, preparing presentations, creating plans and taking minutes at meetings, I continually search for new contexts in which these graphic systems can save time, clarify thinking and generally support learning. And yet, in spite of this focus, I have had some spectacular blind spots. One such instance was with my son, Pascal.
>
> Pascal has Down's syndrome and at the time of this event was 9 years old. He is able to take interest in most subjects and concentrate for prolonged periods of time. He has a remarkable visual memory. His one cognitive difficulty, in relation to his ability, was not being able to organize information. Consistent with other children with Down's syndrome, Pascal found reading both easy and captivating from an early age. Indeed, he soon used to read independently for periods of time. Stories were read again and again. Returning to the same story repeatedly, I was later to realize, was a strategy he adopted to become better acquainted with the meaning of the text: comprehension increased cumulatively.
>
> It was a surprise, therefore, when his class teacher at his mainstream primary school reported that Pascal was merely 'barking at print'. I knew this wasn't true and certainly wasn't convinced by the explanation that he couldn't answer

comprehension questions based on the text. I set about solving this misidentified problem.

I am a headteacher of an SLD Special School with a background in Thinking Skills, having been trained to lead such programmes as Feuerstein's Instrumental Enrichment (Feuerstein et al., 1980) and de Bono's CORT (de Bono, 1986). Indeed, in response to repeated pleas from Pascal, I have used both programmes with him. This was interesting but didn't seem to afford any insights into identifying Pascal's level of comprehension of his current favourite book – only when I started looking through The Wizard of Oz with Pascal did a method begin to emerge.

As we talked about aspects of the book, I drew pictures of the characters and added words to describe their qualities. Almost absent-mindedly, I organized these doodles by drawing a circle around different groups of sketches with the agreement of Pascal. What developed was a map of the book that accurately illustrated Pascal's understanding. The map was based on the mind mapping technique first developed by Tony Buzan (Buzan, 1974).

Having realized what had occurred before my eyes, I redrew the map adhering more strictly to the organizing principles of mindmapping. This entailed asking Pascal questions about categories relating to such concepts as hero, villain, setting and so on. In retrospect, I found out that we had engaged in co-operative story mapping (Mathes et al., 1997).

My intervention was also a classic case of a mediated learning experience for Pascal, one where an adult supports the learner to expand the complexity of his understanding of the world (Feuerstein et al., 1980). I had entered Pascal's 'zone of proximal development' (Vygotsky, 1978) and, through showing him what he understood, had promoted his thinking. This thinking involved developing the schema Pascal had of both The Wizard of Oz in particular and stories in general.[6] The map was a concrete and visual representation of Pascal's schema. Being in front of both of us, its details were readily available for manipulation, the structure easily understood and above all it was a shared construction and discovery.

By applying the rules of mapping, we had helped Pascal learn to organize information. We also went back to practising categorization. There remained, however, another aspect of understanding of the story that this particular mapping technique was not best suited to illuminate. Stories have two fundamental aspects – the internal structure and the 'episodic system' (Rumelhart, 1981). In other words, we had not talked about the temporal features of the story; for example, 'what happens next?' Here, I used a flow-chart structure and, by asking Pascal the 'what happens next?' question, arrived with him at an accurate sequence of events.

This whole process, whose description may sound rather complicated and academic, lasted no more than thirty minutes and was a fun experience. It became abundantly clear that Pascal's teacher had been inaccurate in her judgements and that Pascal had demonstrated a clear understanding of both the structure and the sequence of the story. Mapping, or graphically organizing information, had provided the means to both 'test' understanding and to develop it. Throughout, Pascal had practised describing his own thought processes and demonstrated conscious awareness of those processes (see also Blagg, 1991; Flavell, 1977; Flood and Lapp, 1991). Moreover, mapping had helped Pascal to read like more competent readers.

With this success, Pascal now asked for more. And so we shared other mapping experiences. Any areas of study that he found confusing or too novel were transformed into graspable, visually organized categories whose rationale was spatially demonstrable. Pascal came to be so familiar and at ease with the mapping routine that he used this format to support a five-minute talk he had to give in class. With my direction, he started to map himself. Mapping soon became a regular, indispensable and always reliable strategy to clarify the world. Its construction provided an engaging way of developing the skills of organizing information that we had earlier identified as being Pascal's 'weak' point. That maps provided uniquely visual 'hooks' that literally shaped memory was a perfect addition to what increasingly appeared to me to be the best support for thinking and learning I had yet encountered.

Oliver's experience with his son shifted his own thinking to such an extent that he began immediately to look for ways of transferring his experience into his own school. This is how he proceeded.

As a professional educator, I reflected on this and wondered how far I could use the lessons learned to my own context – a school for pupils with severe and profound learning difficulties. Literacy for pupils with SLD had quite recently become more accessible through the use of symbols. These symbols are a development of signing systems first designed to be used with adults with SLD. They are now successfully built into word processing software. As a word is typed, so the corresponding symbol appears above or below. However, there are inherent limitations to this strategy. By forming bridges between pictures and words, symbols were initially used as keywords. Now, with the universal use of the symbol software in special schools and increasing use in primary schools, we have definitely reached the point of diminishing returns (Detheridge and Detheridge, 1997). If pupils can read symbols for every typed word, surely these skills of decoding could be put to better use in reading the typed words? The fact that symbols are communicated in linear fashion, as in text, means that the reader still has the same job of accumulating information gathered from the left-to-right reading, processing it and constructing meaning. This is a private and abstract mechanism occurring 'in the head' of the reader. Symbols, in themselves, and especially if only used in linear fashion, do not transcend the complexity of this process. Mapping offers the possibility of accessing concepts at a level higher than linear text alone allows.

Specialized programmes for children with autism such as TEACCH (Mesibov, 1985) have identified a hierarchy of levels of communication from objects, through photos and symbols to the word itself. Working with a colleague, Carol Hariram, I pursued the use of maps with any of the above levels of communication. In the context of library lessons, Carol used group discussion, supported by visual clues, to come to an agreement on the meaning of aspects of the focus of the lesson (Wells, 1990). Later, she came to define explicitly the elements of a story (Idol and Croli, 1987) – character, setting, problem, events and outcome. Always, the visual structure was the reference against which pupils could check their judgements. The grouping of items within each element was a physical and visual representation of a concept. To communicate these concepts through linear text, supported with symbols, would be too abstract a task. The spatial aspect of mapping is significant as it taps into a kinesthetic intelligence we all have.

From very early on in our development, we give significance to our spatial experience. We 'understand what it means' when objects are near or far – mummy being far away is a danger and therefore upsetting while her being near is safe and consequently comforting. The sophistication of these spatial interpretations increases as we grow. Infant teachers intrinsically know this to be true, as they demonstrate by their use of physically grouping objects to illustrate concepts ranging from colours (the red table) to more complex, even overlapping, categories (using Venn diagrams). The visual and spatial element has an 'ordinary' power that puts children at ease with the obviousness of the physical 'explanation' (the precise placement of the items within the various groupings). This is seen most clearly in the way that children will not tolerate the placement of any item in an inappropriate category (grouping). It is as if the incongruity is intolerable to their growing sense of order: it upsets their schema!

After discovering this capacity for categorization and its application to fiction, we applied it to the demands of the National Literacy Strategy. There are many techniques to develop both Word and Sentence competencies. It seemed that the inevitable comprehension questions were, by default, the only technique to both teach and test competency in understanding at text level.

Story mapping provided the means whereby text could be examined at a level hitherto considered inaccessible to our pupils. The very means of developing these maps of understanding were also providing a method of including all pupils in mixed ability learning. Given the growing impact of inclusion in mainstream schools, mapping promises to be a powerful means of making differentiation come alive, moving from rhetoric to practice. Mapping puts accelerated learning to work for all.

We have made a conscious effort to make this book differ from the vast majority of books for teachers. Using our own and Oliver's experience, we decided to help exploit your innate visual and spatial intelligence and map this book. Next we explain how.

How do we map this book?

Each part of the book is mapped for you so that you can use it to pre-process your understanding and gain an overview or Big Picture. You can also use it as a reference tool to plot your progress through each chapter.

We map the book this way because we hope that you will also begin to use the methods in your own teaching and in your preparation for teaching.

If you are keen to follow up the mapping techniques and improve your skills, details of useful publications are provided in Part Four.

Review of Introduction

We described a typical 'day in the ALPS'. This was a composite based on schools we have worked with. In what ways did the ALPS classrooms we visited differ from those in your school? What were the similarities?

The accelerated learning cycle has six stages and a pre-stage. How does the accelerated learning cycle compare to what you currently do in your own classroom? What stages do you follow? What stages may be missing?

Few, if any of us, know much about the brain. To what extent did our explanation of the 'four brains' of Nisha, Eddie, Amrit and Annie help explain some of the learning behaviours you see in your own class? Which of our children most resemble those in your class?

'Nine principles for brain-based learning' is a lofty claim. In what ways would we see these principles being followed in your classroom?

In what ways might the development of the 'new three Rs' – resourcefulness, resilience and responsibility – happen in your classroom? How would a visitor notice it was happening? How would the children experience the new three Rs?

A map is a visual tool to structure thinking. How do you map? What, if anything, do you map? How do you convey directions? How do you plan your working week? In what ways do children map their learning?

Part One

Establishing base camp

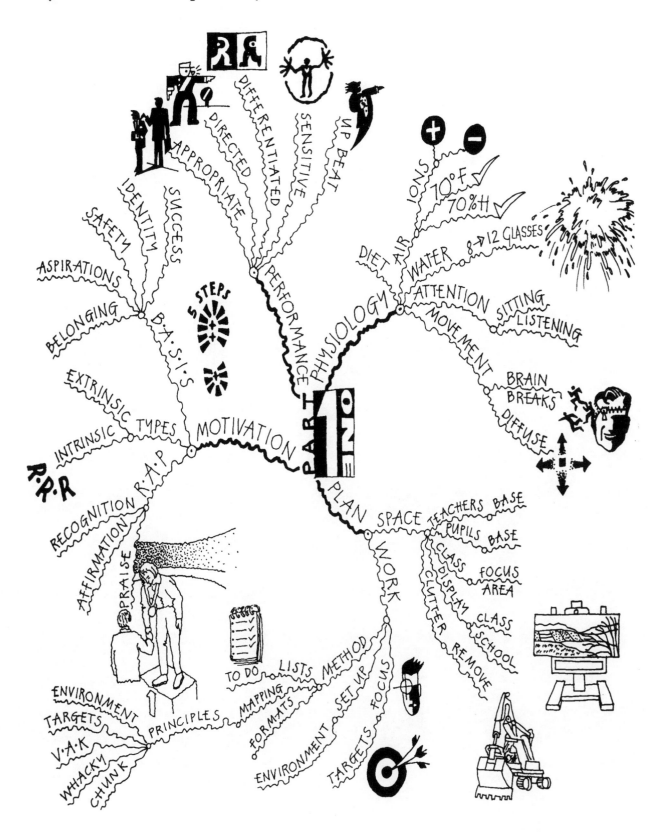

the alps approach – Accelerated Learning in Primary Schools

Preview of Part One

Establishing base camp

In part one you will:

learn about the physical aspects of learning.

find out how to build high expectations and have the learners exceed them.

find out about the five steps to building a 'base camp' for learning and the best use of classroom space.

learn about the RAP method of motivating for achievement.

be given twenty ways to keep learning positive in your classroom.

the alps approach – Accelerated Learning in Primary Schools

Establishing base camp

the alps approach – Accelerated Learning in Primary Schools

1 Preparing for a learning journey

Physiology and learning

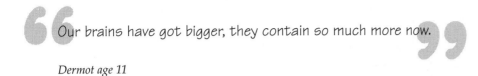

Our brains have got bigger, they contain so much more now.

Dermot age 11

IN THE ALPS CLASSROOM WE TRY TO ESTABLISH the optimal conditions for learning and maintain those optimal conditions.

The brain develops best in environments with high levels of sensory stimulation and sustained cognitive challenge. The ALPS teacher creates environments for learning with high levels of learning-related sensory stimulation. She encourages other colleagues, support assistants and parents to do the same. She makes learning interactive and rich in language exchange.

Along with cognitive challenge, the optimal conditions for learning must include a low-threat environment. The ALPS teacher makes it safe to take risks and to learn from those risks. She encourages positive interactions and ensures that children experience working in a variety of groups. Intellectual and social challenges will be unduly difficult for the children in your class if they are not in the best physical state for learning.

The psychologist Abraham Maslow developed what he called 'a hierarchy of needs' that must be met in succession in order to optimize human performance. Lower order needs in the hierarchy have to be met before someone can advance to higher order functioning. Let us look at this in terms of optimizing learning environments.

For Maslow the first order of needs concerned physical things such as food, clothing, shelter, sleep, exercise and physical comfort and space.

The child needs to be in the best physical state for learning. This may include a diet that is high in protein and trace minerals and low in carbohydrates. Research into diet progresses continually and teachers need to pay attention to the latest proven information and relate it to the children in their schools. Some schools have introduced breakfast clubs and mid-morning snacks to help in areas where children may not have an adequate diet. A London junior school described a ban on fizzy drinks and crisps as a significant contributory factor in its success in improving its league table position. Since the ban on unhealthy snacks and their replacement with fruit and purer drinks, the success rate in KS2 SATs tripled (*The Times*, 20 May 1999).

The optimal physical temperature should be near 70 degrees with a humidity level of near 70 per cent. If it is too hot or too cold, or if there is too much or too little humidity, then the child starts to experience stress. If the classroom becomes too hot and airless, then it is time to pause what you are doing and change the physical conditions or build in a brain break. Overheating causes a decrease in all-round performance in tasks requiring concentration, accuracy, physical dexterity and sensory acuity.

The more negatively charged the air in the classroom, the better. Higher levels of focused attention, mental functioning and cell replenishment are linked to better quality air. With emissions from smoke, dust, smog, pollutants, chemicals and heating systems the air becomes highly electrified with positive ions. Robert Ornstein (1997) reports that rats exposed to negative ionization grew a 9 per cent larger cerebral cortex. The ionization of the air affects neurotransmitters in the brain such as serotonin and can also alter electrical rhythms in the brain.

Maybe look on page 151 to find some ideas for brain breaks

Our brain is about 2.4 per cent of bodyweight. At rest it consumes 20 per cent of the energy in our system. The brain gets about 35 litres of blood each hour. It needs to be hydrated. Water provides the electrolyte balance for proper functioning. Dehydration leads to inattention, drowsiness and poor learning performance. The fluid-to-electrolyte balance in the body is adversely affected by dehydration and by some high-sugar drinks. A simple solution to dehydration is to have water available in the classroom and set up systems for children to drink when they are thirsty. We need 8–12 glasses of water a day for optimal functioning (Hannaford, 1995). Howard Kennedy's description of Holy Family Primary School (see pages 248–258) shows how attention to physical and environmental variables at whole-school level can be planned and sustained.

Our attention span tunes in and out naturally. There is a cycle that includes focused attention and peripheral attention and this can be internal or external, relaxed or vigilant. Teachers seek focused, external, vigilant attention although humans are not biologically well disposed to giving much of this. Some researchers suggest that humans have natural attentional highs and lows throughout the day, which occur in cycles of between 90 and 110 minutes: sixteen cycles of highs and lows within a 24-hour period. Further research points to the shift in our cognitive abilities between verbal and visual processing efficiency (Jensen, 1998b). The periods of alternating efficiency correlate with what is known as the 'basic rest–activity cycle' (BRAC). At some points we are better attuned to making sense of spoken communication and less of visual. As our verbal acuity declines so our visual acuity improves. The VAK (visual, auditory and kinesthetic) model described in Part Three explains how to match different types of input with the range of individual learning preferences and possible mismatched attentional cycles in your class.

At Brown University in the USA, Dr Mary Carskadon researched the internal sleep clocks of adolescents. She discovered that during these years the pineal gland, located in the limbic system, alters its clock and moves it forward. Teenagers had a physiological change that caused them to stay up later in the evenings, yet they were still required to get up at the same time for school. REM (rapid eye movement) sleep, a phase of brain activity that is essential for recovery and rest, was proportionately reduced from within the 3am to 7am essential slot. Teenagers who fall asleep in classrooms may be helped by a later start and finish at school. If this is not possible, Amrit's secondary school teachers need to at least pay attention to the suggestions in Part Two for regular brain breaks, before shaking him to wake him up!

Light and deep sleep patterns also follow the high and low arousal cycles that we experience during waking hours, with the brain shifting its cognitive processing on these cycles. With higher arousal cycles, blood flow and oxygen to the brain increases and contributes to our being alternately better at processing visual–spatial versus verbal information. At different points in this 90-minute cycle we are better at paying different types of attention. We are also better at different types of cognitive engagement. Be aware of the designated 'hour' slots for literacy or numeracy and consider how their timing impacts on the different highs and lows of attention in your class. Could they be shifted over the course of a year to different slots? The cycle of arousal also provides evidence to support an argument for using modes of assessment such as coursework, portfolios or project folders, which are built up over time.

In 1997, Cold Spring Harbor Institute researcher Dr Alcino Silva discovered the importance of 'downtime' in learning. Experiments with mice showed that their learning improved with short periods of rest during training sessions. Silva speculates that the brain uses this time to recycle CREB, a protein necessary for the formation of long-term memories. Regular physical breaks, which are coincident with opportunities for reflection or re-engaging, aid recall. These moments are called 'diffusions'.

For how much of any of these cycles can the teacher expect to be the exclusive point of a child's focused attention? As a general rule, the younger the learner, the less focused external and vigilant attention you can expect. So the answer is – not much! This does not mean that the child is not or cannot be learning in other physiological states. It means that teachers need to plan for attentional changes. The model that we recommend is

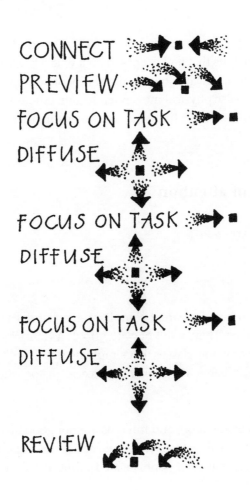

CONNECT

PREVIEW

FOCUS ON TASK

DIFFUSE

FOCUS ON TASK

DIFFUSE

FOCUS ON TASK

DIFFUSE

REVIEW

As a crude rule, we commend chunking down tasks into smaller or manageable units and allowing diffusions or 'downtime' where a different and additional form of learning takes place. The child stays engaged with learning but is perhaps allowed to do so through a different activity. This is explained in full in Part Three.

Studies by Thayer in 1989 suggested that short, brisk activity increases energy levels. If Nisha went to bed at 9pm and woke at 7am, then her energy level will be at its lowest at 2pm. It is therefore essential that you build movement into your teaching, especially in the afternoon sessions. According to 1996 research by Pollatscheck and Hagen,

> Children engaged in daily physical education show superior motor fitness, academic performance and attitude toward school as compared to their counterparts who do not participate in daily physical education.

Pollatscheck and Hagen, 1996, cited in Eric Jensen, 1998a

We need to move. That is why we have brains. Trees do not have brains: they do not need brains. They do not need to move! To avoid turning your class into trees, and possibly even into dead wood, build in physical breaks. During these 'brain breaks' do some concentrated physical activities that involve controlled cross-lateral movements. Each diffusion activity is a chance for two or three minutes stretching or an energizing activity, which will release natural neural growth factors in the brain. Watch the motivation, energy levels and subsequent focused attention skyrocket.

In 1996, University of California at Irvine researchers (Brainwork, 1996) discovered that exercise may be the best brain food. Rats that had exercised on a wheel had elevated expression of BDGF (brain-derived growth factor), which enhances the ability of neurons to connect with another. In Part Two we discuss how to use physical movement to gain attention, maintain attention and re-gain attention in your classroom. But first you need to ensure that children in your class know how to pay attention.

Teaching the skills of attention

> Alistair, what are you doing?
> Thinking, Miss.
> Well stop thinking and start listening! Pay attention!

How many times have you heard a parent complain: 'He just does not listen to me' or 'I wish that she would just sit still' or 'They won't pay attention!' As a teacher, you probably hear many complaints about children or whole classes that simply do not sit and listen. A quiet child is often seen as a good child, and a baby who uses his voice is all too often plugged swiftly with a dummy.

There are different modes of attention, and humans are not good at staying in one for extended periods of time. Despite this reality, teachers often seek a particular form of attention when in fact this is difficult even for the most sophisticated adult audience. Think about an occasion when you have attended a long and intensive teacher training session. Have you honestly ever concentrated through a complete session, without your mind wandering occasionally to dinner plans, or to think of the coming weekend or holiday? It is the same for the children in your class. However brilliant your teaching, at times their thoughts will naturally stray to the next netball match, or Nisha's coming birthday party.

Attention can be focused or diffused. It can be given to a specified and narrowly defined range of activity, or it can span over a number of stimuli. Attention can be directed – 'now watch this' – or dispersed. It can be internal or external – 'pay attention to me when I'm talking'. It can be vigilant or relaxed. All of us tune in and out on natural cycles that are partly dictated by our level of perceived interest in the stimuli that confronts us. Downtime or 'processing' time, when we internalize attention, is also important to learning. Diffusion activities aid learning by creating a space for such processing.

Focused, directed, external, vigilant attention needs to be taught. Listening and sitting are attention skills that need to be learned just as reading or writing. It is part of our role as teachers to help children learn to sit and listen, not simply to stay still and hear. Hearing is not the same as listening. Remaining still is not the same as sitting.

Some people are more effective learners when a lesson is presented in aural format, while others prefer one of the two other styles, visual or kinesthetic. However, all children need to be able to sit and listen effectively when it is necessary to do so. The ALPS teacher takes the time to teach 'good sitting' and 'good listening' and to reinforce this learning regularly. She does this right up to the top junior years, when children sometimes become adept at appearing to listen, while in reality they are merely hearing. Listening involves thinking; hearing simply requires you to be in the same room as the speaker!

With the very youngest pupils, even Nursery pupils, you can begin by referring to listening effectively as 'doing good listening' and sitting attentively as 'doing good sitting'. This was something that we observed being used extremely effectively by a speech and language therapist working with a group of special needs pupils. The talk of the adults in the room was strictly positive and clear. Instructions were given concisely and consistently.

> That's good sitting Sarah. You are crossing your legs, well done!
>
> Daniel is doing good listening. He is looking at me and concentrating.
>
> Kirsty, please do good listening. Look at me, hands in lap – super. Now I'll begin the story.

The principles of 'good sitting' were taught explicitly and displayed in pictorial cartoons on the wall, just above eye level. Children practised 'doing good sitting' for short periods daily, in addition to being reminded of the rules at every sitting activity. In the same way, 'doing good listening' was taught and continually reinforced. All the children could tell us the rules for both 'good sitting' and 'good listening'. They had heard the rules, seen the rules and kinesthetically practised following the rules. These were the speech and language therapist's rules for 'good sitting' and 'good listening':

To do good sitting on the carpet yo[
   Put your bottom on the carpet
Face the front
   Cross your legs
Put your hands in your lap

To do good sitting on a chair you must:
   Put your bottom on the chair
Face the front
   Keep all four chair legs on the floor
Pull the chair in to the desk

To do good listening you must:
   Keep your hands still
Look at the speaker
   Hear what is said
Think about it

This work of teaching listening skills can be applied to all children in mainstream classrooms. Do not assume that children have an inherent skill to listen and that any failure to do so is through choice. All children need to be taught how to listen. Listening in a room of thirty peers is different to listening to a parent on a one-to-one basis. While Nisha's parents may have taught her to listen without being conscious that they did so, Annie's parents may not have been so successful. She needed her teacher to teach her these skills in Reception class, and still needs some reinforcement now. If you wish to accelerate your pupils' learning, teach them how to sit and listen effectively, rather than leave it to chance that these skills will develop.

One teacher we observed taught listening skills by turning himself into the slider controls of a stereo amplifier, so that when he moved his right hand down, the right half of the class progressively went quieter. When he moved his left hand down, the left half of the class quietened. He practised with the class turning the volume up and down.

Another method for teaching listening skills is to have a large clock face prominent at the front of the room with different types of activities described on it: listening (silence), paired discussion (quiet talking), pole-bridging (murmuring your thoughts), and so on. The teacher turns the clock face to the activity and thus the noise level that she wants.

In a Year 6 classroom a group of children talked to us about listening and their preferred methods of learning. Some knew that listening was a skill that they still needed to develop, while others knew that listening was one of their strengths. They had all developed such self-awareness that they monitored their own performance. They had been taught techniques to help them maximize their learning when the teacher's style did not suit their own individual style. This is an extract from a conversation that we recorded:

Eric: I'm a hearing sort of person, I remember things when people tell me rather than reading it. I like it when the lesson is one where the teacher talks, because the information is clear to me.

Claudine: I prefer seeing because if I look at something and read about it, the learning really sinks in. I like it when my teacher puts diagrams on the board.

Heather: I'm a seeing person, although I like doing as well. I know that when the teacher does something that requires listening, I need to listen really carefully. I know that this way I still won't learn quite as much, but the teacher then teaches the same thing later using seeing or doing, so I try hard but I don't worry about it, because when it comes to seeing it I'll understand it properly.

James: Sometimes I know that one part of the lesson is not my best way but I try to get better at it.

Whitney: I find it easier if I take notes during a listening session because I like to see things as well as hear them.

Antony: Yes that's what I do. I listen for the key points and I put them down as she talks. Some people don't do that because they prefer to just listen. Later I make my key points into sentences but while she talks I just write the key points, in one or two words. I learned to do this from accelerated learning.

The ALPS teacher ensures that each child has the skills to listen. She recognizes that each individual will have a preferred method of learning, but she ensures that all the tools for learning are supplied through direct teaching of such skills. She teaches the skills of sitting and listening, and she organizes the classroom environment in a way that is conducive for learning.

Using the space provided

The average five year old in the UK spends five hours a day in the classroom. That is twenty-five hours a week, thirty-eight weeks per year. That makes a total of 950 hours per year. The average time spent watching television is 11 hours 45 minutes a week, six times longer than is spent reading.

Between the ages of 5 and 16 a pupil will spend 15 per cent of their lives in school. It is not a lot, but it is a significant chunk of time and can place a responsibility upon you, the classroom teacher, to utilize your classroom to create only positive experiences. Overleaf are five steps that will help you create a positive 'base camp' for your pupils.

In order to follow the principles of the ALPS method™, you need to create a secure environment within which your pupils can work. You then need to create space in which they can move freely whenever necessary and a base for yourself that ensures that you are accessible to your pupils. Remember that you are the leader and your team need to know how and when to find you.

Five steps to creating a 'base camp'

The five steps needed to create your base camp are:

✓ One: create a base for each pupil – ensure that they have their own recognised space.

✓ Two: create your own personal base – demarcate your space and the protocols for pupils to access it.

✓ Three: create a focus area around the board – around the board becomes a place for a special sort of learning.

✓ Four: clear out the clutter – get rid of rubbish that does not enhance learning.

✓ Five: organize the space that you have created – use different spaces for different activities.

And in detail as follows:

Step One: create a base for each pupil

As humans we act by habit. We all like our own personal space, and we adapt our environment to meet our perceived needs. Think of your staffroom. If you went in there at any time, would you know who to find in which area? Do people have their favourite areas, chairs or mugs? Many of us were warned as student teachers never to sit down in a staffroom until all others were seated! Think of this as you lay out your classroom, then take it one step further and create name labels for each desk, even for the oldest junior class. Make no mistake, even Year 6 pupils will welcome the feeling of having a specific, secure place at base camp. Each child will create his own personal comfort zone around this seat. This is the place where he should sit for most of the day and for all sessions that are emotionally challenging. Of course, if you organize groups for ability in maths or any other subject, you need to move children around, but try to create specific bases whenever possible. The adrenaline created by unfamiliar seating and social interactions for key lessons will only act as a block upon learning.

It is important for children to learn to socialize and work in different groups, but when you move them around, be direct with them about your reasons and give them the Big Picture. We discuss different group-work strategies in Part Three. Some teachers give children individual name cards to put on their desks when they move to different places, or try to ensure that they usually use the same seat for maths or science when the class moves around. Never underestimate the power of forward planning for children. If you had to teach in a different way tomorrow, would you not prefer to know in advance? A teacher we interviewed commented on this:

I taught one boy in Year 6 who decided for a few weeks that he would be better to take his work outside the classroom whenever the class was grouped in friendship groups. He could play happily on the playground, but, at that point, he could not co-operate with his peers in the classroom. He recognized his own emotional state at the time and that this was causing a block to his learning. He worked independently for a few weeks, and then was able to rejoin the class and co-operate happily.

Step Two: create your own personal base

You need a personal base within base camp for yourself. Your pupils need to know that this is where they can find you and what your expectations are about them seeking you there. Make rules about your personal base: how long you expect pupils to wait there, what you expect them to do before seeking your attention, and what they are allowed to fetch and organize for themselves. Encourage independence, but be specific about your expectations. Display your expectations so that there is no mystery.

Also, remember that what you put on and around your base tells your pupils all about you. Do your pupils know your family is important to you? Pictures of your family, a photograph of your parents or your partner give unspoken messages to children: 'People matter to me'. A photograph of you, or your daughter or son, at graduation gives a clear message: 'Education is important to me.' These two messages contribute to one very important principle: 'You, my pupils, and your success, are important to me.'

The more secure you are about your own teaching, the more willing you will become for your pupils to know you, to respect your own personal feelings and aspirations, and to feel a bond with you that will never be forgotten. The influence that a teacher can have is phenomenal and should never be underestimated or taken lightly. Do you remember a special teacher from your own life? Take a moment to think about what was actually special about that person. Give your pupils a direct message that you care for them and they will amaze you with their response!

Step Three: create a focus area around the board

When you become aware of the importance of VAK (visual, auditory and kinesthetic) in every lesson that you teach, you will also become aware of the importance of a focus area for pupils to expect to see you and to expect you to give visual stimulus.

Refer to page 190 for more about VAK

A whiteboard or blackboard is ideal, but you also need a stack of resources nearby: pens and chalks of differing colours, a selection of cards with large, bold coloured pens and vast amounts of blu-tac become essential to the accelerated learning teacher. Try to create space in front of the board, because active participation is another key principle and children ideally need to be able to stand in groups around the board. Somewhere near the board and your own base, you need to keep your cassette or CD player and supply of music and relaxation tapes.

Step Four: clear out the clutter!

Think about the furniture and equipment in your classroom. How much of it is actually used on a regular basis? When we ask this question of teachers, it is remarkable how much furniture and equipment is not really needed in each classroom. Much of it can be centrally stored, creating space for active learning in the classroom. Clear out the clutter, and label everything clearly. Insist on tidiness at the end of each session. An orderly environment leads to a focus on learning. Tidiness gives a message that the base camp is important and valued.

Step Five: organize the space that you have created

As all your lessons will now include some movement out of seats, if only for regular brain breaks, you need to create space around each table. However you seat children, in groups, pairs or singly, ensure that there is enough room for each child to get out of her seat, stretch, turn around and take a step forward or back. Obviously, the more room you create around each seat, the more adventurous your brain breaks and kinesthetic activities can be. When every pupil knows the rules for moving around the room, and has her own personal space within it, you can create the right atmosphere for learning.

We have seen imaginative use of space in many of the classrooms that we have visited around the country. Many have been organized with 'learning centres' arranged around different 'intelligences'. There was a site for work to do with nature and the environment, another for music, another for sharing activities such as circle time and story-telling, and another for quiet reading or work in silence, art and so on. Another school classroom that we came across had different zones:

Z 'Come on in' zone: a space where pupils can store personal belongings to create a positive feel – plants, artwork, today's schedule, lists of achievements.

Z 'Busy' zone: a number of spaces that adapt for whole or small group-work and may have learning 'islands' organized by the type of work that happens there.

Z 'What's new' zone: items of topical interest, photographs, messages, cards, today's birthdays.

Z 'Homework' zone: an area for children to display the work they have undertaken at home.

Z 'Library' zone: classroom reference materials.

Z 'Soft, safe and stretch' zone: an area for sitting and working together, free of desks for story-telling, circle time.

Z 'Moving and learning' zone: for energizing activities including dance, drama and role play.

The space you work in is yours. It should say something to your pupils about how you value them and their learning.

The school environment

We have highlighted the need in classrooms to clear out the clutter that all teachers tend to gather around them as they teach, and we now need to think about how to organize the materials that are left. In our visits to schools, we have seen a wide variety of classroom arrangements, each reflecting the personalities of the teachers who organize them. It is important to take time to look critically at classrooms and think: 'What subliminal messages, intentional or unintentional, is this classroom giving about education?' Then schools need to think beyond the classroom, to consider the wider school environment.

One school started work on their Teaching and Learning policy simply by analysing the book areas around the school. This generated discussion about their beliefs and values that then could be applied to larger issues. They wanted to ensure that the message given to children was that books were exciting, accessible and to be enjoyed by all. At that time, many reading areas were dull and full of uninspiring, old books. By the end of the project, the staff had planned a new school library and had created a list of practical requirements for all classroom book corners:

Each area must have a carpeted area.

Each area must have at least two comfortable seats or cushions.

At least one rack of books must face with the cover outwards.

All torn and tatty books must be discarded.

All out-of-date books must be discarded.

Children must be actively taught how to return books tidily.

Two boxes of books must be exchanged in the library each half-term.

Books must be sorted and sections labelled; for example, by author, subject, genre.

Children must be taught to sort books and understand these categories.

The categories must change at least once per half-term.

The area must have colourful displays of posters encouraging reading.

Children must have access to materials to make their own books and display them.

All teachers must keep an inventory of basic stock.

All teachers must create an ongoing list of desirable books.

The next step was to create a 'wish list' and cost it. Targets were set for both financial and time commitments. The 'wish list' was ambitious and exciting and, once it was created, staff began to think of ways to fulfil it.

Teachers need to seize every opportunity to challenge children's thinking and utilize their time in school. This means that they must consider the use of the entire school environment. Some schools reserve only areas such as the entrance hall for the traditional display of children's work, while in areas where children regularly work and sit, the wall space is used to challenge, remind and inform. One Reception teacher we saw used the corridor ceiling for the display of the letters that she was teaching using Jolly Phonics. The children looked up at the letters as they went to assembly, while another teacher displayed keywords from the reading scheme in the same way, which children read as they walked along. She set challenges for her class such as: 'Count the number of cards with the word "said" on the way to lunch.' In other schools, positive messages about achievement and behaviour are posted around the building to create a shared feeling of recognition and success.

It is essential that the subliminal messages given to children by the environment within the school are positive and show that learning is valued. You can work from any starting point: book corners, outdoor areas, corridors or the cloakrooms. Focus on one or many areas, but work until every aspect of your school environment is portraying only positive messages – including the staffroom.

Designing your day

Teachers are always under immense pressure to meet all the demands upon their time. It is essential that they take time to prioritize tasks and organize their time effectively. Here are some suggestions of ways to utilize your time effectively. These are five habits of effective time managers:

1   Use a 'To Do list'. A To Do list is a regularly updated visual schedule for reminding you of priorities. Use a termly, weekly, daily cycle, with the latter being more of a prompt sheet.

2   Prioritize your list using the ABC123 method: A must be done, B ought to be done, C could be done, and put the tasks in order within each category. Stick to the priorities.

3   Use the Pareto principle to decide which are 'As'. The principle says that 80 per cent of your time is consumed by 20 per cent of your responsibilities. So, for example, 20 per cent of the children could consume 80 per cent of your time – if you allow them. Choose the 20 per cent of activities that will give you the 80 per cent of return: the essential one-in-five things.

4   Be aware of your own energy levels and do any planning activity when they are at their highest.

5   Use the 3-Dplus method. The three 'Ds' are: do, delegate or dump. They are labelled 'plus' because they are positive interventions rather than 3-Dminus: delay, defer or displace. Delaying, deferring or displacing are all good avoidance techniques.

It is clear that effective planning is essential if teachers are to meet the demands of the modern classroom. Lesson planning is one of the most important aspects of the teacher's role. A badly planned lesson is a bad lesson. So how can the ALPS method™ help you to plan your lessons more effectively?

Lesson planning in the ALPS

Planning for the ALPS classroom should not be more time consuming than any other method – if anything, it should take you less time. What we offer is simply an approach to teaching that takes into account current knowledge about learning. The method is intended to be creative yet simple and logical. All teachers are busy meeting the demands of the modern classroom and need to manage their time effectively. We certainly do not want to create more paperwork!

The ALPS method™ of teaching demands that your planning is highly creative. Many planning formats are tightly structured but do not lend themselves to creative thought. However, it is possible to incorporate the ALPS approach into existing planning systems. A few simple additions mean that any lesson-planning sheet can become meaningful to the ALPS teacher.

It is possible to find a balance between creativity and the demands of your school planning systems by memory mapping your lesson plan before transferring the information to a planning sheet. Memory mapping the initial lesson plan enables you to be creative and to see connections to other lessons. Creating a memory map should not be time consuming. A memory map is written swiftly. It uses symbols, keywords and codes. It only has to be meaningful to its writer, and it certainly does not have to be neat! Once teachers have developed memory-mapping skills, they have found that the planning process becomes quicker and more effective.

Memory mapping your lesson plan is a creative activity that will prove to be rewarding and satisfying. There are a few principles to follow as you do this activity. These are:

1 Create the right environment in which to work. It is important to ensure that you are in the best psychological and physiological state to work effectively. Planning when you are tired or distracted will not be effective. This is one of the most important aspects of a teacher's job, and she should give it her full attention. You might wish to use the music lists on pages 167–171 to select some music that will help the ideas to flow. If you plan in groups or pairs, utilize the power of multiple brains!

2 Plan to meet targets. You will find in Part Two an ALPS model for target-setting. You will need these targets beside you as you plan. There is little point in planning if you do not have goals and targets to work towards. If you plan in your classroom, you may find it easier to recall those targets as you work. If you plan at home, you should spend a few minutes reading through your class target cards before you begin. As you create your memory map, you will now be conscious of these targets, and ideas will develop to ensure that you achieve them. Our system of RAP will help you motivate your pupils and achieve your goals.

Try page 86 for more about RAP

3 Think VAK. Imagine ways that you can present a concept visually or teach facts aurally. It is often possible to learn kinesthetically by role play. Think of a way that children can act out the content of a lesson. Can they pretend to be Queen Victoria? How did she walk? How did she hold her head? How did it feel to be her? If you have felt how Queen Victoria felt, you will gain a greater concept of her history, and you will feel more motivated to learn more about her. Think of the posters that will help visual learners and the practical activities for kinesthetic learning.

4 Think whacky. If key facts need to be learned, think of slightly absurd ways of teaching them and installing them in memory. Children remember things that have something unusual in the way that they were taught. Think of music that can be used to learn facts, of key letters that can make acronyms, or of visual images that can aid memory. For example, in one science lesson the teacher had a giant 'thumbs-up' fist that she had bought at a sports event. When she turned it to thumbs-up, the class stood up and chanted 'UP WITH EVAPORATION' but when it was thumbs-down, they sat down and chanted 'DOWN WITH CONDENSATION!' Using this method, important science vocabulary was taught in a way that would certainly not be forgotten! On this teacher's memory map, she had drawn a fist with the word EVAPORATION.

5 Plan for brain breaks. We discuss how to create brain breaks in Part Two. We also know that it is sometimes difficult to think of a brain break activity during a lesson, so we recommend that at first you plan for them. Include them on your memory map. You may introduce a new brain break activity in a lesson, or you may re-use a part of a previous lesson. The thumbs-up whacky activity above became a brain break activity for the next few days. All that the teacher needed to do was glance at her memory map when her class was drifting off task. Rather than use sixty seconds asking them to refocus their attention, she used sixty seconds to refocus and to reinforce learning.

Once you have created your memory map, you will need to organize the information onto a planning format. Some schools have adapted their formats to accommodate the principles of VAK, brain breaks and the multiple intelligences. Some have created planning documents from the accelerated learning cycle. Others have found that simply adding the initials VAK or the multiple intelligences as a checklist can ensure monitoring of the delivery of their lessons. Many teachers have created a section for brain break activities on their lesson planning documents. We saw one teacher who had a brain break menu on the wall, so that whenever the class needed a break they could choose an activity from the menu.

Teachers who have developed this flexible approach to planning have found that the process of transferring information from memory maps to school documents is straightforward:

> I used to struggle to think of what to write on planning documents. It was a real chore. I often felt helpless and that I lacked imagination. When I discovered memory mapping I rediscovered my creativity. I can memory map my lessons easily, in a lively way, and it is no longer a chore. I have no difficulty translating this information then into any school format.

Year 4 ALPS teacher

After the lesson has ended, your memory map should not be discarded. Memory mapping helps you be creative and see links between concepts. Your memory map should grow and build up. Your next lesson can be planned on that same memory map. Use colours to highlight the items that have been covered, add new ideas, incorporate new targets, and lead into the next lesson with a more detailed memory map. As you teach, add to the memory map as ideas occur to you. Later, simply translate this information onto school formats. An outsider can read the planning sheet and see what is planned, but you can work from your own creative memory map and add to it as your lessons progress. Continue in this way until a whole subject area has been covered, and then use the memory map as a personal record of what has been learned.

Diana, a Year 2 teacher, always found it easier to deliver a fast-paced and ambitious lesson if her original memory map was pinned at eye level throughout the lesson. Often the memory map would continue to develop over several weeks as she saw further possibilities after each lesson. She added ideas about how to help children to reach individual targets to the map, which was a vibrant working document. The information from the memory map became a record of what had been taught and the connections that had been made. The essential point is that the process of memory mapping enabled her to be creative and ambitious. In her school, teachers worked in pairs to plan their lessons. This is what a younger teacher who worked alongside Diana said about this method of planning:

> Before, I would plod along using the school's existing scheme of 'boxed' planning – a non-creative form which, to my mind, didn't seem to allow for any imagination or free thinking.
>
> At first, I found planning with her was a nightmare. I found that pinning her down was fairly impossible as mentioning the 'P' word would throw up a 'rigid system' wall in her brain; it seemed to block her creativity. I used to read categories from the planning sheet to her, but she seemed stifled by the structure.
>
> After a while, Diana would wander around the classroom, not looking at the planning sheet, but simply talking about one idea, then another. I'd be sitting, trying to fit her ideas into the boxes, until she'd start to write keywords on the whiteboard, hitting upon one amazing idea after another, and I'd have to screw up the paper and start again. Then I realized that if I went along with her and memory mapped the ideas, later I could fit them into the boxes.
>
> Memory mapping was the only obvious way!

Memory mapping was used extensively in this school as a tool for assessment and for connecting concepts. Another teacher recalls a memory-mapping session with her class:

the alps approach – Accelerated Learning in Primary Schools

One of the most remarkable moments in my teaching career was when I was teaching photosynthesis with my Year 6 class. We memory mapped our understanding on the whiteboard. Each child came up and took a pen, adding a keyword or symbol to the memory map and talked his or her thoughts aloud. Our memory map grew and grew as we saw the connections between photosynthesis and the work that we had done – rain forests, the ozone layer, respiration, habitats, the human body, smoking, digestion, the water cycle, the planets, the elements, the periodic table, and so on. By the end of the afternoon we had a memory map that represented to us the wonder of the universe. One of the children commented: 'This is so amazing, who made it work so well, and why does Man try to destroy it?' Connections had been made that had never occurred to me. It was so exciting, a time of revelation. The power of memory mapping became so clear to me. I could see where other connections could be made for future learning and that nothing needed to be learned in isolation.

If you are creative in your planning, you can transfer the information into any format. The layout of a school's planning documents is a matter of individual choice, but the process of memory mapping allows each individual teacher to draw upon her creativity and plan how she will deliver a lesson that is based on the ALPS principles of learning. If you wish to teach the ALPS way, you need to plan for the essential elements such as VAK and brain breaks. With the powerful tool of memory mapping, you will find that you can quickly and easily plan exciting, ambitious lessons that will help you accelerate the learning of the children in your class.

❷ Exceeding expectations

Our motivational model

HOW DOES OUR METHOD FIT IN WITH THE ENDLESS DEBATE about what constitutes an acceptable or desirable school discipline policy? As we wrote this book this debate emerged as significant to the ALPS model. We had shared concerns about the preponderance of models of discipline and reward that emphasize targets, tick marks, stages of reprisal and chains of consequence. Such schemes did not fit philosophically with what we believed, namely that extrinsic motivation, however carefully defined and ring-fenced with caveats, does not advantage the lifelong learner. Instead we believe that it can create a chain of dependency that leads to less resilience, resourcefulness and responsibility – our new three Rs.

Alistair initiated a discussion with Nicola by emailing her in San Francisco and asking her to consider some of the research and reflect on it in the light of her experience. Here is her reply.

Alistair, here are my thoughts re: intrinsic/extrinsic motivation

I believe that there is a shift in orientation between intrinsic and extrinsic motivation as children progress through school. It would seem to me that the gradual shift through the primary age range is due to a combination of factors such as experiences with different teachers, a growing awareness of external factors such as ability levels within the class, and parental and external influences. It is not really surprising that this shift becomes most significant between Years 6 and 7. The causes are quite probably a combination of adolescence, peer pressure, a move to a new school and social group, a focus on streaming and grading, and the difference between primary and secondary schools.

I believe that it is the job of the primary teacher to send each child on to secondary school with every possible advantage that will help him or her to withstand the different experiences that he or she will encounter, in particular the possible feelings of anonymity and lack of personal teacher interest. The ideal is to have developed strong intrinsic motivation. Many children will need a considerable input in order to become intrinsically motivated, as they may have lost intrinsic motivation very early in their school life. Can a system of reward and recognition help to develop intrinsic motivation?

It is interesting that all the children whom I interviewed regarding reward systems agreed that the specific reward is not important, it is the recognition and approval that comes with the reward. Class approval rated highly, as did teacher approval, and going home to tell your parents. Harter (1996) found that 'classmate support correlates most highly with self-esteem. Parents' support follows closely. Teacher approval also correlates significantly, reflecting the importance of teacher support to child and adolescent self-esteem'.

In a study of children progressing from Year 6 to Year 7, Harter found that the significant factor in whether children gained or lost intrinsic motivation was whether or not they felt that they were intelligent. 'Increases in perceived competence were associated with increases in intrinsic motivation, decreases in perceived competence predicted declines in intrinsic motivation.' The factors that made the pupils feel academically competent or incompetent were: grades, competition, control, choice, lack of personal interest in pupils, social comparison, boring/irrelevant work, and feeling stupid.

It seems to me that the problem with grades and competition in secondary school is usually the misuse of them. However, we need to be careful to stress the positive use of grades and competition in ALPS to avoid misinterpretation. I see grades, competition, rewards and recognition as tools for raising the child's perception of himself as academically competent. I think that this is why my pupils were so successful. Through these methods I developed a self-belief in each child that he or she was clever, which in turn developed strong intrinsic motivation, so that the learning itself became the motivator, if it wasn't already. I don't believe that children who were already intrinsically motivated lost that motivation because I used these systems. I believe that they became increasingly motivated because the systems were used to increase thirst for learning. Once you get to Year 6 you are battling against peer pressure as adolescence approaches, so you sometimes have to be more explicit in your systems. Affirmation and life mapping are vital components, as are praise and celebration. I see all this as a package that maintains intrinsic motivation where it may otherwise have declined, or creates it where it has already diminished.

It is interesting that the rewards that work best are the whacky ones that everybody wants to gain so that they get recognition. (I think Dinesh said that – 'you want the class to clap and you want to tell your mum'.) Yet the class are motivated by anyone gaining the whacky reward – in the right climate it is a shared celebration. Everybody is recognized frequently as they reach goals. It is the same with the humour of the Brain Box, which is full of stupid items. Getting to choose from the Brain Box is making a statement that a pupil is clever. Hence the success of the Brain Box approach is that there is a shared joke. It is the social thing, the humour, and the novelty that counts. It is essential that the reward is tied in with target-setting – it acknowledges that you have met a target, it celebrates it, there is a moment of public recognition, you have something clear to show that you did it, to say that you are academically competent.

Look on page 89 to learn about the Brain Box

The trouble with grades is that an E says that you did not achieve as highly as an A. Grades and competition can be used positively, but are also open to being misused. I believe that the teacher needs to make positive statements about intelligence in as many ways as is possible. If a child is Maths Superbrain five times, she has solid proof that she is good at maths. This personal perception leads to high self-esteem that leads to more success, which in turn leads to intrinsic motivation. It seems that children who begin secondary school believing that they are academically competent are more likely to maintain intrinsic motivation. It is difficult to say which comes first, motivation or competence.

If research shows that intrinsic motivation and self-belief in one's own academic competence decreases rapidly from Year 6 to Year 7, perhaps RAP along with target-setting and positive feedback can halt that decline. With self-esteem comes motivation, and I feel that reward can contribute to a building of positive self-image. I agree that 'Recognition' is more relevant as a label than 'Reward'. I am also aware that my kids were amongst the lowest in motivation and self-esteem, and therefore needed more explicit techniques than maybe some other types of schools. However, it has always seemed to me that teachers rarely praise enough or effectively. Approval of significant others is a highly charged motivator, and teachers often fail to recognise this. I find it interesting that classmates are the most important 'significant other' to children – hence the success of class recognition and celebration.

My perspective was that children may in the first instance behave and study in a certain way to gain my approval, but that this extrinsic motivation would become intrinsic as the success and joy of learning became a motivator in itself. By the time the class left for secondary school, I had maximized their perception of themselves as academically competent, and had hopefully developed enough intrinsic motivation to withstand the onslaught of their secondary experience. With some children it lasted, whereas the pressure on others was strong enough to alter their self-perception and presumably alter their motivational orientation. With children like Shaun, a lucky encounter with his form tutor re-established the work that I had done, through setting targets and showing a personal interest in him. It is interesting to me that he used to constantly say that he was 'thick' and that school was 'boring' yet now is highly motivated at his new High School – this came across in his interview as strongly intrinsic.

I agree that we need to think this all through very carefully and that we must not lay ourselves open to misinterpretation. It is a huge area for debate. Hope my ramblings make sense! I'm sure that we can find a way through that will work!

Nicola

We decided to include this email in full because it summarizes best the position we advocate via the ALPS method™. Our discussion as co-authors and educationalists led us to one conclusion: that teachers need to be acutely aware of the purpose of any extrinsic methods that they use for motivating their students and have a clear rationale about how they foster intrinsic motivation.

Fostering the 'can do' attitude

The ALPS teacher builds a classroom characterized by learners with 'can do' attitudes derived in part from the BASIS model of building and maintaining positive self-esteem. On top of that she uses a positive feedback loop, called RAP, which engages learners individually and allows them to progress against targets.

BASIS = Belonging, Aspirations, Safety, Identity, Success. Turn to page 79 to discover more. For RAP turn to page 86.

At the same time it is important for teachers to remember the longer-term aspirations that they have for children. In our model it is articulated through 'the new three Rs': resilience, responsibility and resourcefulness. When the teacher holds the longer-term aspiration in sight and has motivational tools and flexibility in how she uses them, she has a powerful model.

Our motivational tools operate along a continuum defined by the degree to which they are externally or intrinsically motivating. With some children you may begin with a situation that requires a heavy extrinsic emphasis but you should not want to stay there. A child may need tangible rewards for staying on task while in Reception class, and may need reinforcement during Years 1 to 6. But if he reaches secondary school and is only motivated by vouchers for attending classes, you have not helped him to develop intrinsic motivation. You have simply bribed him.

As the ALPS teacher advances on the learning journey, she aims to increase the autonomy and intrinsic motivation of her team of learners. Here is how one teacher wrote to us and described her experience of such a journey. We have re-named the 8 year old that she describes as Danah.

Danah moved to our school at the start of Year 4. She had attended several other schools and had a record of non-attendance. Intervention from various agencies had failed, and her mother described her daughter as 'school phobic'. On her first day Danah crawled around the office for over an hour, screaming and yelling. She clung to her mother, who needed strong persuasion to leave. This was clearly a habit of some years. Her mother mentioned that Monday mornings were always the worst, as Danah feared having to read to her teacher and do a spelling test.

Information from screening and test results showed that Danah had high IQ scores, but quite possibly a specific learning difficulty. She liked to be withdrawn from class, and so would be disruptive in order to be removed. Once she reached the classroom, she spent the day under the desk unravelling paper clips. By the end of the day she had copied just three letters 'M-o-n' from the date on the board and had not spoken a word.

The obstacles that blocked Danah's way were removed. Danah's anxiety would build the minute that she arrived on the playground. Her mother agreed to walk to school with another child in the class, and deliver both girls to the classroom to do jobs for the teacher. When the other children came into school, Danah and her new friend would leave the class and visit the office, where she would put a sticker on a weekly chart for 'coming to school'. How Danah came to school was immaterial, and whether she screamed, kicked or yelled, she earned a sticker for being there. At the end of the week, she could choose a reward. Danah chose to visit the local newsagent with one of the classroom assistants to choose a chocolate bar to share with her friend.

Danah's academic targets were intentionally simple and designed to reduce stress. Every activity that she was asked to do only involved copying, followed by a practical activity that she did not associate with 'learning'. Every piece of copying that Danah completed was reinforced with intensive RAP. Her sticker charts were placed on her desk, she gained continual rewards for just sitting and copying words from a worksheet. The focus was on putting pencil to paper, not on the content. When she was called to read to the teacher, the teacher read to her. She was given free choice of books from the library, not a reading scheme book.

Obstacles were simply removed and Danah's day was designed to avoid situations that she found stressful, while ensuring that she watched the other children do the activities that she found challenging before being asked to participate. For example, Danah would not go to PE, because she was anxious about getting changed. The teacher arranged for her to take off just her shoes and socks. She would not attempt written maths, so she took part in practical activities, then copied sums with the answers already worked out into an exercise book. During spelling tests, her task was to recognize her words on flashcards, then copy them into her book. If she recognized them all, she achieved 100 per cent. At breaktimes she could stay in with a friend to tidy the book corner and read by the window. She went to watch swimming lessons. When the class lined up to go to assembly, Danah would go with a friend to take the register to the office and join the class in the hall. As Danah participated in this programme, each step was directly rewarded. Star charts, certificates, smiley faces, stamps, handshakes, pats on the back and hugs were continually part of Danah's school diet, and she responded dramatically.

Within six weeks, Danah overcame her difficulties with school routines. She asked for a reading book. She chose to change into her PE kit for lessons and she joined the class in the swimming pool. She went out to play at breaktime. She said that she no longer wanted to have a sticker chart and rewards for coming into school. She went onto the playground in the mornings. She lined up with the class, and began to write her spellings before she copied them. Once Danah's emotional obstacles had been removed, she began to learn. She became receptive and co-operative, and special needs intervention became effective. Her attendance for that term was 100 per cent. The greatest sign that Danah had overcome her 'school phobia' was when she began to smile.

This is how Danah recalls her first term at her new school:

'I remember when I had a sticker chart and I went to get sweets if I came to school. I liked to come to the office to visit and get my stickers. I liked it when you told me to smile! I liked it when you told me I was pretty. I liked it when I read to Mrs Jones because I am a good reader. I liked it when I could read 'The Meanies' on my own. I like doing my spellings and when I get clapped for getting 100 per cent. I remember when I filled my book with sums and everybody cheered!'

When considering Danah's story, one can see that the ALPS system of removing obstacles and RAP radically altered her attitude towards education. Intensive reward systems were used for six weeks, because her difficulties were so severe, yet Danah then rejected the systems that she had previously been dependent upon. Flexibility is an essential consideration when developing direct reward systems for children with severe difficulties: the teacher must ask herself what she aims to achieve and how she aims to remove the reward system while maintaining the desired behaviour. So too is the longer-term aspiration of developing the new three Rs: resilience, resourcefulness and responsibility. In Danah's case, the system was removed because she had begun to develop intrinsic motivation.

In the next section we consider ways to help build and maintain positive self-esteem and help children like Danah equip themselves for life's journey.

The beginnings of achievement: starting to fill the self-esteem rucksack

> Twenty-five years of study has convinced me that if we habitually believe, as does the pessimist, that misfortune is our fault, is enduring, and will undermine everything we do, more of it will befall us than if we believe otherwise.

Martin Seligman, 1991

> Research shows that infants' sensory experiences and social interactions with supportive adults advance their cognitive abilities.

Bornstein and Tamis-LeMonda, 1994

In the first months of a baby's life, it continually receives positive feedback. The first smiles are met with smiles, and the first gurgles met with encouraging noises.

The baby is quick to develop responses to external stimuli, and the parent plays a part in shaping this pattern of responses. Babies whose mothers are suffering from clinical depression are often less able to demonstrate a normal range of emotional behaviours. Children's personality development is, in part, a reflection of the adaptations they have learned in the formative first three or four years of childhood.

As the child enters primary school, there is a personality shaped by the sum of the interactions that he has experienced so far. This could be positive, or it could be negative and inhibit a propensity to learn. Amrit sometimes finds a maths lesson more difficult than Eddie, and he knows that sometimes he will need a second or a third explanation, but he doesn't mind. By contrast, when Annie finds a concept difficult, she is resigned to failure. After all, her mum says that she too was bad at maths and science at school, so Annie accepts that she has inherited this 'badness'.

From time to time when we run training programmes in schools, we ask an open question of teachers such as: 'How many of you are no good at maths?' Alternatively we may ask about music or art. These are all disciplines in which individuals seem to have hardened views about a given level of ability. Hands shoot up! The next question is: 'For those of you who had your hand up or were tempted to, when did you decide to become no good at maths?' Unprompted, animated and engaged discussion follows. Individuals raid the cupboards of their past and come out with the evidence: 'I'm no good at maths ... when I was five the teacher made me stand up in front of the class and say my two times table. Since then I've hated maths.' This comment was from a headteacher of a secondary school who manages a budget of nearly £2 million. Our early perception about who we are and what we can or cannot achieve is influenced by our response to everyday experience. These everyday experiences are shaped by the people in our lives who help us interpret each event. It is also shaped by our emotional response at the time. We remember what we felt, not what we learned. We do so for years later – if we allow ourselves.

Most of us can recall an experience that shaped our self-perception in some way. A teacher edged towards Alistair at a training session and said: 'It's not maths you know, it's cooking.' After Alistair performed a double-take, she went on to describe how a school experience twenty-five years before had rendered her unable to remain in the presence of self-raising flour or bacofoil: 'When I was thirteen I changed schools and got a new cookery teacher. It was in a girls' grammar school. All the class was lined up in a row and the teacher said: "Now I'm going to find out who can cook." She came along the row and the girls responded in turn: "Vol au vents miss", "Victoria sponge miss", "Fairy cakes miss". As it got nearer and nearer to my turn my sense of panic went up. My heart was in my mouth and I was close to tears. I couldn't think of anything. I blurted out "Egg and chips miss" and the class dissolved into laughter. After that I used to beg my mother to write sick notes for cookery. I've hated it ever since.'

No doubt every reader of this book could dig into the depths of their childhood and find some similar experience. After we have initiated this discussion on teacher training courses, the room buzzes for several minutes as each teacher receives a little 'therapy' from the colleague next door for some damaging incident many years ago. These incidents may seem amusing as adults recount them years after the event, but teachers need to be aware of their significance for the children in their care. No child should grow up to believe they are 'useless' at maths, spelling, singing, or even cooking. Teachers have a phenomenal responsibility to ensure that children grow with the confidence to go out into the world to achieve in whatever field they choose.

A major review of research into the connection between assessment and learning (Black and Wiliam, 1998) shows a tight correlation between how pupils perceive themselves and their performance as learners. It suggests that pupils whose self-esteem is eroded by negative feedback and adverse comments soon learn that it is better not to try. They learn instead that they can avoid the seeming humiliation of 'failing' by simply avoiding the task. In a long-term study of individual primary pupils conducted by the University of Bristol,[7] the research team documented how the pupils gradually come to view themselves in a certain light. The report states: 'even before they leave primary school, a significant number decide they are not brainy and have largely stopped trying'.

Occasionally on our visits to schools we hear staff say things like: 'Children who come to this school do not' or 'Children who come to this school cannot'. Teachers sometimes talk of ability as though it were some sort of 'gift'. Terms such as 'the able child' and 'giftedness' can, we feel, allow some teachers to see failure as a sort of inherited deficit. The heavy industry that has been built around the notion of 'the able child' has overlooked the possibility that an individual's capacity to perform cannot be separated from their willingness to. A child's 'willingness to' is predicated on their self-esteem. Research has shown (Pollard and Filer, 1996) that children's efforts vary from year to year depending on their relationship with their teacher and how successful that teacher is in making them believe in their own ability. Every teacher could delve into her teaching history and tell of a child who was labelled 'weak' in some area, yet achieved highly with a different teacher who had a different perception of the child.

While it is imperative that work is differentiated because some children will need reinforcement when others need further challenge, the ALPS teacher guards against the tendency to fall into the trap of seeing 'giftedness' as being written in stone. She recognizes individual needs while holding the belief that the intelligent learning behaviours of every child can be developed. She also acknowledges that intelligent behaviours can only be developed if the child has the self-esteem that gives him the willingness to learn.

The ALPS method™ of learning depends very much upon building a solid base of positive self-esteem in every pupil. This is obviously going to be easier for some children than others. Amrit, Nisha, Annie and Eddie are all differently motivated. Think of each child being born with an empty rucksack, which gradually fills over the years with both negative and positive feelings. This rucksack has a label that reads 'SELF-ESTEEM'. Comparisons to siblings by parents, teachers or the child himself can be enough to put a heavy rock into the rucksack. A few thoughtless comments, such as 'How many times must I explain this?' can add a few heavy pebbles. Each negative experience loads up the bag until it can slow the mountaineering child to a snail's pace, or even stop him completely. Children cannot unload the bag unaided, and many wait until adulthood to do so. By then, for their educational success, it may be too late.

In comparison, every positive experience adds a useful tool or piece of equipment to the rucksack. This also aids the child in unloading some of the negative weights that he has collected along the way. It is possible to reload the rucksack and restart even the most overloaded child up the mountain. The ALPS teacher ensures that every child's rucksack is filled with the useful tools and attitudes that will bring success. Any excess pebbles and rocks are removed from the child's self-perception.

The rucksack of self-esteem

the alps approach – Accelerated Learning in Primary Schools

The story of one of the students who Nicola Call worked with before writing this book clearly illustrates this point. This is how Nicola describes her work with Shaun:

I met Shaun when he was in Year 3. From Year 3 to Year 6 he had a history of challenging behaviour, minor misdemeanours and poor punctuality. Shaun was one of the brightest pupils that I have ever taught. He was also one of the most challenging. I realized that I had my work cut out when he spent our first lesson up a tree, refusing to climb down and take a spelling test. I read the test to him while he sat up in the tree. We spent subsequent lessons under the climbing frame and in the lavatory, each time with me following him and taking the lesson, even if he covered his ears! This was particularly difficult for him when he was in the tree, as each time he covered his ears, he came perilously close to falling out.

Shaun had a negative attitude that pervaded the classroom and strongly influenced all the other pupils. He was popular and witty, and led the class in thwarting any effort that the teacher made to teach. His attendance and punctuality were extremely poor. I would imagine that his teachers in the past had been relieved when he did not attend for a day or two! When I decided to introduce the individual affirmation work, I struggled to think of positive adjectives for Shaun that would not be rejected by him and the class. For several days he removed his desk labels, and I replaced them.

Nicola continued to work with Shaun in a very direct way. By the end of the year, Shaun had a 100 per cent attendance record and spoke of himself only with positive language. Nicola doubted that Shaun would attend school during the SATs week. In fact he attended throughout and attained two Level 5s and one Level 4. This was a child who had refused to put pencil to paper at the beginning of the year.

A year later Nicola decided to trace Shaun and interview him, to find out if this improvement had been sustained and if he recalled any of the work on self-esteem that had been done with him. By now Shaun was in secondary school and had completed his first year there. Here are some extracts from the interview:

Find out about the desk label activity on page 97

Do you remember the affirmation labels on the desks?

Yes. My first ones were 'humorous', 'lively' and 'active'.

Do you remember the first session when we used the labels? Can you remember the kids' reactions when we did it?

Oh yes, Sam put his head back, like this, and went: 'Oh, that's not me. That ain't me, is it?' He put his head back and started laughing.

Did it have any effect on you, having the positive affirmations on your desk?

It made me feel better, somehow. I thought: 'If I'm lively then I can do my work.' It made me think.

What about coming into school in the mornings? I remember that your attendance improved enormously. What made this happen?

I think it was because I had positive thoughts about the SATs and about work. I thought: 'I've got to go into school because if I do not go into school I won't be able to do well.' Because I wanted to do a good job in my SATs, so I could get a better future, so I could do well when I'm older.

What about in secondary school? How is your attendance now?

98.46 per cent attendance. I got a certificate for it, and a Headteacher's Commendation for good work and attitude.

If you hadn't had the experience of using accelerated learning and getting those grades in your SATs, what do you think would have happened to you?

I'd be below my levels. I think I wouldn't be in that school anymore. I'd be in a different school, because I'd have been expelled or something.

You thought that your future was going to be –

Low.

Very low?

Yes, McDonald's manager or something like that – or not even a McDonald's manager – a toilet cleaner.

So what do you think your future holds now?

I think I'm going to have a decent job. The job that I want at the moment is to work in an office block.

Doing what?

Using computers – I'm good at ICT and stuff like that.

Is getting a good job important to you?

Yes, very. It is, because it's my future. I do not want my future to be rubbish.

One of the fundamentals of the ALPS approach is that the school deliberately and self-consciously creates a positive and supportive learning environment. ALPS teachers work to give every child the skills and confidence that will enable them to make choices in their lives. It is unacceptable for any child to leave school feeling that there are few, if any, options open to them. Whatever career path a student chooses, the fundamental issue is that he chooses and does not have to take the only available option. The ALPS approach worked for Shaun and allowed him to continue to make autonomous choices in his life.

The five essentials of positive self-esteem

Recent studies of infants raised in orphanages in Romania, illustrates the importance of social interaction in the development of emotional regulation and in the development of the sense of self.

Mary Carlson, PhD, Associate Professor of Neuroscience in Psychiatry, Harvard Medical School, 1998

Self-esteem levels are the key to the future for a teenager. How they feel about themselves affects friendships, their approach to the new and unknown, and whether they are prepared to take the risk of learning, which involves revealing ignorance or making mistakes.

'The Leading Lads Report', Sunday Times, 21 March 1998

As children like Shaun grow, they become increasingly sensitive to the evaluations of their peers. Some researchers (Harris, 1998) argue that peer conformity is a more powerful influence in shaping attitudes than the nurturing of parents. In the ALPS classroom the teacher bans put-downs. Make your class a 'no put-down zone'. Promote and actively model the behaviours and relationships that you want and be explicit about outcomes. The aspirations wall that we discuss on page 100 will help to motivate the class so that the peer conformity exerts itself to be working towards achieving high standards.

As educators we need to pay professional attention to the factors that influence a child's willingness to become a learner. A poor self-concept will inhibit this willingness. Strategies to build and maintain positive self-concept are at the heart of the ALPS classroom. We call it the BASIS model. It was described originally in *Accelerated Learning in the Classroom* (1995). The five elements of **BASIS** are:

☺ Each pupil is part of the group and his contribution, whatever its nature, is valued – he feels a sense of **belonging**.

☺ Every pupil is encouraged to work towards his own achievable goals and reflect on his progress as he does so – students are learners with **aspirations**.

☺ The classroom and the learning environment are safe havens for learning where there is consistency in expectations and standards – children learn with **safety**.

☺ A realistic level of self-knowledge is supported by the belief that individuality is not threatened by undue pressure to conform – students build an identity and a recognizable **individuality**.

☺ Mistakes are valuable learning tools in an environment where children can take risks and achievement is valued – teachers reinforce **success** and everyone learns from 'failure'.

The principles behind the BASIS system underpin all motivational systems and all learning activities in the ALPS school. If the affective domain is neglected, children will not meaningfully engage with the cognitive. While doing practical maths, Eddie is in his element. His teacher has some respite from 'corridor duty' – Eddie stays in the room! This is a fast-paced session with plenty of movement. Eddie knows what his target is, and he believes that he is going to be successful. He works in a small group where children listen to one another, and his teacher values his contribution. He is not worried that he may make a mistake, and he certainly feels safe to answer and ask questions.

The affective dimension is often overlooked. BASIS will help you to address the affective dimension alongside the cognitive. Imagine asking the teachers at your school to stand at some point on a line to represent their position on a continuum between the cognitive domain at one end and the affective domain at the other. At what end might the emphasis lie? If they were bunched up at the cognitive end, then you have a hothouse with a high regard for work and little for people; if they were at the affective end, then you have a high regard for people but little for work. Each individual teacher, and then the school as a whole, needs to find a balance between the affective and the cognitive domains.

Opposite is a quick profile for you to use with the children in the class. It is not so much for diagnostic purposes but more a prompt and stimulus for some of the issues related to self-esteem. Using it allows you and the children to reflect more carefully on the elements of BASIS described in detail in subsequent pages. It can also be used as a self-perception inventory at the beginning and the end of a term or academic year.

The BASIS self-esteem questionnaire

	never	sometimes	always	do not know
1 Do you ever want to answer a question but do not in case you look foolish?				
2 Do you like to do well at school?				
3 Do the others in the class listen to you when you have a suggestion?				
4 Do you like reading?				
5 Do your parent(s) like to hear about what you are doing at school?				
6 Do you often feel lonely at school?				
7 Do the others in the class ever pick on you?				
8 Does pleasing the teacher make you try harder?				
9 When you close your eyes can you imagine yourself being really good at something?				
10 Do you like watching television?				
11 Do you think of things about yourself you would like to change?				
12 Do you often feel sad because no one wants to play with you?				
13 When you try hard at school do you get better?				
14 Do you enjoy doing maths?				
15 Do you ever dream about being someone else?				
16 Are the others in the class pleased if you do well?				
17 Do other children often break friends with you?				
18 Do you like to join in when there are group games in class?				

Questions 4, 10 and 14 are mask questions and should be disregarded.
For information:
Questions 6, 12 and 17 relate to belonging.
Questions 5, 9 and 13 relate to aspirations.
Questions 1, 7 and 18 relate to safety.
Questions 3, 11 and 15 relate to identity.
Questions 2, 8 and 16 relate to success.

Scoring table

	never	sometimes	always	do not know
1	2	1	-1	0
2	-1	1	2	0
3	-1	1	2	0
4	mask	mask	mask	mask
5	-1	1	2	0
6	2	1	-1	0
7	2	1	-1	0
8	-1	1	2	0
9	-1	1	2	0
10	mask	mask	mask	mask
11	2	1	-1	0
12	2	1	-1	0
13	-1	1	2	0
14	mask	mask	mask	mask
15	2	1	-1	0
16	-1	1	2	0
17	2	1	-1	0
18	-1	1	2	0

Belonging

When teachers ensure that each pupil is part of the group and his contribution is valued, they generate a sense of belonging. Many children do not get this strong sense of belonging in their lives. They may come from home environments where there is inconsistency in the demonstration of affection. There may be little or no consistency in the outward manifestations of belonging: no sense of family, no protocols over behaviour, mealtimes, or bedtimes. If such children do not get this at home, where will they get it? Some children seek a sense of identity through inappropriate friendships, through cliques, through gangs or through taking sides. In what ways does a classroom offer a sense of belonging? Here are some suggestions to generate belonging by:

♥ using a structured variety of individual, pair and group activities;

♥ teaching 'taking turns';

♥ teaching playground games;

♥ welcoming every child at the door using his name;

♥ taking the register using the desk labels game described on page 97;

♥ ensuring that every pupil has the opportunity to work with every other pupil each term;

♥ using circle time and applying the principles which it promotes;

♥ monitoring your distribution of attention;

♥ providing opportunities to increase awareness of classmates' families, backgrounds and interests – use, for example, a 'getting to know you wheel' and a 'class discovery book'.

Aspirations

In situations where we feel out of control, we become stressed. If we feel that we cannot direct or influence the events in our lives, we become stressed. Where there is little or no perceived choice, we become stressed. Stress leads us back to our comfort zone and we develop avoidance strategies. When pupils are encouraged to set and work towards their own achievable goals and reflect on their progress, so they become learners with aspirations. In your classroom you can develop aspirational thinking by:

★ constantly affirming the positive;

★ using role models from the school and local community to promote positive views about what can be achieved;

★ working hard to create an 'it's cool to be clever' culture;

★ building in the use of personal performance targets as part of lessons;

★ using the language of progression;

★ providing parents with a small feedback card on which they can confidentially write a concern for their child on one side and a hope on the other;

★ reinforcing the positive by catching limiting self-talk and helping re-frame it – turn 'I can't' into 'I can';

★ modelling positive behaviours as a teacher, creating high expectations of what teachers will do for pupils;

★ using the aspirational wall technique of sharing 'life' maps described on page 100.

the alps approach – Accelerated Learning in Primary Schools

Safety

Ensure that the classroom and the learning environment are safe havens for learning where there is consistency in expectations and standards. Make sure that in your classroom pupils learn with safety. Do this by:

✚ following the strategies for positive performance described in the ADDS UP model;

✚ teaching older pupils the skills of peer mediation and then setting up a 'buddy' system so they can be role models for younger children;

✚ monitoring instances of bullying and taking affirmative action to prevent them;

✚ actively involving pupils in school council activities and acting on their contributions;

✚ paying attention to basic hygiene needs;

✚ declaring the school a 'no put-down zone' and posting reminders in every classroom;

✚ using trust-building activities;

✚ making it safe to get something wrong by emphasizing that learning is often messy, creating frequent feedback loops, showing how people need feedback in order to progress;

✚ marking work in a way that gives maximum feedback;

✚ applying class and school rules fairly and consistently;

✚ seeing your pupils and getting to know them in different contexts;

✚ reinforcing positive behaviours by deliberately praising children for them;

✚ anticipating disruption, dealing with it immediately or signalling when and how it will be dealt with calmly;

✚ separating any problem behaviour from the person.

The ADDS UP model appears on page 104

Identity

Value your pupils as individuals. Teachers do this when they differentiate classroom learning. They do this when they individualize feedback. When a child hits her personal target and the rest of the class cheers, they are recognizing individuality and affirming identity. A strong sense of identity means that children have the beginnings of knowledge of their own strengths and weaknesses, and emerging value and belief systems. They have an inner-resilience, which makes them less susceptible to becoming disillusioned and self-doubting. They achieve more. Continue to build a sense of identity at classroom level by:

! promoting and acclaiming individual and class successes;

! developing regular one-to-one reviews and individual target-setting;

! creating feedback loops that are educative and safe;

! encouraging individuals to take on responsibilities within the school;

! turning consultation evenings from retrospective to prospective events by sharing your target-setting activities and the outcomes of life mapping;

! using the names of pupils as you ask questions or invite contributions;

! finding something unique and positive about every pupil and letting him know it;

! sharing your outside interests and enthusiasms and taking an interest in students' enthusiasms;

! exploring the concepts surrounding identity using time-lines, autobiographies or scrap books;

! providing opportunities – especially for boys – to express emotions and develop an affective vocabulary.

Success

Fear of failure paralyses performance. Mistakes are valuable learning tools in an environment where children can take risks and achievement is valued. Reinforce success and learn from failure. Change 'cannot' to 'can' and 'not' to 'not yet'. Replace the concept of failure with the concept of feedback. Reinforce success and build coping strategies for learning from failure by:

✓ 'talking up' achievement of different sorts in assemblies;

✓ sending pupils to the office ... when they are successful!

✓ discouraging comparisons with other pupils' work as the only mean of performance measurement;

✓ focusing on personal performance improvement via target-setting;

✓ breaking down steps to improvement into small realizable chunks;

✓ providing feedback on performance through a variety of means;

✓ using strategies such as hobby days or talks for pupils to display their real interests;

✓ fostering an identity within your class by emphasizing collective achievements;

✔ using co-operative learning techniques to build team skills;

✔ using class team certificates for different types of contribution;

✔ teaching active listening skills for giving and receiving feedback;

✔ explaining the effects of negative self-talk and teaching children how to deal with it;

✔ finding an area where each pupil is guaranteed to succeed and promoting it;

✔ avoiding grading for effort without discussion beforehand – only the pupil genuinely knows the correct grade for this!

The ALPS teacher is not afraid to confront negative feelings and deal with them, but she only ever uses positive language in her classroom. Incidentally, she also only uses positive language when speaking of her pupils:

> I know that one or two of my colleagues were sometimes irritated by my refusal to speak negatively about my pupils. I will not fall into that 'this is the worst Year 6 class ever' routine. If complaints were made to me about the behaviour of one of my pupils, I would listen and take action, but would always make it clear that I disliked the behaviour, not the child. I would also ensure that at some point thereafter I would mention a positive achievement of that same child. I think that was what often irritated certain colleagues, generally the ones who had little that was positive to say about their own pupils, and who consequently had difficulties with behaviour in their classrooms. My classes have always been filled with delightful, motivated children. I do not think that this is a coincidence!

Year 6 ALPS teacher

❸ The motivational loop

Recognition, Affirmation, Praise (RAP)

> Emotional states, particularly negative ones, have powerful – often reciprocal – effects on our cognitive processing as well as on our social relationships. Not only do our emotions affect our thoughts and relationships, but these effects, in turn, can influence our emotional state.

Susan Mineka, PhD, Professor of Psychology, Northwestern University, Co-director of the Panic Treatment Clinic at Evanston Hospital, 1998

THE ALPS CLASSROOM IS CHARACTERIZED by a positive and supportive learning environment. There is high and sustained cognitive challenge but low stress. The feedback system is one containing recognition, affirmation and praise. The method for providing positive feedback in the ALPS classroom depends upon three principles, which can be remembered by the acronym RAP:

R ECOGNITION

A FFIRMATION

P RAISE

The ALPS teacher utilizes all three principles on a continual, sustained basis. They become second nature to her as they combine to raise the self-esteem of all children until their rucksacks are full of positive qualities that help them to stride up the mountain. RAP deliberately attempts to create a positive feedback loop that involves both teacher and pupil in a formative exchange.

Recognition

Sit down with a piece of paper in front of you. Now write the full names of all the pupils in your class. In what order did you remember them? Where were the boys in the list? Where were the girls? Did you omit any? Were some more difficult to remember than others? What helped prompt your memory? Eddie's teacher wrote his name first, but forgot Amrit and Nisha. We have conducted this activity as part of staff development sessions, and have watched staff cringe as they struggle to remember all the names. Few teachers recall their entire class list, and most realize through this simple activity that there are some

RAP: Recognition

children in their class who deserve more attention than they demand. Recognition of oneself is an important dimension of the feedback loop for all learners.

Now take a few minutes to think about your last day's teaching. Were all the children in your classroom motivated and eager to learn, throughout the entire day and in every lesson? It would be an unusual day if you could say yes, yes and yes! Think about the pupils whom you feel could have applied themselves a little more enthusiastically. Perhaps for some of them the block to their learning was caused by factors that are outside your control. Do not allow yourself to be limited by this. You cannot control these external forces, but you can minimize their effect on your pupils' attainment.

One of the keys to motivation is Recognition. The ALPS approach talks of recognition rather than reward, due to the concern about reward becoming an end to itself. When we talk to teachers on training courses about how they motivate their pupils, they are all quick to say that they continually recognize the contributions of their pupils. Before we started to work as teachers ourselves using the ALPS method™, we would have responded in the same way. Yet the ALPS method™ of recognition as a tool for raising self-esteem and academic attainment runs much deeper than the typical use of reward in the primary classroom.

The ALPS approach depends upon direct recognition on a continual basis. The teacher has already set clear targets, and so the pupil is clear about the goals that he is to achieve. She then recognizes each success as it occurs. She smiles, shakes hands, pats pupils on the back and looks them in the eye. She tells them directly that she is pleased with their performance and why.

Wow! Find out how to make a Said Tree on page 202

A Year 4 class has been working on creative writing, making a 'Said Tree'. Tom's work shows a marked improvement and his ALPS teacher responds: 'Tom, I'm delighted with this piece of writing. You have used three different words instead of "said". Well done!'

She then sets him a new target: 'A good target would be to write six more words from the "Said Tree" without looking at it on the wall, do you think you can do that? When you do it we'll put your words up on the wall beside the tree.'

Tom completes this task. But this is not the end of his recognition for success, because when he arrives at school the next day, up on the wall is a poster:

The ALPS teacher then uses Tom's success to motivate the rest of the class. She sets a challenge: 'If you can all bring me a list tomorrow of words that could be used instead of "said", we will then invite the headteacher to read our list. Let's see if everyone can bring more than ten.' The next day she is presented with 'said' lists from every child, as everybody wants the recognition.

Tom certainly learned from making the 'Said Tree'.

He knows fifteen words that can be used instead of 'boring said'.

Well done Tom!

You might be surprised at the recognition of just sending the list to the headteacher for completing a voluntary piece of work at home. Yet our research has shown that ALPS children are not particularly concerned about what the recognition is – they just want to be among the pupils who gain the recognition.

Dinesh's teacher uses a Brain Box, a box full of small joke items such as balloons containing messages, for shared celebrations. When children achieve their targets, they choose an item from the Brain Box. This is Dinesh's view:

the alps approach – Accelerated Learning in Primary Schools

> The clapping is one of the best rewards. If you do brilliantly, you choose something from the Brain Box. It is full of silly stuff, like from free things at McDonald's, and funny things from the cheap shops, or bits of paper with a good reward or a naff reward written on it. It's not the toy that is good, it's going in the box that's fun, because everybody watches you and everyone laughs at what you choose and they all say at playtime, 'Dinesh got to go in the Brain Box today!' You can go home and tell your mum.

Dinesh age 9

The ALPS teacher learns to motivate and recognize continuously until every child is recognized directly every day, and in every lesson. Recognition becomes an integral part of class life, and the classroom becomes vibrant with enthusiasm and celebration of continual success.

In the ALPS classroom children recognize one another, for example, by clapping spontaneously when a success is announced. The teacher teaches them fun ways of giving and receiving feedback – short songs or raps, drumming on knees followed by a cymbal clap with the hands, extravagant gestures. The idea is that the recognition is participative, it is immediate, physical and fun. The Brain Box contains unimportant trivia, and the more trivial or outrageous, the more the children seem to enjoy it. The best moments in an ALPS classroom are when a child's name is sung or chanted and at the same time there's some clapping or a physical gesture like pointing. The best fun you can have is when the children devise their own chants. They steal them from football matches!

Each incident of recognition is placed in the child's self-esteem rucksack. With a rucksack that a child enjoys carrying because it is full of useful tools, the journey is so much easier. Using the ALPS method™, you can answer the question 'Were all my children eager to learn, throughout the whole day and every lesson?' with 'Yes, yes and yes!'

Affirmation

Individual affirmations
The ALPS teacher uses positive affirmations to create the environment of success. She repeatedly affirms all her pupils' best qualities. She acknowledges even the slightest improvement and develops positive affirmations. These serve to confirm in each pupil's mind that the success was not incidental and that it will be repeated. These affirmations are made directly and explicitly.

Children are not born with a positive or negative self-image. It is up to us to create a positive self-image for every pupil. The ALPS teacher actively introduces a language of success for each individual child in her classroom. We all know children who have been diagnosed with special needs and then allowed that diagnosis to paralyse any chance of improvement. A diagnosis must not be allowed to become a straitjacket. Some children may wear a specific badge such as 'dyslexic' or 'ADHD'. Others are sometimes 'labelled' with some tag such as 'slow' or 'a plodder'.

The ALPS teacher ensures that the child's special needs are met, but that, in the meantime, the child labels himself with a different sort of vocabulary. Notice symptoms, diagnose specific difficulties, consult experts, and then draw up a programme and teach! Label children with affirmative descriptors such as 'intelligent', 'conscientious' and 'resourceful'. This way the child's self-image is positive, with a special need being an incidental factor that the child understands to be a part of his identity but not a factor that will stop him from learning. The ALPS teacher believes that every child has the potential to be conscientious, studious and successful. She affirms this over and over again.

RAP: Affirmation

Class affirmations

Whole-class affirmations are an excellent tool for instilling a positive work ethic in the classroom. One of the simplest ways to affect all your pupils is to use positive affirmation posters. These should be discussed briefly then displayed around the classroom. The posters should directly refer to the types of behaviours and attitudes that you wish to foster. You should not feel concerned if some of your pupils do not yet fulfil these expectations; if they see it and hear it often enough, they will become a walking, living proof of your affirmation.

Eddie's teacher used the affirmation, 'We are all good at stopping work when given the signal' when she practised raising her hand to gain the attention of the class. For several weeks, Eddie found it difficult to stop work and would continue to fiddle or chatter. Yet in the end her continual affirmations paid off and Eddie became good at stopping work when she gave the signal. As each individual learns to believe each positive affirmation, he is being provided with a useful self-belief to put in his self-esteem rucksack. Every positive feeling that he has about himself will aid him on his learning journey. Eddie believed, for the first time, that he could be attentive and exercise self-control. He believed that he could overcome any obstacle in his path.

As soon as you and your class are accustomed to using these specific affirmations of particular behaviours, you can start to introduce some more conceptual messages. These serve a more general purpose in building upon the work ethic to create an expectation of success in every field. We were amazed as we did the research for this book that children who had left their ALPS primary classroom for secondary school could recall these positive messages and speak of how they have influenced their lives:

> On my desk I had the message 'Winners never quit and quitters never win'. I thought that was clever. I sometimes think of it now when I play football and we are losing. If you give up, you give more goals away. Now I never quit, I keep trying to win.

Kevin age 12

Be creative with positioning your positive messages. We all know people who stick messages about healthy eating on their fridge doors! Think of the places where your pupils often gaze during lessons or 'dead time'. Use the cloakrooms, the corridors and the coat pegs. In their subconscious, the children will absorb the messages and will begin to assimilate and respond to them. Use every available space, including the inside of the windows. After all, that is where children frequently gaze towards the end of the day!

Put the affirmations to music. If you were asked to recall the words of a poem some two pages long, you would probably struggle. Yet as you drive to school, if a popular song comes onto the radio, it is quite certain that you will hum along to the tune and know most of the words, even if you have never consciously listened to that song. Positive affirmations to music make use of the fact that it is easier to absorb information when it is set to music.

Find some useful ideas in our section on music on pages 160–174

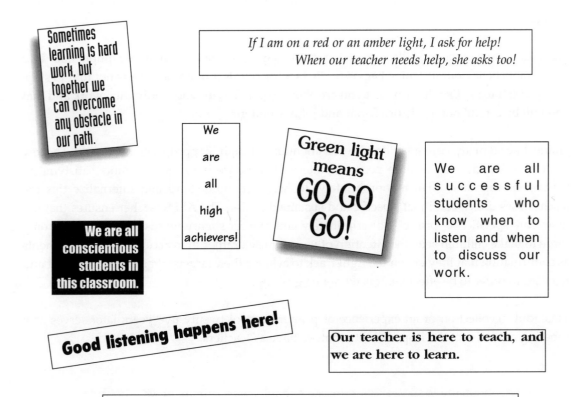

Sometimes learning is hard work, but together we can overcome any obstacle in our path.

If I am on a red or an amber light, I ask for help! When our teacher needs help, she asks too!

We are all high achievers!

Green light means GO GO GO!

We are all successful students who know when to listen and when to discuss our work.

We are all conscientious students in this classroom.

Good listening happens here!

Our teacher is here to teach, and we are here to learn.

We are all great readers in this class. Watch out for the bookworms in our book-corner

91

Praise

Children who have been taught using the ALPS method™ have been clear about the importance of praise when we have interviewed them. Even four year olds told us that they like to know that their teacher is proud of them. Effective verbal praise needs to be Precise and Personalized as well as related to Performance. So there ought to be lots of Ps in praise!

RAP: Praise

Imagine that Janine is in your class. She finds it very difficult to concentrate for more than a few minutes on any task. For her, brain breaks are extremely important and need to happen more frequently than for her peers. The ALPS teacher recognizes this and gives Janine an activity that she can do when she has completed her short maths task. She does not want Janine to come to her once her maths task is finished and neither does she want Janine to distract the other children around her. She monitors Janine from a distance. When she sees Janine close her book and look around, she speaks directly to her, giving her eye contact and a smile: 'Brilliant, Janine. You have finished your task and I am so happy to see that you are about to start your individual work. Well done!' A few minutes later she reinforces the message by saying: 'Good concentration Janine. Fabulous.' A positive affirmation comes later: 'You are so good at concentrating on your work, Janine.'

The ALPS teacher never falls into the trap of negative-speak, even if her pupil falls into undesirable behaviour. If Janine begins to distract the pupils around her, she is not told to stop, but is told: 'I really like the way that you are about to get on with your individual work and that you will be careful not to disturb Sarah and John. Good girl, Janine.'

Janine, like so many young children, seeks attention through inappropriate behaviour. The key to helping her develop a more positive pattern of response is to make it more satisfying to behave appropriately than inappropriately. To help her understand and internalize this the teacher uses direct, continual, specific and sustained praise. The ALPS teacher ensures that her words are specific. To 'praise' indiscriminately and to offer sugary words as rewards will only serve to make children seek the attention of your 'praise', rather than accepting your comments as confirmation that they are on the right track to achieve their targets. Praise must be direct and relevant in order to be effective. It need not be gushing!

This adult recollection of an experience at primary school twenty-five years later serves as a sobering reminder of the responsibility that we have as teachers:

Throughout my last year at primary school, I was brimming with confidence about my own intellectual ability. I had passed the 11plus exams and had been offered a place at one of the most prestigious schools in the area.

92

I knew that I was among the brightest pupils in my class, and I looked forward to my parents attending Open Evening.

That evening, twenty-five years ago, I sat up until late to hear what my teacher had told my parents. She maybe said some positive things about me, but the word that stuck with me until this day was 'dogmatic'. I looked it up in a dictionary. I was devastated.

That word affected my whole life. I eventually went on to be very successful in my own field, but found myself in meetings making a point, then thinking: 'Shut up, you're being dogmatic.' On occasions I even let colleagues make serious mistakes rather than speak up, for fear of seeming to be dogmatic. Eventually I realized that I would have to rethink the meaning of that word 'dogmatic' and rephrase it in my mind as a positive attribute, meaning determined and strong.

I often think that I'd like to meet that teacher and tell her how serious an effect one derogatory comment can have on a child.

When I get my maths right I tick my name on the board and everybody claps me so I smile and smile.

As important as verbal praise is the approval or disapproval that can be exhibited through body language. The non-verbal is as important as the verbal. Children are extremely adept at knowing if praise is genuine. The ALPS teacher gives non-verbal cues that are as positive as her verbal praise. Eye contact is one of the most vital of non-verbal cues that human beings read and interpret with great accuracy. We have all taught children who find eye contact difficult, and we know that it is essential that we make a point of giving clear eye contact to pupils and teach them to reciprocate. One of the easiest ways to begin this work is to insist on eye contact whenever you call the register. This ensures that you give a clear welcome to each pupil, and if you combine this with memorizing the desk label adjectives, you will start each day with an extremely positive atmosphere.

Well maybe you could turn to page 97 for the desk label activity

Just consider the difference in your response if you walked into the staffroom one morning and received either Welcome A or Welcome B from a colleague who had covered your class the day before.

WELCOME A: (with no eye contact) 'Mrs Smith.'

WELCOME B: (with eye contact and a smile) 'Good morning, Mrs Smith. By the way, the children in your class were fantastic yesterday, particularly the Orange Group. I really enjoyed teaching them!'

It is sometimes easy to forget that children have the same desire as adults to be acknowledged. One of the most common complaints from teachers is that their good work is never acknowledged, that being a teacher feels like you have a continual school report that reads 'COULD DO BETTER'. The adept ALPS teacher develops the ability of utilizing every moment to make positive affirmations and to acknowledge every achievement. This is an extract from the morning register of an ALPS teacher:

> Good morning, conscientious Henry.
> Good morning, attentive Samuel.
> Good morning, creative Partha. By the way, Partha, I noticed yesterday how neat your handwriting is in your homework book – great!
> Good morning, peaceful Sheila. Let me see your eyes please – a lovely smile, thank you!
> Good morning, careful Jumoke.
> Good morning, athletic Jason.

Calling her register may take two minutes longer than using the method of Welcome A, but she will recover that time because the remainder of her day will be more productive. The atmosphere in her base camp is now totally positive and every pupil is ready to learn.

66 An inspector once told me that I praised children 'too much'. She had observed me teaching Daniel, a five year old, who liked to spend most of his lessons sitting under the desk. I had taught him what 'good sitting' meant, and I praised him whenever he did it. If he was about to crawl under the table, I would say: 'I like the way that you are about to do "good sitting", Daniel. Well done!' Daniel would invariably change his plan and sit down rather than crawl on the floor.

My response to that inspector is that it is impossible to praise a child too much. 99

Reception Class Teacher

The ALPS teacher expects to provide specific praise to every child at some point in every lesson. She expects every child to remain motivated and follow agreed class rules, and she expects to recognize this verbally and non-verbally on a continual basis. She recognizes achievements continually and specifically. When she does this, she has no need for punishment or sanction, or even the Assertive Discipline consequences for poor behaviour. There should ultimately be no requirement for rewards and consequences, only for praise and recognition. There is certainly no place in the ALPS for punishments such as writing lines that visually reinforce a hundred times the concept of bad behaviour. Imagine being told to write a hundred times 'It is naughty to spit at other children and the teacher.' What a great way to remind yourself a hundred times that it is possible to spit at other children and the teacher! Moreover, what message does it give if you make writing into a punishment? ALPS teachers want children to have intrinsic motivation, to have a love of reading and writing. If writing for punishment is a part of your school repertoire, at least make the children write positive statements. Ideally, find an activity for a child to do that will reinforce positive feelings about himself, not the idea that he was genetically programmed to spit at teachers.

This is what ALPS teacher Kate Barnes says about the use of praise and recognition:

In my class we agree rules, rewards and consequences. I would find it impossible to list all the rewards that I use, although the bottom line is that the children want recognition – that is their real reward. I can honestly say that I never have to use the sequence of consequences.

On one or two occasions I have had to shortcut to the final consequence and send a child to the office for a calming-down period, but I never allow this to be a negative experience. I try to phrase it positively. For example: 'Joseph, I know that you are feeling quite tense today. Sometimes I feel like that myself. I really would like you to go downstairs and complete this piece of work in peace and quiet, then I'd love to read it with you at break-time. I know I can trust you to go down on your own and explain, because you are always so reliable. See you later with some fantastic work!'

I try to troubleshoot all the time, and I never verbalize a misdemeanour. If you remain only positive, you really have no need to use consequences, as *children only make the right choices. I suppose that this is RAP at its best, but I'd now prefer to not have to even mention consequences, as I have no expectation of ever using them.*

The discipline models that rely on structured systems of reward, warnings and consequences need to be viewed with caution. Certainly, these systems might give inexperienced teachers a structure for classroom management and discipline. But the aim should always be to move towards RAP and away from the need for consequence or extrinsic reward. This is the next step on our journey as an ALPS teacher, to be able to jettison the extrinsic reward and the notion of consequence, and develop intrinsic motivation on the shared journey of learning.

Non-verbal praise comes more naturally to some teachers than to others. We have observed teachers who feel comfortable hugging their pupils and others who give frequent handshakes and thumbs-up signals. Others create their own fun messages that demonstrate approval. One infant teacher uses a pat on the back, but she makes the child pat his own back while she pats her own. It is not important which particular types of non-verbal praise you use with your class, but it does matter that you use some! In particular, language-impaired children will gain from non-verbal praise, as they may not fully comprehend the emotional message behind pure verbal praise.

The younger the child, the more imperative it is that feedback is given physically in addition to verbally. The wider the variety of non-verbal praise you give, the more responsive your class will become. From a purely practical point of view, non-verbal signals like giving a thumbs-up sign or a wink can increase the feedback that you give to your class ten-fold. You can give either while talking to another pupil, or while marking a book. As long as the non-verbal praise is either preceded or followed by a specific verbal praise, it can strongly reinforce the desired behaviour.

This is one of our favourite quotations from a book that was presented to a teacher by the children at her school when she left. The book was a leaving present and contained messages from the children.

> **Mrs Hammond has a trendy smile.**
>
> James age 4

Although James had only been in Reception class for one term, his perception of Mrs Hammond was as someone who gave him only positive feedback. He will not recall the specific messages that he was given, but will recall clearly the emotional one, that he is an intelligent and loveable little boy.

So we see that the ALPS teacher follows a continual cycle of

R ECOGNITION

A FFIRMATION

P RAISE

These combine to create a vibrant atmosphere where only appropriate learning behaviours are displayed and only positive statements used. The ALPS teacher fulfils her role in actively developing positive self-images for all her pupils. She acknowledges that there are some factors in a child's life that she cannot control, but she also recognizes the power of positive reinforcement.

There is no room for excuses in the ALPS classroom. Positive conditioning begins with the teacher. She must believe that she can achieve her goals. She must believe that she can teach every child to read, that the whole class can learn key spelling rules and that her target percentage can reach particular national curriculum levels. Her language about herself must be positive, in the same way that she is positive about her pupils.

Desk labels are the business

A simple but very effective activity to start building an expectation of success for pupils is the 'Desk Label' activity. It takes ten minutes to complete in the first instance and can become an integral part of classroom practice, being repeated as often as necessary.

Copy and cut out labels bearing positive adjectives, with at least one appropriate label for each pupil. Tell your class that you are going to celebrate and recognize all their best qualities as individuals. Read out the adjectives on the labels and display them so that the class can see them. Explain the meanings as you do this and give examples of children who best match each adjective. For example, if Patricia is particularly witty, talk about her as you display that label, or if Rahul is known by the class to be extremely thoughtful, talk of how this label would suit him. After a while, begin allocating labels to individual children. Encourage the class to help by making suggestions. In some cases one word may suit two or three children, but in this first session ensure that a wide range are used and that children feel individually recognized.

Here is a sample list of fifty positive adjectives for your desk labels

able	committed	energetic	industrious	persuasive
active	compassionate	enterprising	intelligent	polite
alert	confident	enthusiastic	kind	quick
articulate	conscientious	forgiving	lively	resourceful
artistic	considerate	generous	loving	reflecting
athletic	creative	gentle	mathematical	scientific
bright	determined	gracious	musical	studious
calm	diligent	hard working	original	thoughtful
caring	diplomatic	humorous	outgoing	warm
clever	empathic	imaginative	peaceful	witty

By the end of the session every child should have one label. Attach them to the corner of their desks neatly. Ensure that the labels are valued in the way that you want the children to value themselves and one another. Tell them that you will repeat the activity until they all have many labels. Some teachers ask the class to allocate labels to the adults who work with them too. This creates a feeling that everyone has attributes that are worth celebrating.

Refer to the children's labels frequently. Think of different ways to work the adjectives into your daily routine. For example, try to remember each one when calling the register, such as, 'conscientious Amy' and 'patient Andrew'. Use the adjectives when you mark work and use them for affirmations. When another adult asks for a child to volunteer for a task, decide which attributes would be useful for the task, then ask the class to decide who would best carry it out. When you give the Big Picture for a lesson, list the attributes that will be necessary for success.

When you feel ready, spend another session giving a second or third label to each child. You can do this as a daily or weekly activity, or just when it fits with your weekly plan. Think carefully about what adjective you assign to each child, and remember the power of labelling – you can create a conscientious pupil by publicly labelling him this way, as long as you mean it!

In subsequent lessons, when you notice a positive development, give an individual label to a child. You can enclose a new label in an exercise book when you return it after marking, or ask a child to stay back at break for some individual attention and recognition, or you can make it a very public event. However, you must ensure that everybody begins to collect a selection of positive and valid labels on their desks. Eventually the class will begin to attribute labels to themselves and to one another. When the labels eventually become tatty, encourage your pupils to stick them inside homework folders or exercise books. These positive qualities are theirs for life, so do not throw them out!

There are lots of team building and positive feedback activities that can be based upon desk labels. One, for example, involves recognizing feelings. The class stands and then children sit when you describe an adjective that they think matches them. Or, in pairs, children sit when they hear an adjective that describes their partner. Or, each child chooses one of his own adjectives and makes a copy for another child whom he feels also shares that attribute. At circle time, desk labels can be introduced, reinforced and used as an additional tool for positive recognition and self-esteem building.

A secondary school German teacher read the draft of this book before it went to print, and tried out a few of the ideas. This is what she had to say about using the desk labels:

I even had a go at the desk labels today. I thought I would try it with one class. I asked each of them to think of just one positive adjective to describe themselves and write it down in English. It was so interesting — none of them chose intelligent or clever, even though there are some really brainy kids in the class! Nearly all the boys said they were 'sporty' (interestingly, the girls predominantly used words like 'neat' or 'hard working'). A few couldn't think of anything, so we made a list of all the words they could think of and I added a few. One girl who is really very clever, but has no self-esteem would only choose 'punctual'.

They now had their original word, and a second from the list. I then asked them to look up their words in German, and they wrote those words in coloured letters on the front of their exercise books. I then told them that I'd give them each a word from the list — one that I thought described them. At first they were really giggly, but they began to take it really seriously. I got to Elliot, whose behaviour can be immature. I gave him 'diligent', making a big deal of his improved attitude and effort recently. Do you know what, when we went on to the rest of the lesson, he had his hand up the whole time, and remembered some vocabulary from last term — I gave him 'intelligent' as well!

I spent the rest of the lesson calling them 'intelligent Elliot' and 'musical Chris' etc., and they loved it!

The great thing was that in addition to the effect on their attitude in class they learnt new words in English and in German — I'm going to try really hard to keep reinforcing it. I was astonished at the difference in their behaviour just from stressing the positive aspects of each personality. I was also surprised by the effect that the activity had on my relationship with them. I am now working hard to ensure that every word I speak is positive.

I even bumped into Elliot at lunch and he chirped 'Watcha, Miss Reid' rather than just ignoring me, which would be more normal. He went off down the corridor, and as they went, I heard his friend say 'come on intelligent Elliot' and giggle — but it wasn't malicious in any way, they just think it's fun. Magic!!

Motivational 'life' maps

The ALPS approach stresses the importance of clarity in every aspect of classroom life. This extends to being clearly focused on why you are working hard to deliver the school curriculum and helping children better understand what they are doing and why they are doing it. It is so much easier to learn something if you know why you are learning it and that it will be useful to you in the future. Very young children are able to articulate what they wish to achieve.

Adults frequently ask: 'What do you want to be when you grow up?' Yet they rarely follow on with: 'What are you going to do in order to achieve that?' The ALPS teacher asks the question: 'What do you want to be?' But follows it with: 'What do I need to do to help you?' She ensures that she equips every child with every necessary tool to make it up the mountain towards that outcome, and she offers encouragement at every step. She believes that no mountain is too steep to climb.

The most effective ALPS teacher discovers the aspirations of every child at the start of the academic year. A simple and effective way to explore these with the class is to develop a life map. A life map is a memory map of an individual person's ambitions and goals. Life mapping gives children an opportunity to map out their interests and their aspirations and then share them with their teacher and classmates. It is a simple activity to organize and will give you enormous insight into the children in your care. When the individual life maps are placed on the classroom 'aspirational wall', you will have an ongoing focus for your work throughout the year. Creating individual life maps will go a long way to making your classroom teaching more coherent and, as a by-product, it will reduce behavioural problems.

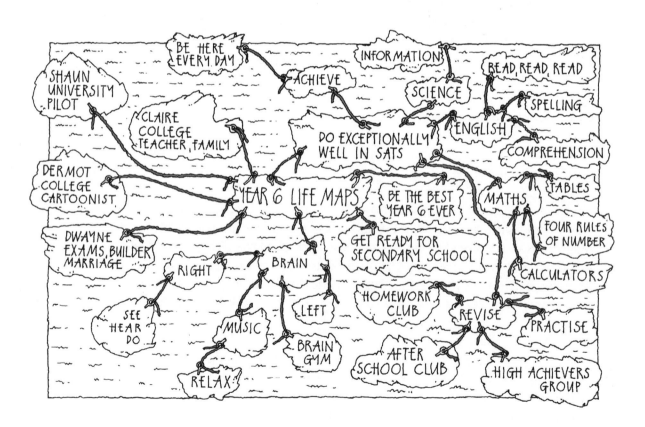

the alps approach – Accelerated Learning in Primary Schools

When you have taught your class the basic skills of memory mapping as described on page 40, set aside a session of approximately twenty minutes. This should be a time when your class will be relaxed and open to ideas, so avoid the twenty minutes before lunch, after a hot playtime, or just before a school football match! Give every child a piece of blank A4 paper and a selection of pencils. Begin a class discussion about ambitions and allow all the most creative and ambitious thoughts to surface. Tell the class that you are going to map out where you each wish to be in ten and twenty years time, then you are going to help them decide what you need to do as a teacher to ensure that they fulfil their dreams.

As the children begin to share their ambitions, start to direct the discussion. If Sam says that she wishes to be a doctor, mention the importance of sciences and maybe Latin. If Rashvir wants to be a computer programmer, talk about maths. If Eric wants to work with animals, talk of the importance of biology if he is to be able to care for animals knowledgeably. Steer the conversation towards higher aspirations and do not allow 'ambitions' that are reinforcements of poor self-image. If necessary, plant ideas, but on no account allow anyone to opt out.

In one such session, Wayne stated that he wished to be a professional footballer. At this point he had extremely poor co-ordination and lacked agility and fitness. He had never been selected to play for any of the school's three football teams. Two weeks after creating his life map he was enthusiastically following a fitness and co-ordination regime drawn up for him by the school's football coach. Three months later Wayne had been selected as a solid and determined defender for the school's 'A' team. This activity certainly focused his efforts and enabled him to make the first steps towards achieving his outcome.

You may be smiling to yourself right now, as you imagine that most of the children in your class will want to be famous sportsmen, models, actors or pop stars. Encourage and show faith but, at the same time, be realistic and practical. Introduce the language of further education and personal development. Deliberately use the language of achievement: 'When you get your GCSEs', 'When you are at university', 'When you have begun your fitness programme'.

When interviewed by a journalist from the *Sunday Times* (*Sunday Times*, 14 October 1998) Ross stated that he was going to be a professional footballer. He followed up swiftly, however, with the comment: 'But that's after I've been to university.' It is a good idea to talk of athletes whose careers have been cut short by injury and who then made successful second careers because they had attained high levels at school first. This enables you to support children in their ambitions, while retaining a motivation towards high standards of achievement in school.

At a point when the discussion is still vibrant and enthusiastic, ask the class to memory map their ambitions individually, then to fill in the details of what they think they will need to do to achieve their goals. Start by listing the keywords on a separate piece of paper, or on post-it stickers, or on the side of a large sheet of A3. Then build out from the centre starting with different categories. For example: 'What I am good at', 'What I like doing', 'What I could be better at', 'What I do not like doing', 'Things I remember from the past', 'Things I plan to do in the future'. For each category there are the possibilities of sub-categories. Develop sub-categories and encourage the children to think of skills that may help them to improve. Ask them to think about this immediate year. If they perceive a weakness to be their spelling, or their listening skills, ask what action could be taken to help them to improve. Decide what commitment they must make and what help you can give.

This activity can be broken up in any number of ways. It can be completed on one day, or in short sessions during one week. We do not advise taking longer than one week to complete it. You can work with individuals, groups or the whole class. A powerful tool is to complete your own life map as the children do theirs. Whenever Nicola has done this activity with a class, she has written her own life map, which for several years has included an ambition to write this book about the ALPS method™. She believes that without this focused approach to creating the paths for her own future, the dream would have remained just that – a dream.

Next, begin to reflect on these individual life maps and create a whole-class life map. Display it in a prominent position, such as on the back of the classroom door. Working out from the centre, stick up clearly written or typed captions, symbols or pictures that show the actions you will all take that year. These could include creating high achiever groups, lunchtime help groups, spelling tests, home reading, handwriting practice books and home study groups. Create a plan of action that will ensure successful attainment of these goals. Work out towards the border where each child's future can be represented with a clear, four or five word sequence, such as:

Polly

↓

Music Grades

↓

Drama

↓

University

↓

Actress

When you have finished, you will have created a powerful plan. You now have a focus. You know where each pupil is heading. Your pupils know how you are going to ensure that they make the journey safely. You must refer to the life map frequently and allow for changes of focus and needs. Add new challenges as they arise, celebrate when an area is completed and allow children to review their ambitions. You will find that they will become increasingly ambitious as their self-esteem rucksack fills with positive experiences.

> At the start of Year 6 I thought I'd be a secretary. Mrs Call told me I was a talented writer and that I could be an author. She loved to read my stories. I got Level 5 at English and I had a go at Level 6. I didn't get Level 6 but it was fun trying. I love to write. When Mrs Call has written her book I will be so proud. I will send her a copy when I write mine. On my last report before I left primary school I wrote: 'You have given me hope for my future.' That was true, I'd never have thought I could have been an author.

Jamie age 12

This is an extract from an interview with a class of ten year olds who had made a class life map for the first time three months previously:

Rashvir: I like to see the life map up on the door because it shows what I am going to do, and so that I know why I am working hard at school. I like to know about the others in the class too, where they are heading.

Nadia: Everyone in the class knows what you are going to do and we all encourage each other to achieve it.

Jumoke: When I started at this school in Year 5 I didn't realize the things that I am good at. I changed my plan on my life map because I realized that I am good at some things that I didn't realize about. I know now that I am good at maths. I thought I was bad at it. I did think I would be a designer, but now I want to do something using my maths.

Rashvir: My dad said I should be a chef and my mum said it too, that I should work in a restaurant. When I went home after doing my life map I said: 'I do not want to be a chef, I want to be something else.' In science I was learning about air pressure and flight, and I started to get good marks. I'm also good at maths, so I do not want to just be a chef. I thought about it and I told my mum and dad that I want to be a pilot. They are really pleased now.

Ellen: I came to this school in September. I thought I was just no good at maths, but when I came to this school I found I could catch up. Now I'm up with the rest of the class. I never thought I could do something using maths, but now I know that I can, I want to be an architect. My mum has asked someone who is an architect to send some house plans so I can see the sort of thing I'd have to do.

Ross: I still want to be a footballer. I have always wanted to do that. But since I went into this class it has changed. When I'm on the football pitch, all I think about is the football. But straight afterwards I start thinking about the work that I need to do at school and passing exams in the future. My thoughts are on schoolwork when I'm off the football pitch.

Mehreen: Once I had a maths test and I only scored 50 per cent, so I thought I was no good at maths. I never had a chance to see what I had done wrong, so I thought it was me, like it was all my fault. Now I know that I can do maths, and I get good scores. If I get one wrong, I find out why. I now want to be a chartered accountant. I'd never have thought that I could do that before!

Life mapping is one of the most powerful tools at our disposal. It encourages pupils not only to reach for the stars, but also to see how they will get there. Try it, and you will find that a whole new world of possibilities will open not only for your pupils, but also for you!

❹ Twenty strategies for positive performance

> There is a need to be explicit about what we mean by better forms of thinking and of educating directly for thinking. If students are to become better thinkers – to learn meaningfully, to think flexibly and to make reasoned judgements – then they must be taught explicitly how to do it.

DFEE Research Report, Carol McGuinness, 1999

A T THE START OF OUR JOURNEY INTO THE ALPS, we have established a positive and supportive environment for learning. We have created a physical space that reflects the regard with which we hold learning and our learners. We have begun to build on real aspirations within safe protocols that encourage risk taking. Children feel positive about themselves and respect each other. We have created a considered learning arena for the development of resourcefulness, resilience and responsibility.

Imagine that Eddie suddenly thumps Annie – hard! This time, he is convinced that she has his paintbrush! What do you do? Mayhem beckons. Intervention is required. The model below shows how this kind of situation can be handled, or avoided altogether.

The ADDS UP model

A simple mnemonic provides our underlying principles for behaviour management in the ALPS classroom. The management of behaviour should be all the following: **a**ppropriate, **d**irected to specific outcomes, **d**ifferentiated, **s**ensitively handled and **up**beat. We call this **ADDS UP**.

A ppropriate

D irected to specific outcomes

D ifferentiated

S ensitively handled

UP beat

Our mnemonic also allows you to check your own behavioural management strategies and ask yourself to what extent they 'add up'.

Outlined below are twenty complementary strategies for positive behaviour and a positive and purposeful learning environment that support the ADDS UP method. The strategies

'No pupil is allowed on the sixth form block roof.'
Headteacher of a Bristol Independent School announcing guidelines at assembly

the alps approach – Accelerated Learning in Primary Schools

are designed to deal with some of the possible causes of misbehaviour and to provide strategies for children to have behavioural flexibility. Eddie should not be thumping Annie when these strategies are in place. If he does, it may be that he needs a programme such as the one for Danah described on page 72. The purpose of an individual behaviour programme is to modify behaviour within the philosophy of the ADDS UP model. Your systems of recognition may have to be more specifically targeted and you may need to include extrinsic rewards. However, you must also plan how you will withdraw them as motivation becomes intrinsic.

The twenty strategies

1 **Describe the behaviours you want.** A lot of misplaced effort is put into describing behaviours that teachers do not want at the expense of clarity about exactly what they do want. Be specific. Teach the behaviours: good sitting, good listening, good talking.

> 'Will the pupils seen on the sixth-form block roof last night make themselves known to me ...'
> Headteacher of the same Bristol Independent School at assembly a fortnight later

2 **Model fairness, consistency and problem solving.** You are a role model for the pupils. Practise what you preach and let them see you doing it.

3 **Stay focused on the larger goals.** Sometimes in the heat of the moment it is easy to stray into unhelpful responses. The 'aspiration wall' helps pupils to remember the larger purpose. If you have your own life map on the wall, it can help. If you choose not to do that, then clarity in your own mind about your own aspirations for that particular lesson, day or week will help you to stay focused.

4 **Make your classroom a 'no put-down zone'.** Write it above the door. In the 'no put-down zone' any sort of put-down is banned. You do not put any child down, they do not put each other down, nor do they put you down.

5 **Start positively and stay there.** Welcome each child at the door and use his name. Make the opening interactions with each child positive.

> 'You are entering the positive zone. No whinging, No moaning, No complaining.'
> Sign outside a classroom, Scunthorpe

6 **Practise outcomes thinking.** Encourage pupils to think in terms of desired outcomes: 'When you have successfully completed this piece of work, how would I know you have done well?' 'How would a visitor to the class know you had done well?'

7 **Provide lots of opportunities for mental rehearsal of success.** Practise thinking in terms of success. Encourage pupils to visualize themselves behaving in a positive way to others. Ask them to notice what is being said, who is saying it, how it is said, and how they feel about it.

8 **Teach and use 'I' messages**. 'I' messages allow the child to reflect back to you how well she understands an instruction, or how she feels about a request for a change in behaviour, or how she feels about something she has done.

A five-part 'I' message for managing behaviour might sound like this: 'When you (describe the action in neutral and non-judgemental language), the consequence for the class is (describe the action in neutral and non-judgemental language) and I feel disappointed because (describe how you feel). So, I would like you to (describe the desired behaviour). How do you feel about that (allow space for a response)? Then clarify understanding: 'Just to make sure that we are both sure, can you tell me what we have agreed?' 'Before you begin, just explain to me what you are going to do.'

> 'No entry without a member of staff'
>
> *Sign outside boys' toilets in a Liverpool Primary School*

9 **Separate the person from the behaviours**. The child will feel threatened by any sort of negative label attached to him. Attach labels to the behaviour. This allows choice.

10 **Set a time or positive deadline**. Use phrases such as: 'Oliver, when you have had a minute to think about this come back ...' 'I know you are going to be ready to begin shortly Kirsty but just take a minute to get yourself ready first.' 'I know you are feeling annoyed Clinton. Take a time out and in five minutes I'll come back and help you.'

11 **Four-to-one classrooms**. In order to effect positive changes in behaviour make your class four-to-one. Catch them being good, catch them being successful and let them know it. Try to have four specific and positive units of feedback for one of every other type. Of course, the fifth comment will not be negative, it will be neutral. Look at your marking and the comments that you've made. Can you apply the four-to-one rule?

12 **Strip down your language and be specific**. Avoid convoluted instructions such as: 'If we haven't tidied up and put our coats on, then no one is going out to play.' What is the message here? What might a small child hear? She might focus on part of the statement and fail to make sense of any of it. Amy and Denise may end up in tears if all they heard was: 'No one is going out to play.' Alternatively, 'Tidy up now, it's almost playtime,' followed by, 'Great! Put your coats on!' then, 'Let's all go out to play!' gives a clear instruction, plus the emphasis on the fact that, in your classroom, all children help to tidy up and all go out to play.

> 'Keep your opinions to yourself.'
>
> *Sign above serving hatch in an Upminster Secondary School dining hall*

Avoid instructions in disguise. A statement such as, 'Is there anyone who's going to run to assembly?' is supposed to be translated as 'Do not run to assembly.' It is an instruction but it is wearing a heavy disguise! Avoid coded language. 'Cheryl, it may have escaped your attention that Tracey is not at the end of the corridor.' The instruction? Speak more quietly![8]

13 Give single instructions. Multiple questions have been correlated with underperformance of response. Questions that demand only simple recall of factual information are only going to achieve limited thinking on the part of your students.

A high percentage of teacher questions are not answered by pupils but by teachers! Mix questions. To minimize the impact of lack of understanding on behaviour, give clear instructions and repeat. Be specific. Seek 'I' message feedback on understanding. Do not accept head nods. Do not ask: 'Do you understand?' Ask children to explain their understanding with their response.

14 Avoid coded language with generalizations, such as: 'There's a little girl who's not paying attention!' The outcome of this is that everyone stops and pays attention, but not to you! The result is a classroom of children each wondering who is it that is not paying attention. Children are not necessarily familiar with this sort of language. The confusion it can cause leads to uncertainty and possible misbehaviour.

15 Provide safe feedback strategies. Make it safe to say: 'I do not understand'. Use fun techniques that are immediate and reflective. Traffic lights and scoring understanding are both methods that work. When using traffic lights, green means 'I'm ready to go', amber means 'I'm uncertain' and red means 'I don't understand – yet'. Scoring understanding means that giving a score of five means 'I'm on a green light' whereas a score of zero means 'I need help!'

16 Teach and use active listening skills. Circle time and forum theatre are good mechanisms for children to experience and learn turn taking, attentive listening, giving and receiving feedback, asking clarifying and reflective questions. Insist on eye contact when you speak to children or when they speak to one another. Role-play how to give clear eye contact. Ask your headteacher to bring school visitors to your classroom for your class to practise welcoming guests confidently.

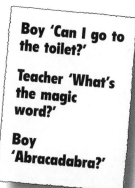

Boy 'Can I go to the toilet?'

Teacher 'What's the magic word?'

Boy 'Abracadabra?'

17 Practise behaviours. For example, practise making noise and being quiet. Turn yourself into a stereo amplifier. When your hand moves up the noise levels increase. When your hand moves down the noise level decreases. A refinement is to have a large clock face with a pointer for different levels of noise marked for suitability: noisy for celebrations; normal for asking questions and giving answers; whispers for paired work and quiet reading; muttering for pole-bridging.

18 Teach children to 'wait for the bus' and 'fly in the private cloud'. These are techniques for anger management. They involve children being able to defer an impulsive response by internalizing their thoughts. 'Waiting for the bus' requires children to imagine that they are at the bus stop and the bus is about to arrive. They are encouraged to see themselves getting onto the bus, sitting down and then moving off. Their immediate angry response – a punch or a kick – is deferred as they conceptualize themselves travelling away from the cause of their anger and leaving it behind. It helps them walk away. 'Flying in the private cloud' is described in detail on page 245.

19 **Time-line for behavioural flexibility**. Ask a child who has misbehaved, without giving negative blame: 'What did you do that was wrong? What would you do if you could do it over again? What will you do in the future?' To help the child learn from an instance of bad behaviour, place him on an imaginary carpet. The carpet represents time. Encourage him to walk back into the past and forward into the future. Practise going back in time and putting things right. Practise the sorts of behaviour that you wish to encourage.

20 **Use names**. Place the name at the beginning of the question or request. So, 'Alistair please open the window' is better than 'Open the window please Alistair' is better than 'Open the window please'.

Review of Part One

List some possible ways in which the physiological resourcefulness for learning could be enhanced among the children in your class.

Can you describe your school's current systems for building self-esteem? Take each of the elements of the BASIS model in turn, and list five things that your school could improve.

For each of the five steps we listed for 'building a base camp for learning', compare your classroom. What further steps can you now take to make your classroom space even more supportive of learning?

Who gets recognition, affirmation and praise in your classroom and for what? For whom might RAP be absent? How can you ensure that your distribution of RAP is equitable?

The ADDS UP method describes some of the best ways to provide positive feedback to keep children in the learning loop. Look at the list. What other methods do you and your colleagues successfully use?

Part Two

Into the foothills of learning

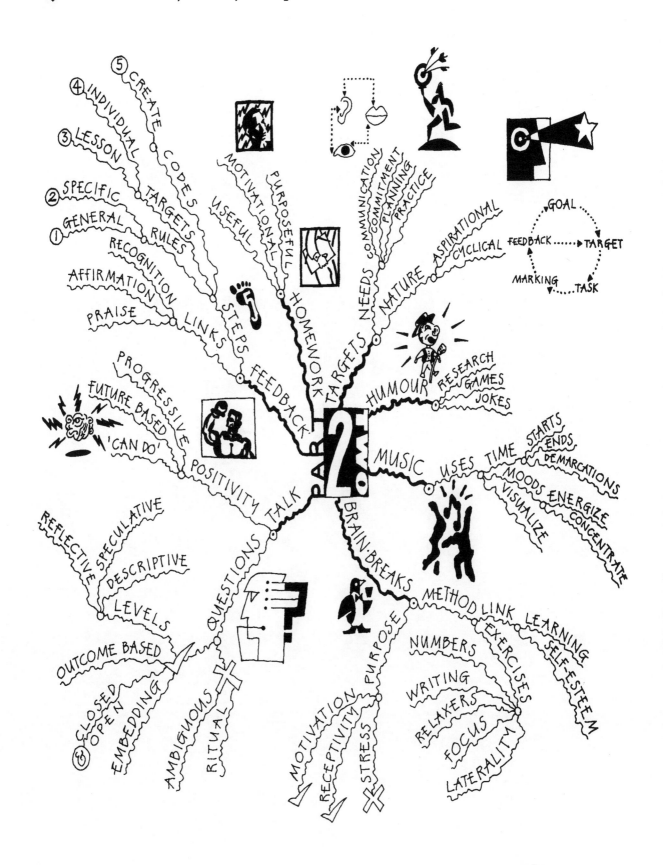

the alps approach – Accelerated Learning in Primary Schools

Preview of Part Two

Into the foothills of learning

In Part Two you will:

find a description of the best way of target-setting with learners.

hear about how teacher talk and effective questioning strategies will accelerate achievement.

learn about target-setting, focused marking and the use of homework.

have the theory behind brain breaks explained and be shown how to use physical movement before, during and after lessons.

find out about music and learning, music and the brain, and how and when to use music in your class.

the alps approach – Accelerated Learning in Primary Schools

Into the foothills of learning

the alps approach – Accelerated Learning in Primary Schools

❶ Target-setting that works

Why target-set?

TARGET SETTING, PROPERLY DONE, CAN BE the main lifelong learning skill that will accelerate the performance of all the children in your class.

Sadly, many target-setting activities are badly done. Often they are a half-hearted attempt to conform to directives passed down from above. A target will only have an impact on learning performance if the individual owns it. When the child owns the target, when it is positively stated so that he can conceptualize the benefits of achieving it, then the child's performance will alter. The capacity to achieve the target must be within the gift of the learner. Targets that are felt to be too abstract, too remote or not relevant to the learner will not engage. Target-setting can help to create a positive and purposeful learning experience, while still meeting any statutory requirement. Target-setting is at the heart of the ALPS experience.

A goal is a visionary thing: a dream with a timescale. Targets are significant landmarks on the journey towards the goal. Setting goals and their related targets is essential to success. When the children memory mapped their aspirations and pinned the maps around the class door, the map was the goal for that child: each strand within the map was an assembly of related targets.

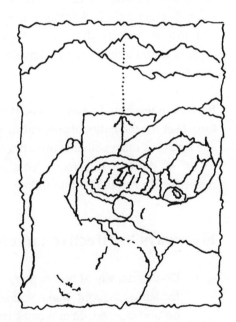

Few of us would make a conscious choice to undertake an activity without an outcome in mind. The outcome may be vague or it may be specific. If it is specific, then there is a well-defined goal and the landmarks, or targets, on route to that goal are easier to identify. The nature of the goals that adults set will vary. The goals may be spiritual or material; they may have a highly principled basis or be morally dubious; they may relate to oneself, one's family or a community or a cause; they may be externalized or internalized. As teachers we concern ourselves with all these possibilities but often neglect the skill of goal-setting itself. Authors such as Daniel Goleman, Martin Seligman, Stephen Covey and Peter Senge all argue in their own way that the capacity to conceptualize a positive goal, to relate patterns of behaviour to that goal and move towards it with self-discipline, can be correlated to success in life – however one may wish to quantify success.

Those people who set clear targets are more successful than those who meander through life. Successful people follow through. If we are motivated to achieve, we set targets. To do less for our children than we would do for ourselves would be treating them as though their progress was less important than our own. A goal requires forethought and those targets that relate to it require planning. The individual needs to commit to the process. If your goal is to have a healthy lifestyle, a target may be to get fit. You join that gym, you undertake a fitness assessment and then you work out according to your plan. If you merely visit the gym and talk of getting fit, that is not a target, that is a diversion.

In the classroom, the ALPS teacher first sets a goal for herself. She has drawn up her life map and is clear about her overall outcome and the significant landmarks towards it. She then has a goal and a series of related targets. When she sits down she can conceptualize successfully achieving that goal. The goal can be vague but the targets need to be defined. Targets give shape and substance to aspiration.

One of her targets may be that each child, whenever asked, will be able to give a clear description of the purpose of any classroom activity. This is measurable. It could be measured by an oral interview, by classroom observation or by the production of a life map. The tasks that relate to this target could include the production of both a class aspiration map and an individual life map by each child. Successfully achieving this will allow the teacher and any child at any time to explain how a classroom activity relates to the map. For example: 'We are learning how to write a letter to a department store because we want to grow up to be adults who can assert their rights.'

There is some terminology that gives us cause for concern as schools go about the business of target-setting. One such word is 'prediction'. This word suggests that the future is written and that a level of passivity can be maintained as each child lives up to, or down to, the expectation of the teacher who is target-setting. If your process can be described as making a prediction, you are not target-setting. Another process that disturbs us is that of setting two targets: one that is 'achievable' and one that is described as 'ambitious'. This process negates the activity of target-setting. If you follow the ALPS method™, all your goals will be ambitious and you will achieve them.

If you are teaching in England or Wales, it is highly likely that at some point you will have to target set for the national curriculum for your class. To the ALPS teacher this is not a hardship; she finds it a most valuable investment of time. Even if this is not required of you, find the time to do it. Without this focus, you will be journeying up a mountain with no idea of the destination, or of the path to follow.

Five ways to effective target-setting

1   Do this activity at home, somewhere comfortable. Make sure that the environment facilitates thought. Make yourself a drink, put on some relaxing music and arrange to be undisturbed. Take a class list and write the subject areas across the top. Break this down further into sections that make sense to you. This may be by statements of attainment, or you may choose to use other classifications. Leave plenty of space down one side for notes. These will be more important than your figures.

2 If you have been given target figures, for example, a percentage of children who must reach Level 2 or 4 in core subjects, forget this until you have completed the first stage of target-setting. Do not begin with the figures, or you will lose the focus. The focus is the children. If you allow your mind to focus on the targets that you have been set, you will develop a negative mindset. Do not despair, if you follow the ALPS method™ of teaching, you will be able to enhance your pupils' performance and meet targets.

3 Work your way down the class list, one child at a time. Take time to think of that child. Let us imagine it is a boy. Visualize him in class, think of how he interacts, how he concentrates, his strengths, his self-image. Now in your mind give him the perfect attitude to learning. Bless him with 100 per cent attendance, immaculate behaviour and excellent concentration skills. Only when you have really focused on that child, with his ability enhanced by those attributes, should you begin target-setting. When you set a target level for that child, set the level that you think he would have the ability to attain, if he were to have every obstacle removed from his path and every positive aid in his self-esteem rucksack.

4 In the blank column down one side make a note of any factors that might hinder that child in achieving the level that you feel he is capable of achieving. These might be poor attendance, low self-esteem, poor listening skills or a lack of concentration. If an obstacle such as poor reading skills has affected your target for him, go back to stage 3 and imagine what he could achieve if his reading skills were accelerated. Re-set his targets accordingly.

5 Now turn your long-term goals into an action plan – plan how you are going to remove those obstacles or, if you cannot remove them, how you will compensate for them. If you need to see a parent, plan to do it. Be honest and upfront. Tell the parent that their child has the ability, show them your figures, plan with them how to remove obstacles. If the child does not complete homework, or if he has poor concentration, use the homework questionnaire to diagnose the problem and help him understand it. If his reading is poor, plan an intense programme to improve it. The ALPS teacher does not accept underachievement. She utilizes every resource available; she will not accept excuses. Do not worry if you cannot immediately see ways to remove every obstacle. Read on through this book and, as you discover more about the ALPS method™, you will begin to devise ways to remove all the learning obstacles for your pupils.

You have done it! You have set your class national curriculum targets for the year. If you are required to set for two years in advance, do it in exactly the same way, but ensure that you also set targets for the end of your academic year, or you will lack direction and focus. Set targets that assume the best motivational levels, parental support, behaviour and attendance. To do less is to make excuses. Your job is to alleviate the difficulties and remove obstacles. As we have said, you cannot 'fix' the home life of your pupils, but you can take any action available and you can raise self-esteem, behaviour, attendance and motivation through following the ALPS method™. In a roundabout way, you may find that you 'fix' aspects of a child's home life through improving his motivation at school.

If you have followed these steps, you should have met any targets that were expected of you. Calculate the figures and do the maths. If you do not measure up, you may have allowed obstacles to remain on your visualized mountain path. If this is the case, you have fallen prey to negative thinking, so go back to stage 3. If you really know that you have put each child in the perfect learning mould and still not fulfilled target figures, talk to the person who set the figures. However, with the types of figures being currently quoted, it would be surprising if most teachers could not set targets that fulfil statutory criteria. The targets will only remain unattained if you allow obstacles to slow your progress.

Sharing the long-term targets with your pupils

There is no value in your setting targets if your pupils have no idea what they are. Obviously, the older your pupils, the more sophisticated your sharing of information can be. We have seen Year 5 and 6 pupils who are familiar with the layout of the national curriculum and understand the levels that they are aiming to attain in Key Stage 2 SATs. They have all been remarkably composed and shown less anxiety about testing than their counterparts who do not share that knowledge. This is how Dermot talked of the science national curriculum:

> MR GREEN is the science curriculum, it's up on the wall. Each letter stands for something. You know what you have to cover this year. I like to look at it and think: 'I know all about magnets, and all about plants, but I need to do more on humans.' I know how I'm doing and I know what to work on. I like it that my teacher gives us the Big Picture, so we know how we are getting on. I can look up things at home if I want to before we do a lesson, or ask my mum and dad to help.

In our visits to ALPS schools we have listened to pupils giving reasoned arguments for their personal national curriculum targets with clarity about their personal strengths and weaknesses. The ALPS teacher shares the destination with her class. She talks of levels and grades honestly, and there is no mystery about the national curriculum or assessments. In our research for this book, we also talked to children who had undergone Key Stage 2 SATs without using the ALPS method™. This is what Claire, now aged 13, had to say:

> I didn't know what would be expected in the tests. I was not confident, I knew that Level 4 was important, but I didn't know how to get it. Our teachers kept telling us to do our best and not to worry, but I did worry. I know they were trying to reassure us, but it didn't work for me. On the day we went into the hall, I didn't have any confidence, I wished I was anywhere but in the test. The first few questions were OK, then I didn't know what I was supposed to do with the rest, I didn't know what was expected. I felt sick. I thought: 'I'll switch off, and ignore it, and do nothing.' Then I'd panic, and think: 'I can't do nothing, I'm supposed to do my best.' But I just didn't know what they wanted of me.

Beforehand all the teachers said: 'It doesn't matter, it's just an assessment.' I believed them, until it actually came to sitting in the exam, then I realized that it does matter. It matters if you can't do your best because you are too nervous to concentrate, and you do not know what is expected of you!

In our research we found that peer pressure adds to the impact of the experience of SATs, in either a negative or a positive way. Between 40 and 50 per cent of Claire's class achieved Level 4 or above in the core subjects. Yet this was what she had to say about her peers:

Almost everybody else achieved Level 4 or 5. When the results came out everyone was going round saying: 'I got Levels 4 and 5.' Some of them got Level 6 and Level 7 too. I felt awful. I wished I had known what to do, then I could have had 4s too. I got 3s for all the subjects.

When we told Claire that, in fact, only two or three of her peers had attained Level 5, and none had achieved anything higher, she would not believe it. Then she became tearful. This is an argument for being explicit about grades. Claire spent three years believing that she had been the lowest achiever in primary school. Quite probably, she also told her peers that she had achieved Levels 4 and 5. More than half of her year group suffered under the same illusion that they were the only losers in this mystery contest. This is the effect that this experience had on her self-esteem as a learner:

At secondary school it took me ages to begin to catch up. I worked hard and my mum encouraged me, but I didn't like to speak up too much in case I was wrong. Some subjects like German were OK, because we hadn't done them in primary school and I found I was good at them. Now I am in the top group of my class at everything, I realize I am bright, but I just didn't do well at primary school. I do not know why. If I'd realized how important it is to try I'd have worked much harder.

Stories like that of Claire are commonplace in classrooms where there is no direct target-setting. We owe it to our children to make sure that they know their destination and know that they will be helped along the way. Contrast her story to this further extract from Shaun's interview:

When I went to secondary school my behaviour and my work slipped for a little while.

Why do you think that happened?

I do not know, except that nobody had set me targets, like you did. It just sort of crept in.

What made you turn yourself back around?

When my mum went to see my form tutor, on one of those days when your mum sees the school, she told him about me. He spoke to me, and then he set me targets. I thought I might as well do them, as it was worth it, really. I knew how much better it is if you meet your targets, like we used to do at primary school.

So targets are important?

Yes. Once they were set I just started doing them. My work and my behaviour improved, and now if I slip, my friends remind me and say: 'It's not worth it, Shaun.' It's not worth it, is it? Because it's all to do with your future. You've got to work hard and meet your targets.

Shaun and Claire both went on the same journey, but one knew the destination and the landmarks on the way, while the other journeyed in a blindfold with no sense of direction. It was not Claire's Level 3 grades that affected her self-esteem, the damage was done by the lack of understanding of how her attainment had been measured and the frustration at knowing that she had been assessed inaccurately. Target-setting is not a paper exercise to keep the authorities at bay, it is an essential element of the ALPS method™ of teaching.

Making the targets work

As we have said, a target without related tasks is merely a diversion. Nobody ever made it to the top without a plan. You have now set your long-term goals. These need to be translated into short-term targets. To extend our metaphor, the expedition needs to be broken down into short, achievable journeys, with plenty of opportunities to set up camp along the way. It is essential that all the members of the expedition know where they are going and what is expected of them. They also need regular feedback regarding their progress. As each short-term target is met, another needs to be set.

Setting short-term targets for the whole class is easy. At the beginning of each lesson you will give the Big Picture, and within that you will tell the class exactly what they are going to achieve in the lesson.

Write your class targets on a large piece of card, such as: 'By the end of this week, we will all be able to write a beautiful letter "S".' Display it on the wall, or by the whiteboard, and refer to it regularly. When Bethany writes a perfect letter 'S', recognize her success; for example, by displaying her letter 'S' next to the target, or by writing her name on a chart. Remember, if you set the target, you need to take action to make sure that everybody accomplishes it – so if Yacob needs additional help, make sure that you plan for it. By the end of the week, every child must have achieved the target.

There are many targets, however, that cannot be set for the whole class, as children all have individual needs. An effective way to accelerate individual improvement is to use target cards with each child. These target cards are a part of a whole package of the RAP model of focused marking and feedback. No individual part of this package stands alone or is fully effective without the others. Using target cards can be a good starting point for focusing your mind on your expectations and can help with the monitoring of performance.

Design a target card and make enough for each child. Use one card for each child per subject area, or for a type of activity. Large cards covering every subject will become meaningless due to a lack of focus. To begin with, narrow your focus and choose one area to pilot the cards, such as story writing. When you mark the next batch of stories, take the target cards home with you. Focus on each individual child, and identify two or three specific points for improvement. Write them on the card. Here is an example from a Year 2 pupil's story targets:

Go back to page 86 for RAP

T Form letter m correctly

T Use paragraphs

T Use four words instead of 'said'.

At the next story-writing session, give the children their previous piece of work along with the target cards. Explain what the targets mean to any child who is unsure. When you first use target cards, it is easier to set many children the same targets so that you can explain to the whole class. As time goes on, they will become more adept at understanding your meaning and setting their own new targets. Once every child understands their own individual targets, begin the lesson, ensuring that target cards are clearly visible on desks. At regular intervals during the lesson refer to targets and make affirmations such as: 'Everybody in this class is looking at their cards and we are all meeting our targets.' Remember that an affirmation is a statement that something is already true, so make your statements strong and positive.

If Sandeep has forgotten all about his targets and is merrily speed writing in his huge script, he will hear your affirmation and steady himself. If he does not, give an individual affirmation: 'Sandeep is slowing down and is writing smaller!' Follow with praise: 'I love that line of writing there, Sandeep, it is so small and neat.'

When you collect in the work, collect in the target cards. When you mark the stories, refer to the target cards and measure how far each individual has met their targets. It is vitally important that you give feedback. With younger children, this is usually necessary on a one-to-one basis, and you may well give feedback as you mark during the session. The important thing is that you give feedback that is directly related to the targets. You may well comment on other aspects of the work too, but there is little point in setting targets if you do not monitor progress. With older children it is usually effective if you give feedback immediately prior to the next story-writing session, although a quick recognition of improvement can be given more immediately such as: 'When I marked the stories last night I noticed how Julian used speech marks consistently throughout. You met your target, Julian. Well done!'

Many schools have set policies on marking. It is worth considering how marking policies are linked to target-setting. Think about how you use your marking to give feedback that motivates your pupils to meet their targets. One school had a rule that no target on a card should be left unachieved for more than three weeks. If a target was not achieved within that timescale, either the target was mismatched, or the teacher was not using RAP effectively enough.

My target for handwriting is to keep it a bit bigger. It's much better now. If it wasn't on my target card, I'll still try but it wouldn't be as easy to remember.

Target motivators

Here are seven simple target motivators.

> **1** If you are marking a piece of work from a child who is failing to meet targets, write a specific reward plan at the bottom. This could be: 'When you use joined up writing for a whole paragraph on Monday, I will arrange for you to show it to Mrs M.' Remind him of the reward as he works on Monday and ensure that he achieves the target.
>
> **2** Write a list with every pupil's grade or score from a previous piece of work. Write at the top the statement: 'This week we are all going to increase our score.' When you announce the next set of scores, allow children to use a fun brightly coloured pen to write up their improved score. In order to focus on improvement rather than raw

the alps approach – Accelerated Learning in Primary Schools

score, you can simply choose to write in the difference between the first score and the second, so both Annie and Amrit may score 12, but Amrit's score went from 48 to 60, while Annie's went from 36 to 48.

3   Make the class or a group race to achieve a target. Put all the names on the wall. The first to achieve it writes FIRST next to his name. Carry on until all have achieved the target and then have a group celebration. If your targets are appropriate and your use of RAP is strong, it will be a close race.

4   Create a 'Target Card Achievers Board' to pin up all completed target cards. Decorate it with balloons and banners, along with positive messages, of course!

5   Create a 'Target Terminator Award'. Design a certificate to award whenever a set of targets is achieved. Have a Target Terminator of the day, of the week or of the month. When the novelty wears off, design another award. Make it fun and a cause for celebration.

6   Create a Target Club for lunchtime work on meeting targets. Send target cards home, and ask parents to help their child to achieve targets. Set little reinforcement tasks for home that will accelerate a child's progress towards achieving his targets.

7   Send certificates to parents of children who achieve targets, saying: 'I'm the proud parent of a Target Terminator.' Be creative, children love to please their parents! Encourage parents to take an active part in target-setting and achievement. Parental RAP is remarkably effective.

Target-setting and marking are closely linked and must form an ongoing cycle:

(goal)
↓
target
↓
task
↓
marking and feedback
↓
revised target

Each short-term target should lead the child further towards attaining longer-term targets and then towards meeting your national curriculum targets for the end of that year and beyond towards your long-term goals. Of course, targets can be set for anything, and the ALPS teacher uses these methods to influence behaviour, attitude, attendance, homework and punctuality. She uses a wide range of target-setting motivators to ensure that the obstacles she identified when setting her annual class targets are removed from the path. Target-setting is at the heart of the ALPS method™. Without goals or targets, you have nothing to accelerate towards.

❷ Positive classroom talk

Self-talk: how to help children stay positive

> People's beliefs about their abilities have a profound effect on their abilities. Ability is not a fixed property; there is a huge variability in how you perform. People who have a sense of self-efficacy bounce back from failures; they approach things in terms of how to handle them rather than worrying about what can go wrong.

Albert Bandura, New York Times, 8 May 1988

> The reality is that the quality of life does not depend on what others think of us and what we own. The bottom line is, rather, how we feel about ourselves and what happens to us. To improve life we must improve the quality of experience.

Mihaly Csikszentmihalyi, 1990

A PRIMARY HEADTEACHER ATTENDING ONE OF OUR COURSES on accelerated learning explained how he and his staff had tried to eradicate the word 'not'. In assessment documentation when a child was being characterized as capable of demonstrating a given skill, 'yes' and 'no' were replaced with 'yes' and 'not yet'. Throughout his school he had tried to develop the 'not yet' principle.

Often a child will give up when confronting complexity or seeming difficulty, saying: 'I can't do this'. If this experience is reinforced by successive 'failures', then the 'I can't do' attitude begins to harden. Such attitudes can persist and can be transferred into other areas of life and begin to limit the child's willingness to take risks. Taking risks is an essential part of learning. Every child needs to develop a 'not yet' attitude.

A preoccupation with comparing ourselves with others, fuelled in part by grades and sets and hierarchies based on external measures, can also lead to the dead-end of making the connection: 'I got a low score, therefore I'm stupid.' The work of Carole Dweck (1988) illustrates the difference between getting pupils to think about what they are doing on the one hand and, on the other hand, focusing on how well they are doing. One of her conclusions was: 'pupils led to think mostly about how well they are doing – or even worse, how well they are doing compared to everyone else – are less likely to do well.' These findings point to the value of absorption learning: learning where the motivation comes from a curiosity and engagement with the experience itself.

Dweck demonstrates a vicious cycle when learning is seen as a means to an end – where the end is a reward or a good grade. A cycle of self-recrimination develops where the learner thinks: 'I failed therefore I'm stupid and if I'm stupid then there's no point in trying harder next time.' In this state, avoidance strategies kick in to help avoid the self-recrimination of failure. The cycle can become more threatening when the learner is surrounded by comments that reinforce the view that intelligence is innate and ability is a gift at birth. Comments such as, 'She's a bright child', 'He's done well but his brother was also very gifted', 'We have more than our share of able children this year' can make a child believe you either have 'it' or you have not. 'It' is perceived as being the fixed commodity, genetically pre-determined and packaged as our life inheritance, of intelligence. As soon as a child begins to believe that intelligence is an inherited commodity, the inevitable end-point is: 'If I don't have "it", what's the point of trying?'

For teachers, it becomes a vicious cycle. There is a heavy industry built around the notion of the 'able child' with all the articles attempting to define the characteristics of such a phenomenon. There are schools that have units, masterclasses or extension schemes for the able child. Apparently, gifted children are 'challenging', so there are books, conferences, staff development programmes and videos to help teachers to meet the challenge.

If intelligence were a fixed phenomenon, what would be the point of trying to develop it? If intelligence is a product of genetic inheritance, then why intervene? This is the underlying presupposition that locks many teachers and pupils into a 'what can be done?' attitude. Caroline Dweck's work looked at the quality of resilience. How had the coping strategies that are learned through accommodating failure actually helped learners? What happened when the coping strategies were not there?

In one of her research studies Dweck found the least resilient group to be 'high-ability' girls. In the face of complexity and adversity these girls showed less resilience and less willingness to persevere. In her observations many of these girls had sailed through the gateways that formal education had provided. As they had advanced through a system that assigned a high value to outcome and performance, rather than learning for improvement, they were accompanied by the reassuring endorsements: 'You're very capable', 'You are bound to do well', 'You are a high achiever'. As a consequence, they were more susceptible to the belief that there are innate abilities. When they confronted genuine difficulty, they seemed to think they had simply bumped their heads against their limit. This highlights the necessity for children to be challenged continually in class and to tackle work that demands that they take risks and learn from their mistakes.

In our observations many girls internalize the blame for failure in such circumstances. Yet many boys, for whatever reasons, externalize blame. Thinking back to Eddie and his painting lessons, we can see that he felt the reason his painting became messy was that Annie had taken his paintbrush. But Annie felt that her painting was wrong because she had used the wrong brush and, anyway, she knows that she is 'useless at art'. When the paintings were displayed, Eddie and Annie both felt that theirs were the worst, which to them proved the point. Eddie hit Annie, and Annie knew that it was all her fault. Nisha, on the other hand, was disappointed with her painting but in the next lesson remembered to use a paper towel to wipe her brush dry. Her next painting was a success. Eddie and Annie repeated the previous experience and their next paintings were messy as well. In every case, the more emphasis that is placed on performance outcomes, the more severely students are set back by what they perceive as failure.

125

So what's the answer?

Part of the teacher's role is to help displace 'not' with 'not yet'. Professor Arthur Costa of the Institute of Intelligence at Berkeley, Northern California identified twelve intelligent behaviours.[9] He identified 'persistence' as his number one. To persist is to behave as though 'not yet'. What does a child in your class do when the solution to a problem is not immediately apparent? Do they persist? Do they give up? If they give up, what happens then? Do they blame themselves? Do they blame others? Circumstances? The equipment? The task? Do you set the example that everyone is challenged sometimes, and that everyone experiences occasions when they 'don't understand – yet'?

Persistence is a lifelong transferable learning attribute that is not best served by doing the same things again and again, each time for longer or with more intensity. Phrases like, 'Put your thinking cap on', 'Think harder', or 'Just stop and think about it' all imply that the speed with which a child reaches an outcome is shaped by some ill-defined and improperly understood physical effort. To develop persistence in a learner is to value the questions as well as the answers. Ultimately it is not how many answers the child knows that will help in life, but what they do when they do not know the answers. Annie finds it difficult to problem-solve. When her teacher asks a question, she immediately panics and makes a quick response in the hope that she is right. Amrit, on the other hand, thinks for a moment and then responds: 'I'm not sure. Could you explain again how?' When a teacher tells Annie to 'think harder' she turns red and resolves to tell her mother that she has a stomach-ache the next time she has maths first lesson. What is needed is a repertoire: 'How many ways can we solve this problem?' is better than 'Who can tell me, hands up?'

The capacity to persist is enhanced by positive self-talk – 'I can do this ... I'll try a different way and then it will work' – and a repertoire of problem-solving approaches. The first stage is to encourage children to develop positive self-talk: change 'low or no can do' talk to 'I or high can-do' talk!

Low or no can do	I or high can do
No	Not yet
Never	When I'm ready to
I can't	I can
I'm no good at	I'm getting better at
It's not cool to be keen	I'm cool and I'm keen!
No one in my family can	I'll be the first in my family who can
I do not want to be different	I do not need to be the same
No one likes me	Sharon's my friend
I got a low score	I'll make sure I get better next time
I'm stuck!	I'll move on and come back to it
I can't do this	What will it be like when I can?

To encourage high can do attitudes, avoid the absolute of avoiding failure at all costs: make failure part of learning. When someone gets stuck, help them experience the temporary nature of it: 'Gather round everyone, Ashley says he's stuck.' Struggling to cope is life itself, so why should not struggle be part of the classroom? You help by citing this moment as part of a learning process. Provide good questions for pupils to ask of themselves when they begin to experience 'stuckness': 'What is another way of trying this?' 'Let me go through it again a step at a time', 'How would a teacher do this?' 'How will I teach this difficult bit to my little sister?'

Positive self-talk

In everyday classroom discussion, use the 'not yet' language. When a child laments that he cannot do something, avoid saying, 'Oh yes you can' or 'You're not trying hard enough' and be surprised and curious. Try saying, 'That's interesting – what do you think has made you stuck?' or, 'I know you cannot do it, not yet anyway, but what would it be like if you could?' Encourage persistence and a 'can do' mindset and open up dialogue about learning processes.

Finally, in your classroom provide educative feedback loops that are safe. Make it safe to say 'I do not understand – yet!'

Using the language of progression

In February 1999, Prime Minister Tony Blair announced his government's intention that by the end of a second term of office, 50 per cent of adults under the age of thirty were to have actively engaged in university-level programmes of one sort or another. Setting ambitious targets has been part of his government's agenda for education. So too is the subsequent practice of talking up those targets in an enrolling manner. Defending national targets for primary school children, he told a conference for headteachers in June 1999: 'Targets, tests and other initiatives such as the literacy and numeracy hour put pressure on teachers: they put pressure on all of us – not least David Blunkett and me, with our commitment to ambitious national targets. And rightly so, for a key modernizing principle of this government is that we are all accountable.'

Setting ambitious targets is part of the current agenda for education. So too has been the subsequent practice of talking about those targets in a persuasive manner. Leaving aside the political arguments about targets and the merits or otherwise of such commitments, the trend is for politicians to actively talk up the possibilities of achievement. The rhetoric is in part about enrolling, but is also about embedding beliefs. In classrooms, when teachers encourage children to set targets, they also need to utilize language to embed belief. If, as a teacher, you are dismissive about the significance of a child's contribution or about the targets she has worked to, you unwittingly subvert your own efforts. In the classroom, talking up the language of achievement goes beyond rhetoric. It influences performance.

In some of the best classes we have been in, we have observed teachers use the language of progression, saying things like: 'When you do well in your SATs we will all have a party', 'When you go on into secondary school you will need to be good at ...', 'At the end of Year 11 you will sit your GCSE exams and ...', 'When you have passed all your GCSE exams, you can then choose to ...', 'When you go to university, you will need to be good at planning' or 'Being able to manage your own time is important for when you get your first job'. For some children they will never hear words like these at home. Perhaps there has been no one at home in full-time, extended employment for three generations. Perhaps there are no role models there, or in the extended family, or even within the community for progression into further or higher education or the world of work. So where would the child ever hear terms like these used? To talk up the language of progression deliberately – the language of personal autonomy – is to continue to extend the horizons of possibility for that child. To do otherwise, at the behest of sociologists or of socio-economic data, is in effect to deny those possibilities.

On parents' consultation evenings we have heard teachers use the language of progression: 'When your son goes on to ...', 'Have you begun to think about what sorts of things your daughter might want to do after school?' Listed below are practical ideas to help children experience the language of progression and develop their aspirational thinking.

 Invite professionals in to talk about their professions; for example, nurses, doctors, vets and engineers. Do remember to prime them to talk about how everyone can achieve – both genders too. Put up displays about these professions and the necessary qualifications alongside photographs of the class with the adults.

 Encourage university students to work with groups – not student teachers, but others who will talk to children about going to university.

 Arrange visits to local universities for one-off lectures or visits to laboratories or museums.

 Follow up with displays in school – for example, photos of inside the university – to reinforce the idea and make it familiar.

 Invite secondary teachers to talk positively to children about their futures, not the usual pre-transfer talk, but before that stage.

 Arrange mentoring links with local sixth-formers.

 Time-line the academic challenges ahead – each set of SATs, GCSEs, A-levels and so on – include stuff like MA and PhD too!

the alps approach – Accelerated Learning in Primary Schools

Set up after-school clubs to widen children's experience. For example, in an Inner London School the staff organized a Pony Club led by a riding teacher. The children learned simple anatomy and had visitors like a vet and a farrier to talk to them, opening their horizons and giving them opportunities to learn about things beyond their immediate world.

 Create a photo board of children outside school involved in their hobbies; for example, gaining medals for swimming, morris dancing, riding or football. When teaching children who have serious outside interests, you may be the first teacher to know about it. Along with the display put photos of people who do these things professionally – this gives the idea that they also started at a young age, so anyone can do it!

As part of the research for this book, the children from a Year 5 class were tracked through Year 6 and then on to secondary school. Listed below are the verbatim comments from the transcript of their interviews. They were asked why they worked so hard.

I work hard for myself. I work hard for the future so that I can get a good job. And I also work hard to pay off my teachers and my mum and dad and everyone who has helped me.
Liam

I work hard to make my mum and dad proud of me. I work hard to make my teachers proud of me. I work hard to make myself proud. I work hard to do well in secondary school. I work hard to show myself and everyone else that I can do it.
Ruth

I worked hard because I wanted to pass my SATs and to get a good grade in secondary school. I also worked hard to get a good and responsible job when I grow up.
Javier

I work hard because I need more knowledge for the future ahead of me.
Mileta

I work hard because I would like to pass all my exams. I would like to get a good degree in university and I would also like to get a good job. I also work hard because I would like to know lots of different things.
Hamida

Well I worked hard because I had my SATs and I worked hard for myself to learn and get a good job.
Lisa

I work hard because I want to get a good grade in work. Also I want to be able to get a good job when I am older. I work hard to show everyone how hard I try.
Russell

Because I do it for myself. So that I can be educated. To make my parents proud. To make my teachers happy. To get a good report. So I'm ready for secondary school.
Rob

To pass my SATs. To teach my little sister.
Mark

For some of these children, clarity about what the future could offer and a sense of self-efficacy in journeying towards it had been the result of encountering good teachers using good methods in a good school. For some of their parents, the school and the teachers whom their children met there had provided a language of progression, so that they too were better positioned to talk positively with their own children about what the future could offer.

How to talk so pupils learn

Teaching thinking skills not only makes pupils more intelligent, it raises standards of achievement.

Michael Barber, Times Educational Supplement, May 1999

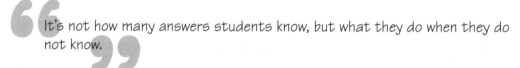

It's not how many answers students know, but what they do when they do not know.

Professor Arthur Costa, Institute of Intelligence, Berkeley[10]

Barbara Maines and George Robinson conducted research on the association between the language of the classroom and children with patterns of difficult behaviour. In 'Teacher Talk and Pupil Behaviour'[11] they concluded with the observation that: 'the importance of an adequate understanding of the language she hears in school cannot be underestimated since she is likely to be required to understand, learn from or obey teacher talk every few minutes of the school day.' The research explored the association between the language of the classroom and the behaviour of pupils with patterns of difficult behaviour. This is how they describe the project:

The study followed a sample of thirty-two pupils in eleven infant and lower junior classes. They had been selected by their class teacher because they were described as restless, frequently off task and often disturbing to other children. Pupil behaviour was observed and incidents of minor disruption were counted before the intervention began and again after four weeks. The eleven teachers were given a short training session and a handout which invited them to make prescribed changes in their language.

These were:

1 Before giving any instruction or information the teacher was asked to pay special attention to maintaining the child's attention by using her name, keeping eye contact.

2 Efforts were made to improve the clarity of the language and avoid classroom jargon and school-based codes which might be misunderstood by some children.

3 Check the child's understanding before ending the interaction.

4 Encourage the child to state in her own language the agreed plan or an understanding of the information.

During the research project the frequency of 'disruptive behaviours' was measured in a selection of pupils who had been described as difficult to maintain on task and often in trouble. The effects of the changes in teacher language were to reduce by 50 per cent the observed incidents of disruption. The outcome was measured by assessing changes in pupil behaviour and in teacher attitude to the intervention. Of the original sample, complete records were obtained from only seventeen children because of absences. Of these, fourteen showed improvements in their behaviour. Teacher attitudes were generally favourable but some found it hard to make and maintain the changes. They did not seem to be aware of the quite dramatic improvements made by some pupils.

If fourteen out of seventeen children were to make dramatic improvements in their behaviour and attitude to learning, would you notice? If you had the formula to make this amount of change, would you continue to use it? Researchers have identified a correlation between the way teachers ask questions and subsequent levels of pupil engagement and achievement. You can influence the behaviour and the levels of academic performance of your class through the way that you choose to ask questions. In the ALPS classroom there are two sorts of questioning strategies: questions generated by the teacher and questions generated by the pupils, with the emphasis shifted in favour of the latter. The next section contains some suggestions as to how you can enhance your questioning strategies.

Improving your questioning strategies

Processing time

Allow processing time. The younger the learner, the more time they may need to assimilate the question, form a range of alternative responses, cue the articulation of the appropriate response and, finally, volunteer their response. The more you rely on questions that reward simple recall of information, the more you may struggle to achieve a properly cued response. Some children will not take the risk of responding to 'Do you know?' questions. Responding to 'Hands up who can tell me?' is a double jeopardy. You take the risk of not knowing or getting it wrong, and the risk of putting your hand up.

Rowe (1996) called processing time 'wait-time' and found that when teachers deliberately waited for the response to the question – three to ten seconds – not only did the length of student response increase, but the probability of clarification, speculation about alternatives and on-task conversation increased. Here is a summary of the findings:

1 The length of the students' responses increased.

2 The number of freely offered and appropriate student responses, unsolicited by the teacher, increased.

3 Failure to respond – 'I do not know' or no answer – decreased.

4 Inflected responses decreased, thus students appeared to be more confident in their answers.

5 The number of speculative responses increased, thus students appeared to be more willing to think about alternative explanations.

6 Children worked together more at comparing data.

7 Children made more inferences from evidence.

8 The frequency of questions raised by students increased.

9 The frequency of responses by students who were rated relatively 'slow' by their teachers, increased.

Remember, a high percentage of teachers end up answering their own questions! They get impatient for an answer because they are keen to progress to the next question. Questioning becomes a devalued currency. The way to avoid this is to ask fewer simple recall of information questions and to use combinations of the following instead.

Processing cues
Provide processing cues. These can be implicit in the question or utilize an external prompt. An implicit processing cue could take the form of any of these examples:

> In a minute I am going to ask you about x. Before I ask you about x let me first ...
> Nicola, I am going to come to you next and ...
> Last week we did x. I'd like you to think of three words we learned to do with x ...
> Alistair, if you were to teach this to your younger brother how ...

The intention behind these questions is that they each contain implicit processing cues that defer an immediate response in favour of a delayed response. This creates a longer processing time and, in some of the examples, a parameter to shape the response. You can also ask children to repeat the question to you to allow time for processing.

Questioning strategies which utilize external processing cues are included in the following examples:

Last week we did x. I'd like you to think of three things we learned to do with x. (Pause) Now say your things to your partner and then listen as they say theirs. (Pause) Now with your partner, see if you can agree on five things to do with x.

Shortly, I'd like each pair to think of as many words as they can that are to do with ... and then, in your pairs, I'd like you to write them down. I am going to play the music and before the music stops you have to write down as many as you can. (Pause) Ready?'

Some strategies combine implicit processing cues:

What would be a good question to ask a Roman centurion if he were here in our classroom today?

And then add external parameters:

Try your question on someone nearby. They have to answer as a Roman centurion would.

Embedding questions

Embed questions at the outset of a learning experience: 'By the end of the lesson we will be able to answer the following questions ...', 'What would it be like if we had answers to the following ...?' 'Before we are finished we will be able to ...'.

Why? The research of Donald Shachter and others into human memory shows that when the curiosity of a learner is engaged, he processes for an answer in a number of ways and at a number of levels. Humans process actively in a conscious way, but the mind also works unconsciously. This is the 'tip of the tongue' phenomenon. For example, you attempt consciously to attach a name to a face. You fail to do so and you give up. Later in a different and non-related activity when you are not actively seeking a resolution, the name comes back to you. Embedding questions at the outset and during a learning experience can engage the same phenomenon.

Positive start questions

Start lessons positively. By utilizing the above questioning strategies you can avoid falling into the negative, fretful and defeatist quality of 'There are three people who are not ready yet', and all the other 'struggling-to-fire-the-lesson-into-life' approaches.

Outcomes questions

Do you encourage outcomes thinking? 'What will the finished piece of work be like?' 'How will you know you have successfully completed it?' 'How would someone else know you had been successful: what would they see, what would they say to you and you to them, how would you feel?'

Closed and open ratios

Change the balance of teacher to pupil talk from 80 per cent teacher talk towards 20 per cent teacher talk, with the maximum of structured on-task pupil discussion. Balance your use of open and closed questions. An open question offers the possibility of a variety of responses and solicits opinion. A closed question has one answer. Do you ask follow-up questions? If so, do they take the thinking to a higher level? How do you cue the response to open-ended questions?

Further ideas

How do you enhance the quality of questions in group-work? Do you use the 'individual, work as a pair, share as a group, present to the class' method to its best effect? Do you provide pupils with the sorts of questions that they might want to ask?

Do your questions motivate? Can you use the motivational numbers – 3s, 5s and 7s[12] – to put challenge within a task? Can you preface your question with an individual's name and a motivational challenge: 'Julie, I know you can give me three examples ...' Can you do so in ways that make it safe to get it wrong?

Do you ask pupils to explain their thinking? What do you do when you ask the question, 'What makes you think that, Rajan?' and get the answer 'Dunno, sir'? Do you provide other extending questions: 'What other alternatives did you consider?' 'Why did you reject them?' 'What makes this choice the best?'

Do you reflect back? 'So, if I'm right what you are saying is ...'

Do you ask children to listen actively? Summarize? Speculate? Do you play devil's advocate? Can you encourage upside-down thinking by asking for the opposite point of view, or an outrageous alternative?

Do you encourage thinking about thinking through your use of questions? Do you provide opportunities for pupils to explain the processes they chose, as well as describe the outcome?

Things to avoid!

Finally, there are things to be avoided. Minimize the amount of 'Hands up who can tell me' questions, and minimize pouncing! When pounced upon – 'Nicola, how tall was a Brontosaurus Rex?' – children and adults pronounce the first thing that comes along: 'It came up to the curtains Miss!'

Ritual questions

In a 1988 research survey into pre-school and early school language use, 60 per cent of the interactions between teacher and pupil took the form of interrogation with many conversations opened and maintained by questions. In many cases cited, what elicited a response was not the words themselves but the surrounding non-verbal and situational cues. In a Scottish infant class we observed, a boy was being asked about his start to the day: 'How are you this morning?' He looked quizzically at the adult before replying 'Donald' and wandering off. He did not understand what he had been asked and took his cues from elsewhere. If he had been required to take ownership and his name had been used, 'Donald, tell me what you have been doing this morning?', it may have helped him engage more meaningfully.

Coded questions

There are codes that are used exclusively in classrooms. Such codes are idiomatic and difficult for many children to crack. Children do not come across the codes out of a class environment: 'Jeremy, feet are not for shuffling!' Sometimes the codes contain heavily disguised instructions: 'What do we not do when we go to the toilet?' The answer for those of us who are deeply baffled is, apparently, 'run'.

Ambiguous questions

Another variant on a coded question is one that is subject to different interpretations: 'Who has not put away their crayons yet?' Or a variant, which causes general confusion, is known as a nominalization and goes like this: 'We're all being very naughty aren't we?' The effect of this sort of vague generalized judgement – 'There's a little girl who isn't paying attention' – is to stop everyone in their tracks while they sneak a look at who this could possibly be!

And the nominations for the world's most useless question are:

Now class, do you understand?

Does everyone understand?

Who doesn't understand?

❸ Providing educative feedback

Focused marking

> ❝Intelligence is a solution system run by an association system alerted by an emotional system.❞
>
> *Robert Sylwester*[13]

LEARNING SHOULD BE A LIFELONG JOURNEY. If we see target-setting as the process that decides each interim destination, we can see feedback as the signposting along the way. Quality marking and feedback are key components of the ALPS method™. Without targets, education lacks purpose and focus. Without clear feedback, progress will be slow and the learner may stray from the path. Children need feedback that provides a clear idea of progress being made towards targets.

The evidence of the 1998 research on improving formative assessment (Black and Wiliam, 1998) showed that much teaching and learning was ineffective because feedback was not of sufficient quality or at the right moment. The findings were derived from a comparison of international research and pointed to three areas for improvement of the feedback loop.

My teacher is saying 'Well done Chloe' and smiling at me. It makes me feel happy so I try harder.

1 Feedback from teacher to pupil:

➡ Give specific feedback about the particular qualities of that pupil's work.

➡ Give specific advice on what she can do to improve.

➡ Do not make any comparison with other pupils.

➡ Avoid giving overall marks – this takes attention away from the qualitative feedback.

➡ Give feedback during the learning process – at the end is too late to guide learning.

the alps approach – Accelerated Learning in Primary Schools

2   Pupils' self-assessment (feedback to self):

➡ Provide training for pupils in self-assessment.

➡ Ensure they understand the purposes of their learning, so they can grasp what they need to do to achieve.

➡ Include self-assessment as an essential part of the learning process.

3   Feedback from pupils to teacher:

➡ When designing every piece of teaching, build in opportunities for pupils to express their understanding.

➡ Actively involve all pupils in reflective dialogue and discussion designed to explore their understanding by using open questioning.

➡ Use regular short tests or exercises to get feedback in order to adjust teaching and learning.

A considerable amount of the feedback that you give is in the marking of work when the child is not present. Marking is most effective when it supports the target-setting process and is an integral part of the cycle:

> Jason attained a Level 4 for his story this week for the first time. We are all extremely proud of you, Jason!

✓ (goal)

✓ target

✓ task

✓ marking and feedback

✓ revised target.

Marking work takes up many working hours for the average teacher and is a common source of stress and frustration. We have all spent late Sunday evenings marking endless comprehension tasks or maths exercises, making the same comment over and over: 'Please write on every line' or 'Join up your writing!' The good news is that the ALPS method™ helps you to be more effective with your marking, but without taking more time.

Below are five steps that will help you to make good use of the time that you spend marking. These will help you to ensure that your feedback has maximum effect on your pupils' learning.

> **Helen's handwriting has improved tremendously this term. Well done, Helen!**

In brief, these steps are:

1 Establish some 'General Rules' for all pieces of work that you mark.

2 Establish some 'Task Rules' for specific types of work.

3 Develop a method of sharing your 'Lesson Targets' with the class.

4 Mark according to pupils' 'Individual Targets'.

5 Develop some marking codes to speed up your marking and your pupils' progress.

In detail, these steps are as follows.

1 Establish some 'General Rules'
Create rules for every piece of written work that your class will complete during the year. Spend time teaching the rules and then display them on a board in the classroom. You may need a few practice sessions to rehearse for success, but make it clear that these rules are to be applied consistently and without exception. If a child does not follow the rules, you will not mark his work until he has corrected it.

Here are some rules that a teacher set for a Year 4 class for written work:

! Names on top left corner

! Date on top right corner

! Underline title

! Use every line

! Use every page

! Join up all writing

! Line across page at end of work.

**Maths
Brainbox
this
lesson
was**

SARAH
RICHARDSON

Once these rules were established and displayed they were all followed. No child broke the rules, as they learned that if they did so they would have to correct them. It is important to be explicit and also to display the list. Visual cues are subconsciously absorbed over time. A positive affirmation such as 'We all follow the work rules' at the top of the display can make it even more powerful.

One teacher also listed her rules on a checklist. For the first few weeks of the year, she placed a checklist in front of each child at the start of each lesson. She then asked pupils to clip it to their finished work after they had ticked each statement to show that they had followed the rules. If they had forgotten to follow a rule, they either corrected their work or, if this were not possible,

the alps approach – Accelerated Learning in Primary Schools

wrote an explanation. Within a few weeks, she had eliminated any need to make repeated comments about presentation.

If you teach young children, be creative with how you teach your rules and display them. Use graphics and cartoons, and put posters where you can point to them and remind children of the rules. A Reception class teacher told us of one of her rules:

> *Fabulous work Karunveer! I was thrilled to mark this. Thank you.*

> I was driven to distraction during the Literacy Hour by the fact that very young children can often not remember instructions. I would set a group to work on a task where I wanted them to write freely without asking me for assistance. Within two minutes I would have a little queue behind me, wanting help and reassurance.
>
> I decided that they needed a visual cue that would remind them that they were to free-write. We developed the saying: 'You can't go wrong on pink!' Now whenever I want them to free-write, we use either pink paper or our pink books. It was so simple, and gave them so much confidence to write freely. They now write a lot more and have developed much more independence, because it's true, in my class, you can't go wrong on pink!

This can be extended. Pale blue means this is a draft; light green means children can use a dictionary; yellow means that children should work in pairs.

Another teacher displayed the rules on children's desks at the beginning of the year. She spent time establishing rules, particularly with children who had slipped into bad habits and were underachieving. Focused, individual attention was given to those children until this improved. For example, Samuel failed to follow the rule to write cursively at all times. He had been taught how to write cursively, but had slipped into bad habits that had gone uncorrected in the previous year. He needed to break this habit swiftly. It was hindering many areas of achievement by slowing him down and by creating untidiness in his books that affected his self-esteem. This teacher reminded Samuel regularly of his target and gave feedback in her marking, no matter what the curriculum area. There was little point in Samuel writing neatly in his English books, but reverting to bad habits in other subject areas. Samuel soon began to use cursive writing and his confidence and self-esteem grew.

> **These students have chosen from the Brain Box this week**
>
> **Correan**
> **Amanda**
> **Zain**
> **Darren**
> **Partha**

2 Establish specific 'Task Rules'

Once you have taught your general work rules, you can begin to develop rules for specific types of task. At the start of the year you will need to devote a considerable amount of space to display these rules clearly and in view of all children. For each type of task, draw up a list of essential requirements. Make your rules specific and be ambitious. Remove the mystery by analysing what constitutes good quality work and teaching the skills directly.

This is an example of some of the rules drawn up by a Year 4 teacher for story writing:

! Write at least four paragraphs, preferably more.

! Use speech marks for direct speech.

! Use a new line for each new speaker.

! Use no more than three pieces of consecutive direct speech.

! Use no more than three friends' names.

! Use at least one exclamation mark.

! Use question marks for questions.

! Do not start sentences with 'Then', 'And' or 'So'.

! Use at least three interesting connective phrases.

By setting and teaching specific rules, you can accelerate learning by avoiding the necessity to correct bad habits over and over again. There is a cycle to setting rules:

★ Teach a specific skill.

★ Set a rule that the skill must be used.

★ Give RAP as children start to use the skill.

★ Limit over-use of the skill.

> A Pat on the Back
>
> for
>
> Kai Chesterman
>
> who completed an excellent science investigation this week

You will often need to set the final, limiting rule after you have taught a skill, because children will over-use it. This is a natural development, but you must then not leave it to chance that they will self-correct. There is no time to be wasted in the ALPS classroom. The teacher does not wait for development – she facilitates it. For example, once you have formally taught the use of exclamation marks and set a target of 'At least one exclamation mark', you will find stories scattered with exclamation marks! Within a few sessions you need to set a limiting rule, such as 'No more than five exclamation marks'. Similarly, there is no point in setting the rule about 'Then, And and So' until you have taught, and displayed, alternatives in the same way that you would teach words for the Said Tree.

We witnessed a Year 1 class at the beginning of the academic year, where their teacher had developed a list of ambitious rules for story writing. Melissa, who had just turned five, was in the middle-ability group for literacy. The teacher later described her as 'Bright, but not exceptional'. Melissa brought her work for marking. As she was about to hand her paper over, Melissa put

See page 202 to learn about the Said Tree

her hand to her forehead and said: 'Oops, I forgot the speech marks.' We watched her go back to her seat and correctly add three sets of speech marks. Her story was clearly defined into three paragraphs. It was structured, amusing and entertaining. When we read those of other pupils, every child had followed the story rules. An ALPS teacher had also taught Melissa in Reception class. The work of the whole class was startling in its high quality.

> **SuperBrain Of The Day Is**
> **Derek Baker**

3 Share your 'Lesson Targets'

Once you have established your general work rules and your specific Task Rules, you will need to set out your lesson target at the start of each lesson. You can do this most effectively as you give the Big Picture. It is essential that you are direct and clear about your expectations. There is no room for mystery. If you wish your pupils to make more thoughtful hypotheses in a science experiment, tell them at the outset. Think of the language that you use as you describe the outcome, and use strong, positive statements:

> By the end of this session you will all understand that ...
>
> You will all be able to ...
>
> We will all be successful in ...

Remember that some of us are visual learners, so write up your lesson target clearly. Refer to it frequently and make positive affirmations throughout the session to ensure that all pupils remember it. Some teachers pin their lesson targets on the board with their General and Task Rules. Find a method that works for you and your class, and stick to it. A class who are accustomed to having targets will remind you if you forget and will make the life of a supply teacher quite uncomfortable if she is not clear in her intentions!

> **Lloyd attained Level 2 Maths today. Brilliant!**

When you mark, have your task and lesson targets in front of you. Do not be distracted from measuring attainment against targets. Soon your General and Task Rules will become ingrained on your memory, but when you make an additional rule, write it up wherever you are marking, in order that you remember to measure progress against it.

4 Set each pupil 'Individual Targets'

If you have already developed the use of target cards, you will find systems that make your feedback individual. A basic principle must be that you have the target card in front of you as you mark work. You are now measuring against four sets of criteria:

> Congratulations to this week's 100% students
>
> Harley
> Jamie
> Paul
> Rashvir
> Jasmine
> Samantha

◆ General Rules

◆ Task Rules

◆ Lesson Targets

◆ Individual Targets

If you have established your first two sets of rules effectively, by the time you come to setting individual targets you will have freed yourself from marking anything from your first two lists of rules. This means that you will no longer have to make those repetitive corrections that can take up so much time. You can focus on what really counts: progress towards challenging, ambitious targets!

Michael Samuels answered ten questions correctly in our science brainstorm on Monday! What a superstar!

In a short space of time you will find that your children will begin to take responsibility for their own targets. If they have learned to use the first five connective phrases on your display in their writing, they can set themselves the challenge to learn to use five more. If they can recite the two, five and ten times tables, they can decide to learn the three and four, and so on.

Targets are only effective if they are shared. Children will often surprise you by their eagerness to set themselves challenging targets, often more challenging than you would have set. This is what a Year 5 child had to say about target-setting:

I like to prove all the things that I know, so I test myself and do my own projects to learn more at home. Once I have learned something new I set a challenge to learn something else and bring it to school. I like having the special display board at school to put up work that you have done at home. It's not work that is set at school, it's stuff that you decide to research for your own interest, like learning more about plants and habitats. I just want to learn more and more, it's really enjoyable.

As children become accustomed to target-setting, you can create systems for them to make their own target cards and write their own targets. They will amaze you in their ability to measure their personal progress, and you will find that they are often more ambitious than you in the standards that they set. In the ALPS classroom everybody, including the teacher, has a set of targets and everybody makes rapid progress towards them.

5 Create marking codes

Now that you have focused on what you are marking, you need to speed up the process. The answer lies in developing short codes that link to your system of RAP. It is essential that your children understand quickly and easily what your codes mean. Many teachers have their own personal systems of marking, such as 'sp' for a spelling error. These systems can be developed so that your pupils become responsible for their own learning and target-setting.

Speediest hand in maths today belongs to SEAN DEACON Hands go up fast in this class!

One Year 6 ALPS teacher used a code 'T' for 'Target' and ticks and question marks to indicate to the child how far he had come to fulfilling the target. 'T?' meant that he should look at his target card and make a correction, while a ticked T meant that he had achieved the target. The code of circling a word and writing a 'D' meant to use a dictionary to find a more interesting alternative.

This freed her time to make comments where they were needed, not to nag about commonplace errors and mistakes. Her children's work was full of encouraging, positive statements about progress. If a child did not follow the General or Task Rules, she did not mark the work until they had corrected it. Her time was fully utilized, and her marking was focused and effective.

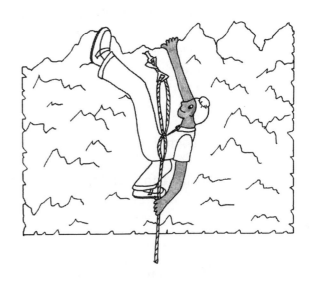

So much of effective teaching depends upon systems that are understood by pupils. The ALPS teacher sets out these expectations and displays them. She links in systems of RAP to her marking systems. In one class we saw children eagerly take back work to see who had earned a Target Terminator certificate. In another classroom, children had a system of gaining 'points' in the back of their book for using mathematical terms correctly. They were in teams, and they raced towards one hundred. The buzz from children as they made corrections and gained points was audible.

As you mark work, think about how you will lead a child towards achieving targets. If he has not met his target of using speech marks correctly, yet you have done all the formal teaching and he understands how to use them, try using a Target Challenge, coded 'TC'. This is what you write at the end of his work:

TC: 10 sentences with speech marks for 5 team points

He understands that if he writes ten sentences with correct use of speech marks, he gains the acclaim of his team. The reward can be anything that recognizes the achievement. You have to fit in with school policies, but you will find that the simplest activities are often the most effective. One Year 6 class loved the class reward of making toast on a Friday afternoon when everybody had attained their targets. This became a time of success and celebration, for relaxation and discussion, and for setting new targets in a positive atmosphere. Another class liked to sit together sociably with the teacher in the classroom to eat their packed lunch each Monday. Find what works for you and your class. Make it imaginative and fun, and the children will respond.

Codes will speed up your marking and enable you to give focused feedback measured against targets. They will not, however, take the place of the human contact that is essential in the ALPS classroom. You will, of course, return work to your class with all the verbal and non-verbal praise that we discussed earlier. Your language will be warm and positive, and your verbal feedback clear and effective. Your class will respond by making rapid progress, and you will continually need to recognize Target Terminators and set new, more challenging targets.

The connection between RAP, target-setting and marking

As you mark work and set new targets, consider how the use of RAP interlinks to provide the climate of success:

Recognition

You have followed the rules and are making progress towards your targets

Affirmation

You always follow the rules and always meet targets

Praise

Well done! You have achieved your target and we will all celebrate!

The ALPS method™ depends upon the teacher utilizing every skill and taking every opportunity to create a successful situation. With focused marking you will find your pupils responding with great enthusiasm, as they can measure their own progress and begin to take responsibility for their own education.

Grades and what to do with them

As teachers we are accustomed to breaking each area of the curriculum into categories and these categories into levels. Sharing this information with pupils and giving grades to provide clear targets and feedback about progress can be a positive tool if managed in conjunction with effective RAP. We know of a number of schools that have begun to develop methods of structuring classroom activities that are based on different levels. At Ninestiles Secondary School in Birmingham, pupils are given explicit and detailed information about the levels of attainment for each subject. They then choose which set they wish to work in, based on a prior knowledge of what levels that group will be working at.

While you might choose to work without giving grades, it is your duty to ensure that no child has the experience of those children who faced statutory assessment in the early days when the majority of teachers shared the philosophy that kind reassurance was adequate preparation. In our research we have seen the effect that this experience had on children who then felt that they had 'failed'.

Before any child is assessed, he has the right to understand what the assessment involves, what the grades represent and how he is currently performing. This can be done in a positive manner with every child. We have spoken to pupils with special needs who have felt extremely positive about attaining levels that were well under the normal levels of their peer group. These children's SELF-ESTEEM rucksacks were so full that they met their personal targets and did not give a second thought to the attainment levels of others. Some children may never attain national target levels by the end of each year, but every child can attain their own individual target level and be a high achiever.

Teachers can only work effectively with systems that make them feel comfortable. It is better not to give grades than to give them in a manner that presents any child in your class with a negative experience. International comparative research published in 1998 by King's College London (Black and Wiliam, 1998) emphasized the power of educative feedback. Educative feedback is specific about what to improve and how to improve it. The research also suggested that raw scores contribute to de-motivating all but the higher achievers. When the teacher gave raw scores and comments, many pupils did not read or give any attention to the comments. They simply took notice of the scores. To give you an insight into how grades and levels can be incorporated into the ALPS classroom, we will share some examples of teachers whom we have seen using grades as a powerful tool. If you use these techniques, you can significantly increase the levels of motivation in your classroom, raise attainment and accelerate progress.

One of the difficulties with national curriculum levels is that each level covers a broad range of attainment. In some schools, for the purpose of target-setting, each level is subdivided into the categories Low and High. A child on Level 2 Low would be only just progressing from Level 1, whereas a Level 2 High would be considered to be on the threshold of Level 3. This gives greater flexibility for targeting and can be adapted to give children and parents a clearer sense of progression. An even greater range can be given by including a Medium standard for each level. At Ninestiles School, children are aided in their choice of which group to join by each level of the national curriculum being broken up into Foundation, Intermediate, Higher and Advanced. Children can then see a measurement of progression that spans less than one year, rather than a two-year step that is quite meaningless to a small child.

We have seen teachers using national curriculum levels to give positive feedback through their marking. In one Year 5 classroom we watched children 'race' to the next level in mental arithmetic. The children were tested several times each week, and their marks equated to national curriculum levels. On the wall were lists of the children who had attained each level, with the levels broken into High, Medium and Low. There were six groups, each of approximately five children. The children's names were on pieces of laminated card and only stuck on the lists with blu-tac. This was an important principle: every child was expected to move his name up from one level to the next as he improved – nobody's name was written up permanently. Once each child had scored at a higher level, he moved his name up to the next list, to the recognition of a round of applause from his classmates.

As a variation the teacher would group the children and have 'Team Races' to the next level. On another occasion she allowed the children to choose their own teams, so that those four friends could race together. It made no difference if they were on different levels, because the race was to improve by one level. At other times, children would decide to challenge one another. There was a board entitled 'I bet I could ...' hung on the wall, which encouraged children to set their own challenges and targets for any task or area of the curriculum.

There are many ways to grade pupils and give feedback other than on national curriculum levels and assessments. Another teacher in the same school preferred to set scores out of twenty as targets. A third teacher gave colour-coded levels of mental arithmetic testing. Children could opt to attempt the harder levels as they improved. The decision to move up a level was in the hands of the child rather than the teacher. This is what the teacher had to say about the children's self-assessments:

> What surprised me was the way that the children pushed themselves. Pupils whom I would probably never have asked to take the challenging tests not only took them, but ensured that they learned the necessary skills to attain high marks. I had never before had children wait to see me after maths lessons to ask for explanations. For example, many of them found it difficult to work out the time span between two times, for example between half-past-one, and two-fifteen. These questions were in the harder tests. A group of children stayed behind after school one day to ask me to help them to answer these questions. We practised in class at each opportunity, from PE to home-time, register to breaktime, and so on. In a short space of time they had mastered the concept and could answer the questions in maths lessons. If there hadn't been a choice for them about which groups they worked in, they would have just 'switched off' when the top group covered this work. Instead, they worked hard until they could attain the next level.

If there is an atmosphere of achievement and success, children can be encouraged to call out their scores from tasks to the teacher. Because everybody has targets that they understand and strive to attain, there is no feeling of anxiety about being public about levels of attainment. Calling out individual scores is a time for reflection and for celebration. This is what Ellen, age 10, had to say about publicly sharing results with the class:

> Sometimes my teacher gives you marks as a percentage. If I knew I'd tried and for some reason I got under 50, I wouldn't be worried, except I'd want to know where I went wrong. But if I hadn't tried, it would be awful. I always try my best. That's the thing, as long as you try, there is nothing to worry about. When you get a lower mark it means you need to understand where you went wrong, so my teacher will ask you what you think or set you a new target to help you to overcome the obstacle. If I only got 25 per cent, then I found out how to improve and then I got 45 per cent, I'd be pleased; it's not the mark, it's how you tried and what you have learned. Everyone in our class tries hard and everyone is a high achiever. Sometimes the marks are for different levels, so someone who finds it harder might still get 100 per

cent because that is at their level. Being a 100 per cent student is the best you can do, that is what everyone wants in every lesson. But nobody laughs if you get low marks, some people get lower marks at some subjects but higher marks at others. We all try to encourage each other. If someone makes an improvement we clap and the class next door hear, and sometimes they all clap too! It makes you so determined to get a good mark in something; it feels so good to be clapped.

In one Year 2 class the teacher had a system called 'The Roll of Honour' for children as they moved up a level on the reading scheme. She colour-coded with bronze, pewter, silver and gold, and children's names were put up as they moved up a reading level. In this way, a beginner reader could reach the Golden Roll of Honour before a more fluent reader; the measure was improvement and every child was soon honoured! The age-old problem of competitiveness over levels of reading books was replaced by competition for improvement, and the question asked by children and parents was not 'What reading book are you on?' but, 'Which Roll of Honour are you on?'

Whole-school systems of recognition for grades can have enormous power to motivate. In one school, children with full marks in spelling stand up to be clapped in class and then in assembly on Monday, where it is to the applause of the whole school. Spellings throughout the school are differentiated, but all classes are tested on a Monday in order that results can be presented to the headteacher for assembly. Every child then takes home a slip of paper with their result each Monday evening to share with their parents.

Many schools use rewards for meeting target grades. All the children whom we have interviewed agree that it is not the reward, but the recognition that motivates them. In one school we watched a Year 1 boy take his 'Top Marks Certificate' for his spelling test out to his mother. This is what he said to us:

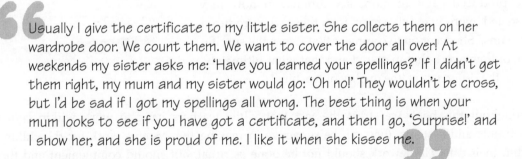

Usually I give the certificate to my little sister. She collects them on her wardrobe door. We count them. We want to cover the door all over! At weekends my sister asks me: 'Have you learned your spellings?' If I didn't get them right, my mum and my sister would go: 'Oh no!' They wouldn't be cross, but I'd be sad if I got my spellings all wrong. The best thing is when your mum looks to see if you have got a certificate, and then I go, 'Surprise!' and I show her, and she is proud of me. I like it when she kisses me.

Sam age 5

For Sam, the powerful motivator is the recognition of his mother and his younger sister. His family have created a fun game linked to his weekly success, helping him to learn his spellings, and later recognizing his success with a game of hiding the certificate, then 'surprising' mummy and celebrating. Linking school recognition to parental recognition can be the most effective motivator for a child. Sam wants his mother's recognition, affirmation and praise. The certificate showing his grades gives him an opportunity to receive her recognition, affirmation and praise.

147

The key to using grades to motivate is to be PC! In the ALPS, the letters PC stand for:

Positive and **C**reative

Be **P**ositive in your target-setting

Be **C**reative in your use of grades.

Grading your pupils will tell them what they are currently achieving. Sharing grades will help them to aspire to higher attainment. Setting target grades will help them to measure their own progress, while focused marking will give them signposts to show them how to improve. Effective RAP will create the positive atmosphere necessary for success. Put all this together in a package and you have dynamite.

Homework in the ALPS

Research can be quoted that shows homework has great value, or conversely, it has no value at all. The key principle seems to be that good teachers set good homework, which has value. Research published by King's College London found that nine year olds who did maths homework once or twice a week did no better than those who did it only occasionally, while those who were never set maths homework improved almost as quickly as those who were.[14] Project Director, Professor Margaret Brown, led the team who carried out research on six hundred nine year olds from seventy-five different classes. She said: 'What is clear to us is that teachers who produced gains in numeracy differed in how they presented maths in the classroom from those who produced low gains.' She went on to comment that it was the specific type of homework that mattered and that what ultimately makes the difference is 'the quality of teaching'.

> Homework is needed if you are going to succeed. It means you revise what you've done, and can come back to the teacher if you want more help. It means you do not waste time watching TV at home – you use your time sensibly. You choose when to play and when to study, you appreciate the time to play and you do not just hang about – you use the time properly.
>
> *Sam age 10*

Throughout this book we stress the fact that while teachers have to work within certain constraints and systems, they can be proactive in making the systems work for the children within their care. Homework should not be done as ritual, but should complement and then extend and enhance good teaching in the classroom. The model of 'do these twenty sums at home' when a child has struggled all day at them in class does not have much to recommend it. So much homework has the imprimatur of 'desperate and dull' marked all over it. There is one common feeling among the children whom we have interviewed, some of whom are set regular homework, some not. They all agree that homework is valuable only if it is connected to the learning that they have done in school and to the lessons that are to follow. If they see the point, they are keen to do the task.

Policies and attitudes towards homework vary, but there are some underlying principles that cannot be ignored. Firstly, within each school consistency of approach is essential. One of the most common complaints of parents is when they have two children in one school, with the older child receiving less demanding homework than the younger. Schools need to ensure that they provide continuity for children as they progress from year to year, and should monitor that policies are followed consistently. Lack of a consistent approach and expectation can potentially do more damage than too much, or too little, homework in one class or another.

If your school has a policy of setting homework, it needs to be planned when you draw up your lesson plan. To set a task that is not planned in connection with the learning that is taking place in the classroom is to waste the potential that homework has in helping your class to accelerate up the mountain. For example, a teacher concluded an art lesson on colour by handing out swatches from a DIY store, each with a range of green shades. She asked the children to try to find a leaf or a piece of grass that closely matched each of the shades of green on their swatch, and bring it into school the following day. The children discovered that this seemingly simple activity was not as simple as they imagined, and the next day brought in lots of snippets of greenery that stimulated a lively discussion.

If a child is not successful in completing homework to the standard that you desire, then you have an obstacle in your path up the mountain. Every time that child fails the homework challenge, he is loading a rock labelled 'F' for Failure into his SELF-ESTEEM rucksack. You need to unload those rocks and remove the obstacle from the pathway.

First ask yourself some questions about the homework that you set. There are a few basic principles that the ALPS teacher considers when setting homework. Each homework task must have a clearly defined purpose, such as to revise, to research, to practise skills, or to challenge thinking. If homework is set merely to fill time, it should not be set at all. Once you have decided that the homework is appropriate and worthwhile, you need to consider how your pupils respond to each task.

Are all the children in your class motivated, independent pupils? Are all homework assignments completed on time and to a high standard? Do the children in your class all complete homework without their parents needing to remind them? Or do you spend inordinate amounts of time reminding children to do tasks, keeping checklists of who has completed assignments, meeting with parents to explain tasks and deal with complaints, and marking incomplete or unsatisfactory pieces of work?

> I still go out to play, but I do not waste time watching stupid things on TV like I used to, or hanging about. I think about how to use the time to do all I want to do in the evenings.
>
> *Dermot age 11*

> I look at my brother's homework – he's in Year 8. I do it with him, some of it is similar to what we have done in Year 6. I like to see if I can figure out what he is doing, and understand it. Usually I can, or if I can't I ask someone to explain it to me.
>
> *Andrew age 10*

> My big brother and sister get work to do like 2,000 word essays, so I do the same. I've done an 800 word essay at home, on stuff we have done at school. Sometimes people think they can't do things, but if you sit down, read, and then concentrate, your brain gets into a higher gear, and you can do it. You have to go to bed earlier so you're not tired. I thought, if they can do 2000 words, so can I, but it will take me a bit longer.
>
> *Sam age 10*

I always used to hate homework. It was so boring! But this year my teacher puts a To Do List on the board. I can understand what she wants to do tomorrow so I see why I need to do the homework. I need to practise stuff and find out new stuff. It's fun if your mum and dad help you. They learn stuff too.

Claude age 8

The likelihood is that many teachers will relate to the second set of questions with a sigh. Homework is often one of the most stressful pressures on a primary school teacher. Setting, collecting and marking homework can be a negative experience. If this is your experience, try using the questionnaire and target-setting activity on pages 281–284 with children. Even if you feel that your class have an excellent attitude to homework, this is a worthwhile activity as it helps children to become more self-aware and develop the independent study skills that they will need in future life.

This questionnaire has been devised to pinpoint four skills that will help children with the skill of completing homework. Section one focuses on organization of materials, section two on time management, section three on listening to explanations and section four on handling distractions. It is important that the children understand that this is not a test and that everyone will score more highly in some areas than others. With young children, the questionnaire can be adapted and read to them. They can use hand signals to indicate how true each statement is to them, or just simple yes, no or sometimes. An adult can record their responses and work out strengths and weaknesses.

Once the children have completed their questionnaires, they should be given the target card for the section for which they had the highest score. This is their main area of weakness. The target cards can be used in a number of ways. Parental involvement is very powerful. The entire process can be shared with parents, with children completing the questionnaire with their parents at home. This will probably ensure that the responses are honest! Parents often speak of the stress that homework can cause within the family, and this is a positive way to work in partnership to help children to become independent learners.

Homework is fun, if you have enjoyed the lessons at school. I think of ways to make sure I can remember key facts, and I like doing extra research to bring into school.

Laura age 10

the alps approach – Accelerated Learning in Primary Schools

Brain breaks

Movement and learning

Robert Sylwester, Professor Emeritus of Education, University of Oregon, writes and lectures extensively on brain-based learning. He holds the view that:

> mobility is central to much that is human. Misguided teachers who constantly tell their pupils to sit down and be quiet imply a preference for working with a group of trees, not a classroom of pupils.

Robert Sylwester, 1998

We do not believe that humans are designed to sit still for extended lengths of time on pieces of plastic (chairs) behind lumps of wood (desks), nor are they designed to sit head-locked in front of glass screens that send out radiation (televisions and computer monitors). And yet many of our classrooms, particularly as pupils get older, are characterized by immobility.

The core purpose of brain breaks is to help keep the pupils in your class in the most receptive state for learning. This may involve regular physical reprieve. Exercise increases oxygen supply to the brain and releases neurotrophins. Neurotrophins are natural neural growth promoters that assist in increasing connections between neurons. Movement also promises some relief from stress. Stress increases cortisol in the system. Increased cortisol can be correlated to an increase in attention problems and a decrease in learning and memory (Hannaford, 1995). Children become stressed if they feel physically 'trapped'.

Learning becomes extremely difficult when there is a variable outside your control. For example, a dog has escaped into the play area, or it has started to snow, or there is a fire at a house nearby and two fire engines are in attendance. After any of these happening, forget higher order learning until you scrape the class back down off the ceiling! Brain breaks can do just that, because it is extremely difficult to continue to be thinking about the dog, the snow or the fire when you have to give your full attention to manipulating the left and right sides of your body in a particular way. The second purpose of brain breaks is, therefore, to equip the teacher with tools to manage the physiology and attention of her class.

The left hemisphere of the cortex contains a motor strip controlling movement on the right-hand side of the body. The right hemisphere of the cortex contains a motor strip controlling movement on the left-hand side of the body. The cerebellum, which is at the back of the brain, is responsible for balance. Brain-break exercises that are co-ordinated, smooth and involve cross-lateral activity can enhance large and fine motor control, improve hand–eye co-ordination and excite the neural superhighways connecting the left and right hemispheres of the brain. Brain-break exercises also utilize different neural circuitry in the brain, thus activating a different sort of memory storage and retrieval system. The third purpose for brain breaks is to engage different neural circuitry in the learning process.

Brain-break exercises can be linked to classroom learning, to social learning and to enhancement of self-esteem. For example, brain-break activities can be used for learning the shapes of numbers and letters, for practising multiplication, division, addition and subtraction, for improvement of handwriting, for awareness of the alphabet and for enhancement of vocabulary. The fourth purpose of brain breaks is to engage with formal learning.

Examples of brain-break activities for specific learning purposes are provided below.

Laterality exercises

Any exercise that involves crossing the mid-line of the body can be described as a laterality exercise. Such exercises can use gross or fine movements and any point between. The principle is to introduce smooth, controlled movements that require simultaneous movement of opposite sides of the body. These exercises develop motor control and engage different sides of the motor cortex within the brain. When a child crawls, this is what is beginning to happen. Some examples of laterality exercises include:

★ *Cross crawl.* In turn, children lift the left knee and touch with the right hand, then right knee to left hand and on. With time you can raise the level of complexity, and have elbow to knees and then go around the back and have heels flicked up to be touched by the opposite hand.

★ *Kneesies.* While crouching slightly, children place their left hand on their left knee and their right hand on their right knee. They move their knees until they touch, then transfer their hands over to other knees. Then they repeat, switching as they go.

★ *Line dancing.* This involves lots of planned cross-over movements in time to music. It is not compulsory to have a pension book to practise line dancing.

Focus exercises

It is very difficult to do the exercises below and be thinking of something else at the same time: so they can be used to displace any unhelpful preoccupation a pupil may have. This allows you to keep your class learning positively. To engage with these activities requires intense focus. Some examples of focusing exercises include:

★ *Nose 'n' ears.* Children put their right hand across the front of the face to hold the left ear lightly. As they take the hand away, they put their left hand across the front of the face to hold the right ear lightly. Then they swap! And again, and again!

★ *Rub a dubs.* Children circle their stomach with the right hand, while the left hand pats their head. Then they change, and then reverse the circling. Then with one finger pointed, they change hands and reverse.

★ *Concentric circles.* Children put their index fingers to touch at the top of an imaginary circle in front of the face. They circle their fingers in opposite directions simultaneously, trying to keep perfect concentric circles. Their fingers should therefore meet at top and bottom of the circle.

Relaxers

All the exercises that we have described so far will energize a group. This is not always desirable! Here are some relaxers, which are exercises that have the desirable physical effect but do not have the same potential for excitability. These relaxers use smooth, controlled and slow extended movements to ease tension and to enhance physical awareness and acuity.

★ *Long limb stretches.* These slow movements encourage stretching and physical awareness of space. To do this, take arms, shoulders and legs in turn. Children stretch their arms forwards and back, and rotate them slowly. They face the palms of hand upwards and down in turn. Then they rotate their shoulders around clockwise, anti-clockwise and then together. After this, point each shoulder up and then down in turn. Follow by stretching the right leg forward on the floor slowly, holding the hamstrings and easing into the stretch. They should then change legs, and then repeat.

★ *Stretchy shapes.* A variant is to learn about shapes while stretching. In pairs, each pupil takes it in turn to practise the stretches as though they were inside a shape such as a cylinder or ball or pyramid. The partner can either copy the movements at the same time, guess the shape, or instruct the other child to make different shapes.

Using music from page 168 can aid relaxation when you do these exercises

★ *Yawns and grimaces.* These exercises relieve tension in the face and neck muscles. Children should slowly make silly faces, exaggerating the movements as they do so.

★ *Ear rolls.* With finger and thumb, tell children to massage their ears slowly. Start at the top and roll around to the ear lobes.

★ *Chop chop.* In pairs children take it in turns to massage a partner's back and shoulders and conclude with the sides of the hands chopping in a gentle firm movement.

Learning numbers, letters and words

Shapes of numbers, letters and words can be practised in any physical location using hands or parts of the body to simulate the patterns. By physically rehearsing patterns of number and letter shapes without pens or pencils, pupils become more familiar with their sequence, their proportionality and physical orientation, and they have fun! This can do a great deal for confidence and familiarity with numbers and letters. The following are examples of activities that can be done to reinforce concepts in maths and literacy:

★ *Drawing numbers.* Children clasp their hands together and, in front of their faces, move their hands in the shape of numbers. Then ask children to write a larger number with their hands; then give a subtraction or a multiplication. Children should work out the answer first, and then when everyone is ready, draw the answer large in the air.

153

This is me doing 6s in Brain Gym.

★ *Decimal places*. Children move a finger and thumb left or right according to multiplication or division and by the correct number of places. For example, multiplying by ten means one 'jump' with their hands, whereas dividing by a hundred means two jumps, in the opposite direction. Or the children can all stand and jump left or right, again according to multiplication or division and by the correct number of places. Draw the digits and arrows up on the board to ensure that everyone jumps in the correct direction.

★ *Writing letters*. You can do similar things with letters of the alphabet as with numbers. Starting with the letter 'a', pupils progress through the alphabet, making the shapes with clasped hands as they go. Then you can play around by starting in the middle of the alphabet or by using just one hand, or noses or ears! Move on then to spell simple words, then write whole sentences.

★ *Alphabet edit*. This is a physically co-ordinated left and right activity first described in Alistair's 1995 book, *Accelerated Learning in the Classroom*. An alphabet is displayed so everyone can see and shout out the letters in sequence. At the same time as the children follow the alphabet they make accompanying hand movements for each letter. The children either raise their right hands, left hands, or both hands together. This is represented by the letters 'r', 'l', or 't' written out underneath each letter of the alphabet.

Handwriting

Fine and large motor control and co-ordination of smooth movements can be improved through carefully chosen physical activity. Ten minutes daily of the following types of activity will enhance the physical skills that aid handwriting.

★ *Double doodle*. This is a simultaneously patterned left and right activity. Children begin with finger and thumb together and with each hand simultaneously draw shapes in the air. The shapes should be exact mirror images left and right: use an imaginary mid-line up the centre of the body. As the pupils get better at this, emphasize change of shapes

154

from large, smooth, rounded shapes to finer, geometric shapes. Experiment: use different types of shapes – triangles, squares, circles – and encourage relaxed, controlled movement. Transfer the activity to a flat surface such as a desktop. Then use a piece of paper folded lengthways and a pen in each hand.

★ *Names in the air.* Practise spellings in the air with one hand or two. Start with pupils' names, and then progress onto keywords or the spellings for the week. Children should use their favoured hand first, then use the weaker hand, and finally use both simultaneously in a mirror image. Ask them to close their eyes and write the words large, small, forwards or backwards.

★ *On the back.* Organize children in pairs, so that only one of each pair can see what you write on the board. Pupil A spells a word on pupil B's back and, as this happens, pupil B writes the word on a piece of paper. For a really good bit of fun do this with a line of pupils. What word is spelled at the end of the line? Is it the same word that you started with?

Chaining material

Children can remember information in sequence when they learn through a sequence of physical gestures that are related to the learning and easy to remember, for example:

★ *Events in sequence.* Any chain of events in history can be remembered in outline form through a sequence of mimed gestures with an auditory accompaniment. When the class then goes through the sequence it can be used as a focal point for further and more detailed analysis. Chaining can be used to aid recall of processes in nature: photosynthesis, the distribution of oxygen in the body, the condensation cycle, forces, chemical reactions, and molecular structure. Anything that can be described through a sequence lends itself to this sort of approach.

★ *Teaching grammatical structures.* For older students, you can reinforce the learning of grammatical structures by giving nine students a laminated word. The nine students stand at the front holding up their words. The sentence could read something like: 'Good behaviour at school is important for the future.' Experiment to discover what happens when a word is removed. What happens when you remove a noun? What happens when you remove a verb? What about an adverb? Can you build up the sentence a word at a time? Can you try alternative words? Continually move students around, turning over their cards or exchanging them for another. On the back of the card you may wish to write the words 'noun' or 'adjective' or 'preposition'. In this way you can reinforce learning through structured physical activity, through visual and auditory reinforcement, and through speculation and prediction.

When to do it

Use your professional judgement! It would be ill advised to attempt to pass legislation for brain-break activities. You will not get a member of the Inspectorate scoring your lessons lower because you did not at any point have the pupils rubbing each other's ears. The physical attentiveness and energy levels of the pupils will vary by individual and by the time of day, depending also on the physical environment that you share together. You can use brain breaks to help your pupils stay at the optimal physical state for learning. The brain-break activities can influence and direct attention, change the heart rate, blood pressure and breathing patterns of the participants, help them improve fine and large motor control and develop mental rehearsal strategies for fundamentals such as shape awareness.

Brain breaks can be used between topics as a physical reprieve and to demarcate a change in experience. Before lessons, brain breaks can be used for changing the physical levels of resourcefulness, preparing the child for a cognitive or physical challenge, or for rehearsing learning in a different mode.

Altering physical levels of resourcefulness can begin to displace lethargy. This can alleviate some of the slow build up of stress arising from lack of opportunity to burn off excess energy. Eddie's teacher finds it essential to use brain-break activities when the weather is bad and the class has not been outdoors at playtime. Sometimes the brain-break activity can help a pupil experience relaxation, perhaps for the first time. Some exercises – double doodle and names in the air, for example – deliberately use physical activities to enhance the challenge to follow. Practising shapes and smooth, controlled motor movements help the brain to anticipate and prepare for the handwriting exercises to follow. The pupil has practised different aspects of recognizing, emulating, patterning and combining the shapes associated with letters in a safe and non-threatening way. This makes the act of writing those shapes easier.

Children can rehearse learning at different time throughout the school day. When standing in the queue for morning assembly, five year olds can still be learning about shapes of numbers by rehearsing them in the air. Brain breaks allow learning to take place in different venues and can aid school discipline by keeping children occupied with positive activity when they may otherwise become bored.

You will find that learning via brain breaks spills over into the playground. Playground games evolve over time. Games are added, some disappear, some are corruptions of older games. When you use brain-break activities successfully, the pupils will practise them in their own time. You then have a learning success.

An extension of the philosophy behind brain breaks takes us into what we call 'laugh a minute' – deliberate use of humour to continue to create a sense of belonging.

Laugh a minute for a sense of belonging

Adults laugh up to twenty times a day, but young children laugh as much as three hundred times a day! Laughter reduces stress, can reduce inflammation and can improve sleep. Laughter and humour are essential elements of the ALPS classroom, where learning takes place without put-downs and pupils take risks and learn from mistakes. Through this a sense of belonging can be created. Humour is a great social lubricant. It can help bond a group, discharge anxiety, alleviate pain and express emotions in a socially acceptable manner. Laughter can help to promote teamwork: it breaks down barriers and aids communication. It promotes creativity, builds self-esteem and creates an environment of sharing and openness. These 'laugh a minute' activities are specifically for instilling a sense of belonging (for further ideas see Loomans and Kolberg, 1993).

Alien Greetings

Write on the board or teach verbally a list of words such as that below, with Alien translations.

English	Alien
hello	objob
how	fliply
are	sloily
you	slopsy
today	climpty
goodbye	blump

In pairs, the children turn to meet one another and give greetings in Alien language. Within seconds you will have a class full of cheerful Aliens! Children can work out ways of greeting one another rather than shaking hands. They will love to develop the Alien language as you give them different challenges: to find out one another's Alien names, to ask what they wish to do when they leave school, or to comfort an Alien with a hurt knee.

Farmyard Friends

Write the names or draw pictures of five different farmyard animals on the board. The children need to each choose which animal they wish to imitate. When you say, 'Animals, find your friends!' each child must start to imitate the animal that they have chosen, making its noise and doing some actions. You could decide on the actions before the activity starts, or leave children to devise their own. At the same time, he must find the other children who have chosen the same animal as him, until all the pigs are oinking together, all the cows mooing, and so on. Once every group of animals is gathered noisily together, the game is over!

Would you rather?

This activity is based on the concept behind John Burningham's book, *Would You Rather?* (1994). Create two 'homes' in the room. Children will go to Home A or Home B depending on their response to the question asked. In between questions, they return to their seats. Ask a question from the list below, give children a few seconds to think before they go to Home A or Home B. They should go quickly, without waiting to see where their friends choose to go. This activity always generates a buzz and is particularly popular with the younger children! Once the class have enjoyed this game a few times, they can start to create questions of their own and a child can call out the questions, while the teacher joins in with the rest of the class.

Would you rather:

A   Roll in a pool of jam, or

B   Be caught in a chocolate hailstorm?

A   Stamp on your teacher's toe, or

B   Break your mum's best ornament?

A   Jump in a bed of stinging nettles for £10, or

B   Be chased by a lion for £50?

A   Find a frog in your soup, or

B   Discover a slug in your pyjamas?

A   Dig a hole in the desert, or

B   Climb a chewing gum tree?

A   Be told off by the headteacher, or

B   The chief school inspector?

A   Be chased by wild buffalo, or

B   Be chased by a thousand angry bees?

The Big Dilemma

This activity is similar to the one above and is particularly popular with older children. This time, create three 'Homes', A, B and C, in different areas of the classroom. Read the dilemma, give a few seconds for thought, and then give the signal for children to go to the home of their choice. Once children are familiar with the format, they can devise dilemmas of their own. Some useful discussions can follow later, although the idea is to create fun and laughter, rather than a moral lesson!

If your five year old brother/sister/friend broke your mum's favourite ornament, would you:

A   Tell your mum

B   Say that you broke it

C   Hide the pieces and pretend you knew nothing about it.

If you noticed that your teacher's trousers were undone, would you:

A   Tell him/her immediately

B   Giggle and tell your friends

C   Pretend that you hadn't noticed.

If you noticed that your headteacher's trousers were undone, would you:

A   Tell him/her immediately

B   Giggle and tell your friends

C   Pretend that you hadn't noticed.

If the man in the sweet shop gave you two bags of sweets instead of one, would you:

A   Tell him immediately

B   Say nothing and eat the sweets quickly

C   Eat the sweets but feel terrible about it.

If your best friend lent you a new pen and you broke it, would you:

A   Own up immediately

B   Say it was someone else

C   Say it must have been broken when he or she bought it.

If you accidentally spilt red ink all over your mum's/dad's best shirt, would you:

A   Try to wash it out before they came home

B   Wait until they came home and tell the truth

C   Blame the dog/cat/goldfish.

Top of the Pops

Tell all the children to stand in a space. Give out a variety of silly props for some children to use as a microphone, such as toilet rolls, wooden spoons or carrots. Then give others hats or wigs, or a cuddly toy to hold. Make it visual, silly, and fun! Put on a favourite pop song that all the children know. For a few minutes, allow everyone to pretend that they are the pop stars. Sing the words aloud, do the actions, dance to the music. When the song ends, your class will be lively and ready to work.

Mystery words

Arrange the children in small teams of about six. One child from each team stands at the front with his back to the group. He needs a pencil and paper. Give the rest of the team a written silly sentence, without him seeing. They take it in turns to go up to him and write a letter from the sentence on his back with a silly prop like a parsnip. He must guess what letter it is and write it on his paper before that child goes back and hands the prop to the next child. They continue until each team has worked out their sentence.

Mirror images

Divide the class into two halves. Give one child from each side a baseball cap or hat to wear. He must stand at the front to make a sequence of actions, which his half of the class must copy as if they were watching their reflections in the mirror. When you blow a whistle or hooter, the leader hands the cap to another child, who takes over at the front. Alternatively, the teacher can lead this activity and determine how much and what type of movement she wishes to create.

Tongue twisters

Write a selection of tongue twisters on the board, such as the list below. Practise saying them together. Then divide the class into teams. Give each team a silly prop or a hat. Children must come to the front one by one, quickly say the next tongue twister on the list, then quickly go back to their team, handing the hat or prop to the next player, who then takes his turn, until everybody has had a turn.

She sells sea-shells on the sea shore. The shells she sells are sea-shells I'm sure.

Sixty-six sick chicks.

A box of mixed biscuits, a mixed biscuit box.

Any noise annoys an oyster, but a noisy noise annoys an oyster more.

Red leather yellow leather.

An ape hates grape cakes.

Around the rugged rock a ragged rascal ran.

Peter Piper picked a peck of pickled peppers.

Toy boat toy boat toy boat.

Three free throws.

Fat frogs flying past fast.

A big black bug bit a big black bear, made the big black bear bleed blood.

Mrs Smith's fish sauce shop.

We surely shall see the sun shine soon.

The sun shines on shop signs.

Black bug's blood.

Sly Sam slurps Sally's soup.

Betty beat a bit of butter to make a better batter.

Sheep shouldn't sleep in a shack, sheep should sleep in a shed.

❺ Music in the classroom

Why use music?

> Millions of neurons can be activated in a single (musical) experience. Music has an uncanny manner of activating neurons for purposes of relaxing muscle tension, changing pulse and producing long-range memories which are directly related to the number of neurons activated in the experience.

Don Campbell, 1983

> "I regard music and the arts as essential, not optional, components of education."

Norman Weinberger, Professor of Psychology, University of Southern California at Irvine, 1998

A teacher's first challenge is to create and sustain a positive and supportive learning environment and to use as many tools in confronting this challenge as she can possibly find. So far we have described ways of building positive self-belief, maintaining 'can do' attitudes, mental rehearsal techniques, target-setting, brain breaks and others. The judicious use of music is yet another tool to bring to the repertoire.

Here are some things that children said about the use of music to aid learning in classrooms:

If a teacher is saying no to music in the classroom, it's like saying that our feelings do not matter. If they say, 'You just have to do this work', they are missing the point. The thing is, if you're feeling bored or not in the mood, you're not going to do the learning anyway. It's wasting time if you're not paying attention — that is wasting time. Using music to relax, or to give you confidence, or to get you in the mood really works — it makes you do the learning.
Ellen

When we did some SATs trial papers we used music and it relaxed us. It stopped us panicking, and thinking: 'Oh no, what's this?' It really helps.
Jamie

We have music every morning, which helps you to relax. If you've had a stressful morning, like a row with your family before you came to school, it helps you to get over it and makes you feel better. During the day you hear the music in your head and think of the words, it makes you laugh. It affects you for the whole day.
Mehreen

I like the uplifting songs, like 'Life' by Desree because it makes you feel so good about what you have achieved and what you want to do next. It sets you up for the day.
Ellen

I like the music at the end of the week, on a Friday, when we celebrate what we have done that week.
Ross

Yeah — we have our favourite song on a Friday — it goes 'Let there be lurve!'
Jumoke

In *The Mozart Effect*, Don Campbell (1997) describes how young children with whom he has worked overcame specific reading difficulties by practising with a metronome on 60 beats per minute and then with some baroque pieces with a similar 60–70 beats per minute structure. As they read, their breathing, phrasing and spacing of sound regularized to the accompanying sounds. Music can be used for very specific purposes such as some of those that Campbell describes, or for more general classroom applications.

When I listen to happy music at school I feel happy and it makes me work much more. It stops me from talking about things that happened at playtime or about what's on TV.

Music should not be used in a classroom as 'bubblegum for the ears' nor as a means of befriending pupils nor as a treat. It should be used to enhance learning. The choice of when and what should remain within the gift of the professional: the teacher in the classroom. Do explain why and how you choose to use music to the pupils. Encourage them to understand that it is to aid and enhance their learning. Some of the uses of music we have observed include the following:

♪ Music with a measured and light quality for entering assembly.

♪ Music with a more purposeful and insistent feel for an exiting assembly!

♪ Start-of-day music to accompany class Brain Gym® or a class review/connect activity.

♪ Music for learning diffusions where, for a fixed period of time within a task, pupils are explaining their work to each other, or summarizing key learning or adding to their learning memory map.

♪ Music for tidy up activities.

♪ Music for timed challenges.

♪ Music to accompany reciting multiplication tables.

♪ Music for concert reviews at the end of the day or at the end of the week.

♪ Music for relaxation and guided visualizations.

The use of music in the classroom is not without its challenges. Some teachers will argue that one cannot possibly study or concentrate fully while listening to music; others, that baroque will make you more intelligent. Some teachers argue that music distracts and impairs the integrity of the musical experience, or causes confusion.

In March 1999, *Hospital Doctor*, the UK medical news weekly, published the 'Op Ten'. These were the pieces of music surgeons preferred to listen to while operating. Here are the top five selections in the UK's operating theatres.

1 *The Four Seasons* – Vivaldi

2 Violin Concerto Op. 61 – Beethoven

3 *Brandenburg Concertos* – Bach

4 The Swan, from *Carnival of the Animals* – Saint Saëns

5 Ride of the Valkyries, from the *Ring* – Wagner

The following titles though nominated were not placed – 'Heaven is a Place on Earth', 'Knocking on Heaven's Door', 'Smooth Operator' and 'Every Breath You Take'.

The previous week the *San Francisco Chronicle* published details of how the municipal court at Fort Lupton punishes noise violators. Once a month they are made to listen to music they do not like – loud! Lounge bar 'musak' is apparently most effective, followed by combinations of the following:

1 'One Cup of Happiness' – Dean Martin

2 'Tie a Yellow Ribbon Round the Ole Oak Tree' – Tony Orlando

3 'I'm Going to Leave Old Durham Town' – Roger Whittaker

4 'Sunshine on my Shoulder' – John Denver

5 'Bill Bailey Won't You Please Come Home' – Wayne Newton

So there you have it. Music for concentration and music for detention.

Music and the brain

Brain scans taken during musical performances show that virtually the entire cerebral cortex is active while musicians are playing.

Norman Weinberger, Professor of Psychology, University of Southern California at Irvine, 1998

Findings from research show that at twenty weeks foetuses can hear *in utero*. Babies learn about their mother's own voice *in utero* and will prefer their mother's voice electronically filtered. At two to three weeks of age they begin to prefer the real voice to the recorded voice. As a species, we are wired for language and this wiring begins to be established prior to birth. Might we also be wired for music?

Anthropologists struggle to find a society that does not have music. Generations of mothers stretching back through recorded history have soothed their children by singing to them. Recent scientific studies have revealed the incredible sophistication with which very young learners behave musically.

Toddlers spontaneously exhibit music behaviours, using music in their play and communication, composing songs, and inventing original musical notations.

G. Moorhead, 1977

Infants can discriminate between two notes as well as an adult can. They can remember the contour or pitches of melodies and, as Professor Norman Weinberger of the University of Southern California points out, they can mentally segment extended melodies into smaller phrases in much the same way as adults (Weinberger, 1998). At the most fundamental levels we are wired for a musical response just as we are wired to acquire and use language.

Heeding Susan Greenfield's dictum to 'think regions and think chemistry' with regard to the structure of the brain, we can see that the brain's right hemisphere processes relationships and patterns of sound, and responds to the melody, while the left is processing language. Different sites within the brain are engaged in the analysis of pitch and timbre. Working memory for pitch entails interactions between the front and the back of the cortex. We can make judgements on whether a piece of music is happy or sad 'even in the complete absence of any ability to identify or recognize a melody' (Blood *et al.*, 1999). At a cellular level, neuronal structures are specifically sensitive to pure tone pitch, complex harmonic relationships, rhythm and melodic contour (Weinberger and McKenna, 1998).

At the University of Southern California, Irvine, Professors Shaw and Leng (1997) conducted research with seventy-four college students. They showed that performance in spatial–temporal reasoning tests – manipulation of shapes, understanding of symmetry, proportional reasoning and mental imagery – improved after students had been listening to ten minutes of music by

Mozart. Subsequent EEG scanning tests showed that the effect did show signs of lasting. In a separate experiment (Rauscher *et al.*, 1993), test scores rose significantly for students who learned new material while listening to music by Mozart. The students' scores rose significantly when tested with the music playing. Scores were slightly less when students were tested with no music. Tests of three year olds exposed to piano keyboard training showed an improvement in spatial–temporal tasks and object assembly above the eighty-fifth percentile.

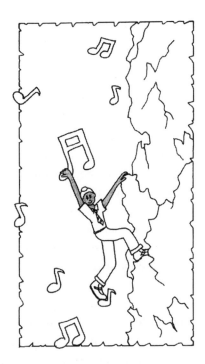

Amrit's father read that music could increase a child's IQ and so he bought Amrit a violin. He had read about the project involving 136 pupils at the 95th Street Elementary School, in one of Los Angeles' poorest neighbourhoods. Shaw found that pupils who learned to play the piano and read music improved their numeracy:

> The learning of music emphasizes thinking in space and time. When children learn rhythm, they are learning ratios, fractions and proportions.
>
> *Rauscher et al., 1993*

Comparisons were made with a 1997 pilot study involving 102 second-year pupils at schools in Orange County who received traditional maths teaching assisted by the use of computer programs. The Los Angeles pupils' results were 27 per cent higher than their Orange County counterparts, and they were able to understand and analyse ratios and fractions, concepts usually not introduced until the sixth year of schooling.[15]

Work done by Dr Susan Hallam at the Institute of Education in August 1998 confirmed findings that music can aid certain types of academic performance. In a small study, three groups of schoolchildren were assessed. A soothing classical piece was played in the background during memory tests for one group, an aggressive piece of modern jazz was played to another group, and the third worked with no music at all. The 'classical' group were better able to remember sentences that had been read to them than both the other groups. Dr Hallam told the BBC:

> We think that the music has an effect on the primitive mechanisms in the brain and directly affects arousal and mood. Then what happens is it enables the children to concentrate better. It really is that simple.[16]

Researchers have shown that music can enhance students' abilities to access, interpret and retain learning content. Learning and performing music actually exercises the brain. Music develops synaptic connections and improves sensory and perceptual systems. It improves large and fine muscle co-ordination and develops the ability to discern patterns and generate novel patterns. Musicians become part of a self-referencing feedback loop where they can apply subtle changes and learn from distinctions related to those changes.

Pitch discrimination is a vital component of being able to manipulate language and to read. Music can prepare very young children to be better readers! In 1975 (Hurwitz *et al.*, 1975), researchers in the USA began an investigation to find out whether music training improved reading performance in five year olds. The experimental group were not taught how to read music but rather how to listen to it. They were taught how to recognize different rhythmic elements. After an input of forty minutes daily for seven months, the experimental group exhibited 'significantly higher' reading scores than the control group. Amrit's mother enjoyed teaching her son at an early age to listen to classical music, and it was not a hardship to her. She was certain that this helped Amrit learn to read; whereas his father remained convinced that it was the violin lessons.

In 1993, Lamb and Gregory attempted to correlate the relationship between musical sound discrimination and reading ability. Their findings established a 'high degree of correlation between how well children could read both standard and phonic reading material and how well they could discriminate pitch' (Lamb and Gregory, 1993). Their findings are of significance because they point towards the importance of pitch discrimination in the phonemic stage of learning to read. First, the child sees words, then he makes a correspondence between visual components (graphemes) and their spoken sounds (phonemes) and finally he forgoes the formative stages and visually recognizes whole words.

Patricia Kuhl (1992) of the University of Washington in Seattle suggests that all babies from all over the world classify sounds and notice sound changes in the same way. In her research she plays computer-generated sequences of sounds and looks for patterns of response. After hearing a given sound repeated a few times, the baby does not respond: it has 'habituated' – it recognizes the sound. At the age of three to four months, babies are taking in most language. In the period from three to six months they start to reorganize the responses according to the language they are hearing. At six months Japanese babies no longer distinguish between the sounds 'R' and 'L'.

Most parents learn and practise 'parentese' without ever having attended a course on it! What is parentese? It is the language of nonsense sounds with accompanying grimaces and wide-eyed stares that parents use to talk to babies. Undoubtedly it features a wide variety in sound changes including changes in pitch. By gurgling and goo-gooing at children, parents are preparing them to become readers!

How to use music

Research suggests that, aside from the obvious benefits of learning to play an instrument or using one's voice to create music, music can enhance learning in any combination of four ways:

♪ Music can carry content.

♪ Music can alter physiology and thus induce a mental state better suited to recall of information.

♪ Music can enhance performance in certain cognitive tasks.

♪ Music can improve language and reading skills.

Many of the teachers we have worked with use music in their classrooms. Their use of it is skilled and judicious. Below we list thirteen ways to use music to enhance learning.

1 Beginnings

Music has a powerful influence on mood and atmosphere. Choose from the following list for entry music on arrival in the classroom to create an appropriate atmosphere.

Beethoven	Symphony No. 5 in E minor – Allegro con brio
Verdi	*La Traviata*, Brindisi – 'Libiamo ne lieti calici'
Handel	*The Messiah* – Hallelujah Chorus
Prokofiev	*Romeo and Juliet* – Montagues and Capulets
Clarke	*Trumpet Voluntary*

2 Demarcation of time on task

You can use music to set up a timed challenge. Set a challenge for the class such as: 'For the duration of this piece of music, I'd like you in pairs to think of as many words as you can about the topic we did last week. The music is the "Theme Tune" to *Mission Impossible*. It lasts three minutes and that's how long you have.' Or use a piece of music to provide a more relaxed time frame for an activity.

Chopin	Waltz No. 6 in D flat ('Minute Waltz')
Ravel	*Bolero* – conclusion
Mozart	*Eine Kleine Nachtmusik* – Allegro
Unknown	*Mission Impossible* – 'Theme Tune'
Elmer Bernstein	*The Great Escape*
Blues Brothers	*The Best of the Blues Brothers* – 'Rawhide'

3 Authentication of a mood

Music can be used to make a qualitative change in the atmosphere in the classroom. For example, when celebrations are taking place in the ALPS classroom, an appropriate piece of accompanying music anchors the experience, such as the pop group Queen and their song 'We Are The Champions!'

Elgar	Cello Concerto in E minor – Adagio–Moderato
Holst	*The Planets* – Jupiter
Albinoni	Adagio in G minor
Bach–Gounod	*Ave Maria*
Giorgio Moroder	'Love's Theme 1978'
Andrea Bocelli	*Canto della Terra* (4.01)
Ella Fitzgerald	'Every Time We Say Goodbye'
Louis Armstrong	'We Have all the Time in the World'

4 Energizers

When you wish to tidy the classroom quickly, Rossini's *William Tell Overture* can help to speed the class along. The pieces listed immediately below are definitely energizing!

Rossini	*William Tell Overture*
Bach	Brandenburg Concerto – No. 1, 1st Movement
Orff	*Carmina Burana* – O Fortuna
Vivaldi	*The Four Seasons* – Concerto No. 4 in F minor (Winter)
Handel	*The Arrival of the Queen of Sheba*
Elgar	*Pomp and Circumstance* – No. 1, Op. 39
Gipsy Kings	*Greatest Hits* – particularly 'Bomboleo' and 'Medley'
Katrina and the Waves	'Walking on Sunshine'
Desree	'Things Can Only Get Better'

5 Relaxers

If you wish to relax after PE, or before the class begins a piece of creative writing, try listening to music to relax and change the children's mood.

Beethoven	Piano Concerto No. 1 in C major, Op. 15 – Largo
Reicha	Wind Quartet in E flat major, Op. 88/2 – Andante grazioso
Bach	Overtune in D major – Air
Mozart	Oboe Concerto in C major
Stamitz	Cello Concerto in G major
Bitty Mclean	'Stop This World'
Annie Lennox	'Why'

6 Music for guided visualizations

Music can be used to enhance the guided visualizations described on pages 241–245. The music provides the background for relaxation and helps children to focus on the visualization.

Debussy	*Clair de lune*
Rachmaninov	*Rhapsody on a Theme of Paganini* – variation 18
Vaughan Williams	*Fantasia on a Theme by Thomas Tallis*
Burgon	Nunc dimittis
John Williams	*Schindler's List* – 'Theme Tune'
Mozart	*Il Andantino* – Concerto for Flute and Harp
Myers	*The Deerhunter* – theme tune 'Cavatina'

7 As an aid to discussion

On a very practical level, music can be used for background to provide an appropriate atmosphere for discussions in class. When you lower the volume of the music, the level of noise in the class goes down accordingly.

Delius	*The Walk to the Paradise Garden*
Mike Oldfield	*Tubular Bells*
Satie	*Gymnopedies*, etc.
Vangelis	'Love Theme'
Jean Michel Jarre	*Equinoxe* – Part 4
Bjork and David Arnold	'Play Dead'
Santana	'Oye Como Va'

8 Evocation of a theme

A theme being explored in class can be enhanced by related music. Period music from the time of the Tudors and Stuarts could be used as a stimulus activity, or as an accompaniment to artwork, or used as part of review of content.

Elgar	Introduction and Allegro for Strings Op. 47
Art of Noise	'Robinson Crusoe'
Incantation	'Cacharpaya'
Capercaillie	'Coisch A Ruin'
Jeff Wayne	'Eve of the War'
Clannad	'Robin (The Hooded Man)'
Salif Keita	'Folon – The Past'

9 Active concert

This is a specific application of music in relation to accelerated learning. The teacher reads information to the class while dramatic and emotionally engaging music is played. The best time to do this is after you have given the Big Picture and before detailed work begins. Your voice should 'surf' the music, rising and falling appropriately while the pupils follow the information in written form. The music creates emotional associations and simultaneously connects the left and right brain. Music by Brahms, Rachmanino, Beethoven, Tchaikovsky and Haydn is suitable, while some more contemporary pieces can be used with effect.

Michael Nyman	*The Piano* – theme tune 'The heart asks pleasure first'
The Edge	'Rowena's Theme'
Billy Taylor Trio	'I Wish I Knew (How it Would Feel to be Free)'
Horace Silver	'Song for my Father'
Dave Brubeck	'Take Five'

10 Passive concert

This is another specific application of music in relation to accelerated learning and it is used following the active concert. The passive concert can take place as a review at the end of the session. The material presented can be the same as the active concert but the method of presenting it and the intended outcome differ. The pupils settle into a state of 'relaxed awareness' while listening to slower pieces of music such as some baroque pieces with less rigorously structured qualities. Pupils should listen to the music, while you read naturally. The passive concert is a concluding activity intended to encode and sublimate the material into the brain.

Bach	Double Violin Concerto in D Minor – Largo ma non tanto
Mozart	Concerto No. 21 in C Major – Andante
Bach	Orchestral Suite No. 3 in D – Air on the G String
Beethoven	Piano Concerto No. 5 in E flat – Adagio un pocco mosso
Pachelbel	Canon in D
Vivaldi	Flute Concerto No. 3 in D major – Cantabile
Marcello	Oboe Concerto in D minor – Andante e spicatto

11 To enhance brain breaks

Music can appropriately accompany the physical activity of a brain break. Any music by Village People, Jive Bunny or the Spice Girls can work here!

12 Endings

There are two possible applications for using music for endings. First, for practical purposes like 'tidy ups' use upbeat and humorous pieces: 'No one can finish doing the class tidy up until the music stops.' Use the music to change the atmosphere, elevate the mood and get the jobs done more efficiently. Second, use music to provide a sense of closure. As you review the day or introduce the To Do list for the next day, ending music can help ritualize the moment. Use familiar pieces to embed this sense of completion.

13 Learning with music to enhance the ability to store and retrieve related information

Content is more readily recalled when learned to musical accompaniment. Primary age children were asked the following question about music and testing: 'When you listen to music during tests, does this make a difference to you? If so, how and why?'

Yes it does make a difference, a very big difference because I find that when we have the music on it helps me think more quickly.
Amy

Yes it makes me more relaxed, and I feel more into answering questions and getting high grades.
Aron

Yes it relaxes my body and I work a lot faster. I think everyone else feels the same.
Lee

Yes because when I am home doing my homework I listen to pop music and it does not help. But when I listen to the calm music at school it makes me feel relaxed and cheerful.
Kighley

Yes it makes me feel as if I am somewhere else and that I can relax and do my best.
Rebecca

Yes this does make a difference because the music is slow and it calms me down.
Laura

This does make a difference because it keeps me relaxed. This is because it is not put on loudly to annoy us, it is not hard music to which we have to rock our heads. The voice comes out and calms us down.
Mehreen

Yes it makes me feel relaxed and confident.
Terry

Yes because it calms me down and gives me a background noise instead of dead silence.
Ellen

It makes me feel like I am at home doing my homework.
Kirsty

When music is used explicitly to carry content, recall is easier. At the Minster School in Southwell, Nottingham, the English Department used music and, in particular, this song to help pupils remember grammar and sentence structure.

A common noun is just a name
  Like book and baby, girl and game.
A proper noun is more precise,
  Like Nottingham or Mrs Price
A pronoun takes the place of noun
  For instance, it instead of town
An adjective describes a noun
  Like yellow ball or golden brown
A verb's an active doing word
  – a football kicked, a noise that's heard
An adverb used to tell us how
  Like slowly, quickly, quiet and now
A preposition shows relation,
  On the bus, or in the station
The list's completed with conjunction
  And joining is its usual function.

I like to relax to quiet music

Sung to the tune of 'As Shepherds watched their flocks by night', this song could be heard being hummed quietly during the A-level English language exam! There is no reason why primary age children cannot learn in the same way.

In order to exploit all aspects of VAK, a large poster or individual word sheets should be used, and actions added to give a physical feel for the information. We listened to one class enthusiastically sing 'Old Macdonald had a body', pointing to the positioning of each organ as they sang. There are many familiar tunes that can be used for learning key facts to music, or you can compose tunes yourself. Once children are familiar with this activity, they can create their own jingles to accelerate their learning. As an example, here is the story of Henry VIII, set to the tune of 'Old Macdonald had a Farm'.

Henry the Eighth born fourteen ninety-one,
  ee-i-ee-i-oh!
Had six different wives, got rid of every one,
  ee-i-ee-i-oh!
With a chop-chop here, and a chop-chop there,
  Here a chop, there a chop, everywhere a chop-chop,
Henry the Eighth born fourteen ninety-one,
  ee-i-ee-i-oh!

Catherine of Aragon was number one,
  ee-i-ee-i-oh!
She didn't last long, he wanted a son,
  ee-i-ee-i-oh!
With a divorce here, and a divorce there,
  Here a divorce, there a divorce, everywhere a divorce-divorce,
Catherine of Aragon was number one,
ee-i-ee-i-oh!

Anne Boleyn was number two,
  ee-i-ee-i-oh!
He soon got fed up with her too,
  ee-i-ee-i-oh!
With a chop-chop here, and a chop-chop there,
  Here a chop, there a chop, everywhere a chop-chop,
Anne Boleyn was number two,
  ee-i-ee-i-oh!

Next Jane Seymour, number three,
  ee-i-ee-i-oh!
She died within a year, RIP,
  ee-i-ee-i-oh!
With a sob-sob here and a sob-sob there,
  Here a sob, there a sob, everywhere a sob-sob,
Next Jane Seymour, number three,
  ee-i-ee-i-oh!

Anne of Cleves was number four,
  ee-i-ee-i-oh!
She was so ugly, he showed her the door,
  ee-i-ee-i-oh!
With a divorce here, and a divorce there,
  Here a divorce, there a divorce, everywhere a divorce-divorce,
Anne of Cleves was number four,
  ee-i-ee-i-oh!

Two Catherines were six and five,
  ee-i-ee-i-oh!
Howard got the chop, but Parr survived,
  ee-i-ee-i-oh!
With a chop-chop here but a PHEW there,
  Here a chop, there a PHEW, everywhere a chop-PHEW
Two Catherines were six and five,
  ee-i-ee-i-oh!

Henry the Eighth born fourteen ninety-one,
  ee-i-ee-i-oh!
Had six different wives, got rid of every one,
  ee-i-ee-i-oh!
With a chop-chop here, and a chop-chop there,
  Here a chop, there a chop, everywhere a chop-chop,
Henry the Eighth born fourteen ninety-one,
  ee-i-ee-i-oh!

Using music to aid recall of facts can be used for any subject and age group. These activities then can be used as brain breaks or to fill 'dead time', such as when changing for PE or waiting for lunch. There are many tunes that can be used for this activity, but to get you started, we have compiled the list below:

Yankee Doodle Went to Town

The Twelve Days of Christmas

Jingle Bells

Here comes the Bride

Frere Jacques

Clementine

Twinkle, Twinkle Little Star

Baa-baa Black Sheep

The Grand Old Duke of York

The Wheels on the Bus

Hickory Dickory Dock

Pat-a-Cake, Pat-a-Cake

Ring-o-Roses

The Farmer's in his Den

Sing a Song of Sixpence

Review of Part Two

As a result of reading our section entitled 'Target-setting that works', what specific things will you now do to improve the quality of the activity in your class? What three recommendations could you make to your school for improved use of target-setting?

Think of your last lesson. For each of the positive classroom talk strategies suggested, how do you score? To what extent have you used or abused your classroom questioning strategies? List each strategy and score yourself 0 to 5: 0 being not used at all and 5 being used skilfully and extensively.

We claim that homework, properly done, can be motivating and enhance classroom learning. Use the homework questionnaire. What are your findings? Share the research with the pupils in your class. What ways do they see of improving?

In what ways might brain breaks enhance an individual child's capacity to learn? How could you use physical movement before, during and after lessons and measure improvement in learning as a result?

Music can enhance learning. Try using some of the recommended methods with music of your choice for a week. What differences, if any, did you notice? Ask the children. What did they enjoy? In what ways, do they think, it might have helped them learn?

Part Three

The learning journey

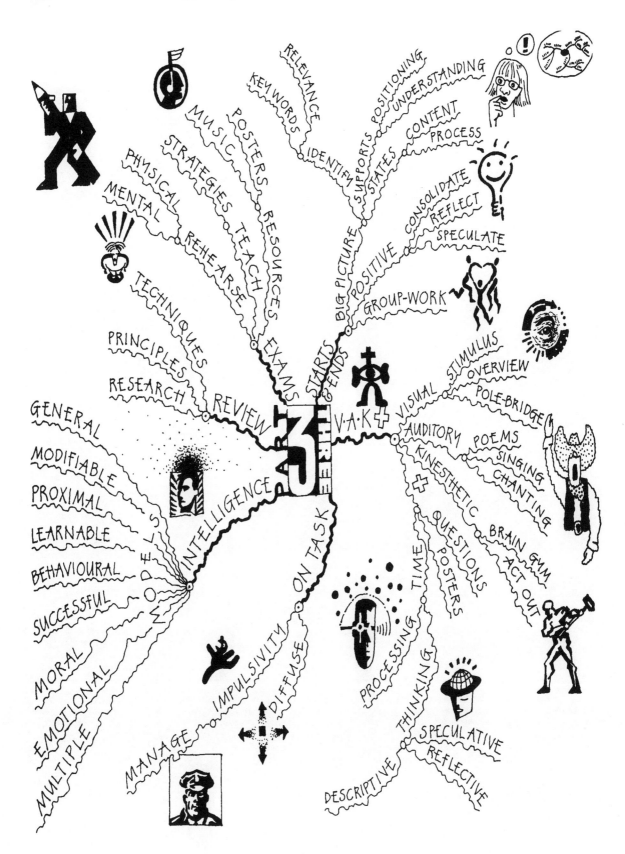

the alps approach – Accelerated Learning in Primary Schools

Preview of Part Three

The learning journey

In Part Three you will:

find out how to start lessons positively and keep them positive.

read about the best way to input any new information so that it is understood and remembered.

consider a model for optimising time on task based on research into attention.

discover how pole-bridging will increase the intelligence of every child in your class.

be given an outline of current theories of intelligence with some strategies for accessing and developing it.

be given eleven ways of helping a child remember.

discover how mental rehearsal will improve performance and how best to prepare for tests and public examinations.

the alps approach – Accelerated Learning in Primary Schools

The learning journey

the alps approach – Accelerated Learning in Primary Schools

❶ Using beginnings and endings

The primacy and recency effect

FOR REASONS WHICH ARE, AS YET, NOT FULLY UNDERSTOOD we seem to assign significance to what is perceived of as the beginning or the ending of an experience. We have our curiosity engaged at the beginning of an experience and derive satisfaction from the sense of its ending. In simple memory tests involving recall of words from an arbitrary list and when participants are told beforehand how many there will be, we find that words from the beginning and from the ending of the list are more readily remembered by a high proportion of respondents. Leaving aside the phenomenon of echoic memory – where we remember the last pattern of sounds we heard – there does seem to be significance in this. Some memory researchers refer to this as the primacy and recency effect and suggest that we do remember things from the 'beginning' and things from the 'end'. Never allow your lessons to stumble into life or run away from you at the end of the day. Clear space for the significant moments of primacy and recency. Give value to beginnings and endings.

Examining this phenomenon of primacy and recency further, it becomes obvious that teachers should align their teaching interventions with the natural human disposition to seek for significance. The ALPS teacher begins lessons on time and positively, and immediately directs children's thinking about what they are going to do and how. She stops her lesson ten minutes early for a variety of short, participative review activities. In between she provides lots of 'mini' beginnings and endings where pupils re-engage their understanding through diffusion activities.

Throughout the ALPS model, the importance of the Big Picture cannot be emphasized enough. To know where the class are going and how the teacher plans to get there is what the Big Picture is about. This helps to separate process from content. Education should never be simply about the storage of information and the capacity for successful retrieval of that information in public examinations. If the teacher does not separate process from content in her own thinking and in that of the pupils she teaches, then there is a danger that education will be driven by the imperative to provide the maximum amount of content in a given time and hope that it can be successfully retrieved later. The ALPS teacher explains the difference between process and content. She makes the distinction explicit and thus helps children to learn about learning. When she gives the Big Picture she identifies both process and content. Here are some guiding principles on how to begin your lessons in the ALPS.

the alps approach – Accelerated Learning in Primary Schools

◆ Always begin with the overview or Big Picture.

◆ Say what you are going to do and how you are going to do it, making explicit the processes that you have chosen to use. Check for understanding as you go.

◆ Begin to embed open-ended questions to engage the curiosity of the learner and to encourage pre-processing at a number of levels. Say things like: 'By the end of this lesson we will be able to ...', 'At the end of the day we will all know about ... and be able to ...', 'What would it be like if we could ...?'

◆ Identify and assign significance to the key vocabulary. Write it up or point it out to the children. Explain what the keywords mean and how you will be using them during the lesson to come.

◆ Use child-centred connecting activities to engage prior understanding and to connect with the previous related learning.

The Big Picture allows the learner to position this experience in relation to those that have occurred and those that are yet to come. It orientates, posing questions related to comparable experiences and allaying anxieties. Separating process from content begins to take the learner away from a dependency loop. In the dependency loop, learning is vested in the teacher. Disabling presuppositions – 'We only learn when the teacher talks' – mean that the learner always seeks a 'correct' answer, always wants approval, is conservative in learning choices and so never develops the new three Rs.

When a teacher separates process from content, the child begins to do the same and then becomes more aware of his learning preferences and can make more autonomous choices. Embedding questions is a method for engaging learning at a number of levels. Closed questions foreclose all but conscious engagement of a focused kind. With embedding questions the idea is to begin to stimulate curiosity. The individual starts wondering: 'What would it be like for me if...?' Humans pre-process understanding both consciously and non-consciously. This utilizes strategies of suggestion familiar to hypnotherapists and counsellors. This is similar to the phenomenon where you attempt to remember somebody's name, struggle and eventually give up. You go red as you mumble under your breath, trying to introduce a colleague to an acquaintance. Later, while driving home and thinking about what to cook for supper, the name comes back to you. You cringe and wonder how you could have forgotten the name of someone who you worked with only two years ago! How can this be possible without some deeper order engagement? That is the power of embedding questions.

Finally, when the teacher identifies key vocabulary and draws attention to where it can be seen on the board or around the classroom, she is aiding the visual learners and giving significance to the points that she wishes the class to learn. The ALPS teacher begins to introduce the words in context, telling the class that during the lessons to follow they will be coming back to these words in different ways.

Having taken five minutes for the Big Picture, you are ready to make a further positive start: you are ready to connect.

How to start positively and stay there

> "You only understand information relative to what you already understand. You only understand the size of a building if there is a car or a person in front of it. You only understand facts and figures when they can be related to tangible, comprehensible elements."

Richard Saul Wurman, 1989

If you put your ear to a classroom door, you might hear the hubbub of high voices and a shushing sound running over it like the lament of a leaking boiler. As you listen surreptitiously, the shushing gets louder. Shush, shush! There is a hint of pain and agitation in there. Shush, shush, shush! Eventually you think the boiler is going to explode! What's happening?

It is called the start of the lesson. It is a seasonal phenomena confined to school terms. It is the plaintive call of the inept teacher. Other recognizable plaintive calls include:

'I'm waiting ...', 'I'm still waiting ...'
'If you are going to behave like you did last time we won't learn anything ...'
'I'm sorry but ...'
'When you stop talking then we'll get started ...'
'Ssh!'
'Is there anyone who can remember?' 'Anyone?' 'Anyone at all!'
'Put up your hand anyone who ...'
'The next person who speaks is in detention.'
'There's a little girl who's still talking.'
'Oh we're very noisy today!'
'Thank you!' 'Thank you!' 'Thank you.'
'Please be quiet', 'Be quiet', 'Quiet.'
'We'll all be staying behind.'

All of us can look back on a bad day when we made one or more of these comments to a class. We need to be self-aware and reflect on the sort of language that we use in the classroom. We are all human, and part of the ALPS philosophy is that teachers, like their students, learn from their mistakes! Take time to reflect on your last day's teaching. Were you positive in all your interactions with children, staff and parents?

A positive start where the teacher quickly and smoothly begins to connect the learning has a number of desirable consequences. Pupils learn that such moments are important and assign value to them. Positive starts can be 'ritualized' so that certain things are always done in an understood order. Pupils then absorb the process and model it in their own learning. A lot of quality learning can be experienced in those first three or four critical moments. When the teacher engages the pupils actively and connects to their prior understanding and to previous lessons, she keeps recall high, and allows patterns of connectivity between the classroom and the world beyond to be reinforced.

To start positively involves engaging different modes of thinking, providing parameters for such thinking to occur and structuring interactions to maximize opportunities for such thinking to occur. A good way to get off to a good beginning is to consolidate, then reflect and then speculate.

Consolidation involves agreement on what children already know and understand individually and as a class. Reflection involves testing some of this consolidated knowledge and understanding against fresh criteria. Speculation involves taking the consolidated knowledge and understanding and applying it to new and different contexts.

You can do any of these in any of three different ways. You can use a timed challenge or a numbered challenge, or use games. A timed challenge is exactly that – a challenge to achieve a task in a specified time. A numbered challenge requires the pupils to achieve a numerical target or achieve within defined parameters. Using games involves participating in an activity where there is a shared understanding of rules, codes of conduct, outcomes and measures of success. You can do any of these as individual activities, paired activities or group activities.

Examples of positive connecting activities that you may wish to use at the beginning of a lesson appear below. They are essentially consolidation activities that can be utilized to give opportunities for reflective and speculative thinking.

1 **Timed challenge.** 'Last week we did work about the physical properties of solids, liquids and gases. List as many words as you can remember, on the physical properties of solids, liquids and gases. You have three minutes starting now!' Or work in pairs or groups and time the task against a piece of music – such as the 'Theme Tune' to *Mission Impossible*, the 'Minute Waltz' or the *William Tell Overture*. You can then take the suggestions and categorize them or map their connectivity on the board. Alternatively, the pupils can write them on 'post-its' and come out to the board, describe the word, spell it, and position it in a category or on the map.

2 **Numbered challenge.** Assign number challenges for individuals, pairs or groups, such as 'List five important things we need to remember about ..., three things that next year's Year 5 should know about ..., the top ten for ...'. Variety in the challenge can be provided by introducing an imaginative element, such as: 'You are the class DJ, introduce the top ten important words of the week in order', or 'List the premier division keywords for the week'.

By providing numbers you can then structure interactions within the class: 'Think of three things you remember as important about ..., then explain your three things to someone else and listen as they explain theirs. Now agree on five important things. Share your five important things and explain them to another pair.' You can enrich this activity by adding music: at each pause in the music a change takes place, then you can pick out seven things that you wish to reinforce with the whole class.

3   **Using games**. Create games that have agreed rules to explore subjects that you have covered in lessons or wish to link to other concepts. Examples include:

♣ *The Earthling Teacher Creature*. Half the class pretend to be teachers and half pretend to be Martians. The 'teachers' produce the laminated keyword list from last week. The Martians are allowed to ask Martian questions of the teachers: 'What does that word mean?' 'How do you spell it?' 'Use it in a sentence please.' Then the Martians move around. Then the children swap places. You can use suitable 'Martian' music to cue the changes!

♣ *Opinion Finders*. Write out a series of statements on a side of paper or on the board. The statements should be opinions rather than facts to encourage discussion rather than 'yes' or 'no' responses. The statements could relate to the topic you have been working on recently or are about to work on, or they could relate to the issues dealt with in a novel or a play. For example, using the story *Danny the Champion of the World*, statements could include: 'Children should be allowed to go to bed whenever they choose', 'Boys are better at girls at having adventures', 'It's wrong to keep creatures in captivity', or 'It's too dangerous to stay out at night without an adult'. Children should be given a statement to research, and told to collect the views of between three and five others. Then they should share their findings with a group and feed back as a group to the class. The activity opens up larger philosophical issues for discussion or consolidates real learning by challenging understanding.

♣ *Autograph Hunters*. Give every child a list of statements with a space alongside each one for an autograph. The statements should relate to an attribute or a skill. Tell the children to interview each other to find people who have the attribute or skills. If someone can demonstrate the skill, for example, 'can spell centurion without looking', he autographs next to that item on the list. Examples of attributes could be 'has a younger sister' or 'lives in a terraced house'. Mix the attributes and skills to encourage interaction, to ensure that everyone can achieve and to encourage pupils to use questioning strategies.

♣ *So you want to be a Millionaire?* Take the format for the popular television show and use it in class. Choose a child to sit in a chair by you at the front. Ask a series of questions that progressively get more difficult. The child can attempt to answer, or can phone a friend, or ask the audience, or be given a 50/50. You will need to stage-manage the session so that everyone becomes involved.

♣ *Noughts and crosses*. Divide the class in half. Half the class earns an X for a correct answer, while the other half earn an O. On the board draw a simple grid and ask questions. The aim is to get a complete line in order to win a point for the team. You can keep the grids up on the board and keep going until the topic is covered or everyone has answered a question. You can ask questions on a topic that you have covered in class, or choose a theme such as spelling, science, or current affairs.

185

♣ *Blockbusters*. This is a more sophisticated version of noughts and crosses. Draw an alphabet or number grid on the board. Divide the class into four teams with a nominated captain who will offer the team's answers. Each team starts in a different corner and has to get across to the diagonally opposite position. You can either limit the turns each team has or allow a team to progress as long as they continue to answer correctly.

♣ *A Question of ...* Organize two or four teams, each with a nominated 'personality' captain. This game can be used for different learning topics over a week. You can have different rounds: a 'spelling the keyword' round, a 'what happens next' round, a 'question for another team' round and a 'finger on the buzzer' round. You set the questions except for the 'question for another team' round, and each team accumulates points towards an end of the week total.

Games such as these are means of organizing opportunities for all students to re-engage with content and to be motivated to continue to learn.

The best group-work strategies

Many teachers, with blocks of time committed to literacy and numeracy and in the face of increasing pressure to deliver content, have adjusted to the default, which is more whole-class teaching and fewer pair or group-based activities. This is, in our view, an error. Effective whole-class teaching requires highly specialized skills on the part of the teacher, which are no less sophisticated than those required to structure and manage effective pupil-centred learning and group-work. Research by Watson (1996) revealed that pupils whose teachers used a more challenging teaching style that actively encouraged reflection, also experienced more group activities. Further research by Watson (1999) observed a dramatic increase in contribution to classroom talk from 5 per cent to 40 per cent as a result of teacher-led group-work alongside questioning strategies to encourage reflective thinking (Watson, 1999). The work of Croll and Moses (1995) demonstrated that eight and nine year olds with moderate learning difficulties in mainstream classes benefited considerably from group-work. In their study the level of engagement of these children increased from 46 per cent when working alone to over 70 per cent in a group.

Group-work

the alps approach – Accelerated Learning in Primary Schools

In the next section we will argue a case for optimizing time on task, based on an understanding of studies in attention. For pupils, an extended diet of whole-class teaching also requires highly specialized skills for effective participation. The ALPS teacher varies the structure of learning.

Our rationale for the judicious use of group-work includes a belief that paired and small group-work can:

➡ provide quality opportunities for pupils to maximize directed and purposeful language exchange;

➡ give an authentic audience and a safe test area for the ideas of others;

➡ offer challenging structures in which learning can be engaged at a number of levels;

➡ extend the quantity and quality of pupil response;

➡ develop the skills of social interaction;

➡ develop the intelligent behaviours of managing impulsivity, empathy and flexibility of thought;

➡ provide a mechanism for differentiation.

Over a half-term period every pupil should have had an opportunity to work with every other pupil in the class and have experience of different types of grouping. Some teachers start with single-sex friendship pairs and move to boy-girl non-friendship pairs. Some argue that boy-girl pairings produces a different type of language and problem-solving engagement, which ultimately is to the pair's mutual advantage. Group-work can start with single-sex friendship groupings and then move to mixed gender non-friendship groupings. When teachers make their professional rationale for mixing groupings explicit, pupils learn the protocols and follow them. Make the learning strategies that you use clearly understood. This way you will help the pupils to learn about learning. This will add to their capacity to be flexible and adapt to different learning challenges.

Resilience, Resourcefulness, Responsibility

Protocols for group-working can be described by the teacher, listed on a class display for all to see, supported by prompt sheets and modelled in circle time. Prompt sheets are laminated cards which give instructions to the group about processes that they should use and rules that they should follow.

You can teach your class the principles of PDR: Plan, Do, Review. Each stage can be broken down further by asking groups to consider these questions at each stage:

1 Plan
- ○ What have you have been asked to do?
- ○ What are some good ideas on how best to do it?
- ○ Choose the best idea and say what you will do.
- ○ How will you know you have done well?

2 Do
- ○ What things need to be done?
- ○ Who will do each of these things?
- ○ How will you each know you are doing well?
- ○ How will the group check that progress is being made?

3 Review
- ○ When you have finished how will you know you have been successful?
- ○ What will you do differently next time?
- ○ Who did what to help the team?

In addition to processes, a prompt sheet could include reference to group skills for things like listening, taking turns, clarifying, building on the ideas of others and taking responsibility.

To ensure consistency and equity in structuring groups, it is a good idea to use a variety of classroom aids. One way to prepare children for group-work is the 'Wheel of Fortune'. Three large pieces of card are cut into circles of different diameter. The larger card is segmented so that it contains a sequence of numbers written around its outer edge. The numbers correspond to those on the desks in the class. The two smaller circles are also segmented and contain the names of every pupil in the class. All three are pinned together with the smallest on top and the largest at the back so that you can rotate them. By rotating the inner two cards, pairings can be changed. By aligning the new pairings with a desk number you can show children where to go.

A large grid with children's names down both sides allows everyone to see the pairings. Another idea is to have group-work bingo where you draw the desk numbers to form new groups. In Part One we discussed the need to minimize stress and anxiety for children in base camp through forward planning. These systems can all help to prepare children in advance for the groups in which they will be working. If you use systems like bingo, be aware that for some children this may cause anxiety. You may want to pair the children before playing bingo, so that Annie knows that she and Nisha will be together with the pair whose names are pulled from the hat at the same time.

One ALPS teacher structures a regular group-work lesson that she calls 'Surprise Groups'. In this session the children are prepared for the fact that they will not be prepared for the groupings, which will be sorted out spontaneously. One of the targets for these sessions is to create a good team from your group and deal with the unknown. It is a good idea to have friendship groups for base camp so that children return to a familiar space when other activities have concluded. If you choose to group base camp in another way, such as by ability, it is wise to pay attention to friendships within those groups. To intentionally seat children where they are least likely to interact happily, is to set immediate limits on the learning opportunities within your class.

Circle time is an excellent method for modelling group-work skills as a whole class. In the circle protocols are learned: taking turns, attentive listening, giving and receiving feedback, building on the suggestions of others, sharing, taking time to talk through 'difficult' things. These protocols, modelled within the circle, then transfer to the small groups. This is a time when it is especially important to give the Big Picture.

When I shake hands with Taylor it makes me feel friendly. If we do good work in our class we shake hands with our group.

For some open-ended problem-solving activities where a range of skills can be used, mixed-ability groupings are safe and effective. For other specific tasks, which by their nature require differentiation, grouping by ability will be effective. A rigid adherence to grouping by ability for all tasks is not, in our view, best practice for either the holistic development of learning skills or the deeper understanding of content. Structured variety can be provided through combinations of the following group-work strategies:

→ **Mixed contribution groups**. Deliberately assign different roles within the group.

→ **Mixed gender pairings**. Ensure that groups include boys and girls. Try seating arrangements that are boy–girl–boy–girl.

→ **Individual – pair – share – present**. Begin with individuals and give them something that they can achieve. They then share their achievement with someone else using descriptive language and responding to clarifying and reflective questions. They form into groups and then the groups present their findings to the class. At each stage the challenge gets higher but every pupil has a contribution to make.

→ **Carousel**. Groups move around different activities.

→ **Snowball**. Progressive accumulation of information: 'Find one fact, now exchange it with someone else so you have two, now exchange your two with someone else so you have four.'

→ **The posse**. The posse is a discussion group where open debate takes place around an issue that has been developed in class. The posse is larger, is informal, is deliberately a talking shop without structure and is used occasionally to promote creativity and passion.

The judicious use of group-work allows us further opportunity to optimize time on task, and that is where we travel to next on our learning journey.

❷ VAKplus

> There is a very important time in a child's life, beginning at birth, when he should be living in an enriched environment – visual, auditory, language and so on – because that lays the foundations for development in later life.

Professor Torsten Weisel, President, Rockefeller University

> Ultimately, a full understanding of any concept of any complexity cannot be restricted to a single model of knowing or way of representation.

Howard Gardner, 1993

THE NOTION THAT EACH INDIVIDUAL ENGAGES WITH AND MAKES SENSE of everyday experience in different ways is at the heart of the accelerated learning message. In the ALPS approach we use the term VAKplus to describe this.

VAK stands for visual, auditory and kinesthetic, or, in other words, seeing, hearing and doing. 'Plus' implies that there is more; the more intuitive or insightful modes of engagement that are prompted by subtle questioning. As you plan and deliver each lesson, ask yourself: 'Am I able to maximize the opportunities for all the learners to access and engage with this new material? In what ways do I exploit the natural disposition to recall the appearance and visual characteristics of an experience? How do I ensure that the sounds will be remembered? How could physical movement and physical rehearsal help? Finally, am I encouraging the learner's questions and engaging curiosity at a more subtle depth?'

Think of Nisha, Amrit, Eddie and Annie. All four bring different skills, attitudes and aptitudes to a lesson. Imagine that the teacher has asked the class to read aloud an extract from a geography textbook, then to answer questions verbally about it, and finally to write a summary in their books. Amrit likes this activity, as it suits him to read aloud and listen to the teacher explain the meanings of new words in the text. This aural aspect of the lesson suits him. Nisha is happy, as she likes to read silently, visually taking in the information from the page, sometimes skimming ahead of the class in the text, sometimes going back over to clarify her understanding. Annie is anxious about being able to read the tricky words in the text and is thinking ahead to the questioning to come. The pace is too fast for her and she tries to go back over the first paragraph. By the time she has done this and looked at the diagrams carefully, the rest of the class has turned the page and Annie is lost. Meanwhile, Eddie is fidgeting within six or seven minutes of beginning the work. He would much prefer to be moving; sitting still is difficult for him. He prefers kinesthetic learning.

Advances in computer and brain-imaging technology have allowed us to watch the brain at work. Scientists now know that different neural structures are used for different modes of learning. When someone looks at a word, scientists see more electrical and chemical activity in the visual cortex at the back of the brain. When someone hears a word, there is more activity in the language centres in the left hemisphere of the cortex.[17] When someone thinks about a word, there is activity in yet another area. When someone completes planned, co-ordinated movements, activity is evident in the motor cortex, and when language accompanies this process, there is even more. Neuroscientists have proved that different sensory inputs utilize different neural processing structures.

The next stage might be to speculate that a combination of genetic disposition, life experience and habituation may result in some of these structures being marginally more efficient than others. Individuals may have better sensory acuity in a given mode. Some of us may be better at remembering the look of something, others the sounds that accompanied the experience and others the feelings it evoked. What might it mean for the classroom and our four children? How could the geography lesson be organized so that it suits Eddie and Annie as well as it suits Nisha and Amrit?

VAKplus is the simplest teaching and learning styles audit you will find. Use it to test that you are conveying learning challenges through these combined modes (for an introduction to representational systems see Seymour and O'Connor, 1990). Learning is most natural and therefore best when the senses are engaged! Children will not use one sensory approach to the exclusion of all others and it is verging on the absurd to say that a child is a visual, auditory or kinesthetic learner. Yet it would also be absurd to say that the geography lesson that we described above suited Eddie as a learner. The good news is that it is not difficult to plan for

VAKplus in every lesson. If Eddie's teacher had added an activity that involved some role play or practical representation of the concept, not only would Eddie have learned more, but the rest of the class would also have had the chance to reinforce their understanding.

The VAKplus tool can be an effective way of ensuring that you balance and broaden your teaching range. Teach children to see it, hear it, do it, and be curious about it!

Guidelines to engage different types of natural preference

Visual engagement

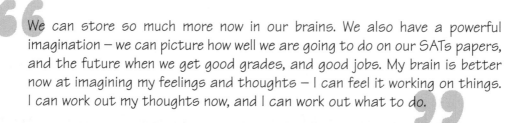

We can store so much more now in our brains. We also have a powerful imagination – we can picture how well we are going to do on our SATs papers, and the future when we get good grades, and good jobs. My brain is better now at imagining my feelings and thoughts – I can feel it working on things. I can work out my thoughts now, and I can work out what to do.

Dan age 10

✔ Use lots of visual stimuli such as cue cards, posters and prompt sheets.

✔ Put a visual organizer, or some sort of visual reminder for the day's work, on the board.

✔ Use peripheral posters with positive messages in your classroom and around the school.

✔ Use teacher-drawn learning posters placed above eye-level in your class to register key learning points.

✔ Ask children to make posters to represent concepts during lessons, or for homework.

✔ Cover up the learning posters and test on the content.

✔ Place keywords around the room and on prompt sheets on the desks.

✔ Put the children's memory maps on the affirmation wall.

✔ Use visual prompts for story writing.

✔ Use visuals and props to enhance and supplement the reading of stories: the story of the Queen's Knickers was enhanced in one classroom by a large bag full of little pairs of knickers, a little wooden wardrobe and a little wicker trunk.

✔ Provide lots of visual references when you give examples or tell stories: 'It looked like ...'

✔ Ask questions through visual recall: 'What did it look like?'

✔ Ask questions through visual imagination: 'What would it look like?'

✔ Use lots of visual associations.

✔ Allow children to gain an overview by first flicking through a book and using structured 'dipping' when reading for information.

✔ Encourage spelling by imagining the word and breaking it down into its constituent parts and seeing this process happen; change the colour of the word; make it big; make it small.

✔ Encourage children to 'see' the spelling in the upper left field of vision with the eyes closed.

✔ Teach and model visualization and guided visualization.

✔ Encourage the children to notice and draw attention to details when pole-bridging. Help children remember the 'look' and organization of information by teaching them to take structured notes using shapes, space and colour.

✔ Use and display individual, group and class memory maps.

Auditory engagement

> I think that everybody is born with a powerful brain, but some people do not use it so they do not do so well. They never listen, they are not taught to listen. They do not know how to use their brain.

Laura age 10

A Establish protocols about noise levels in your class: use the clock face method or practise using the amplifier method described earlier.

A Teach and practise good listening.

A Use circle time or some similar approach to practise active listening, give feedback, practise asking questions.

A Make judicious use of teacher-selected music to complement classroom learning.

A Keep your own classroom talk positive.

A Strip down your own language and avoid adult codes.

A Talk through the learning posters to further register key learning points.

193

A Cover up the learning posters and test on the content.

A Use lots of language activities based on the keywords for the lesson or the week.

A Ask children to talk through and introduce the memory maps on the affirmation wall.

A Encourage children to describe their story aloud to a partner before they write it.

A Make extensive use of singing, chanting and narrative verse.

A For older children with reading difficulties, practise reading with a chronometer or a background tape with a steady insistent rhythm.

A Practise the voices of characters from the books you read: be as melodramatic, quirky and eccentric as your dignity will allow!

A Provide lots of auditory references when you give examples or tell stories: 'It sounded like ...'

A Ask questions through auditory recall: 'What did it sound like?'

A Ask questions through auditory imagination: 'What would it sound like?'

A Use lots of auditory associations.

A Before reading for information, use paired prediction exercises: 'I think this book is about ... and my evidence for this is ...'

A Encourage spelling by sounding the word and breaking it down into its constituent parts and hearing this process happen; change the sound of the word; high voice, low voice, fast, slow, Donald Duck voice.

A Encourage children to say words slowly aloud and listen to each syllable as they say it.

A Teach and practise pole-bridging.

A Set up pairs for taking turns in being the coach: the coach guides and instructs using only verbal instructions.

A Help children remember information by regular diffusion opportunities.

A Encourage children to talk through their memory maps and explain them to others.

Kinesthetic engagement

66 I'd never thought what my brain was like, now I know, and I feel like I can do everything with my brain for secondary school. We are all going to get good grades in SATs so that we do well in secondary school, then after that people will want to employ you, because you are powerful. 99

Sam age 10

K Build in regular planned physical breaks.

K Use different sites within the classroom for different types of activity.

K Put a visual organizer or some sort of visual reminder for the day's work on the board and when you make reference to it make your movements large and extravagant.

K Use lots of 'open' body language: avoid arms folded, shrugs, frowns and the shaking head of disapproval.

K Use Brain Gym® to reinforce learning in the dead time.

K Use Brain Gym® to rehearse motor skills such as handwriting.

K Act things out.

K Provide opportunities for children to learn by manipulating and doing.

K Provide opportunities for children to learn by simulating movements.

K Speak slowly.

K Use laminated letters that can be sorted and organized for practising structuring words.

K Use laminated keywords that can be sorted and organized for practising structuring sentences.

K Allow children to stand beside and describe their memory map on the affirmation wall.

K Use toys and props to enhance story-telling and to prompt story writing.

K Provide lots of kinesthetic references when you give examples or tell stories: 'It felt like ...'

K Ask questions through kinesthetic recall: 'What did it feel like?'

K Ask questions through kinesthetic imagination: 'What would you be doing?'

K Use lots of physical associations and learn through movement, mime or gesture.

K Allow children to gain an overview by first flicking through a book, and teach structured 'dipping' when reading for information.

K Encourage spelling by practising writing the word in the air, on a desk or on someone else's back.

K Ask children if the spelling 'feels' right.

K Teach children to try spellings by first writing them with a finger in the palms of their hands; then with their eyes shut; then saying the spelling at the same time.

K Teach and model visualization and guided visualization with an added emphasis on the physical feelings.

K Encourage the children to notice and draw attention to the 'feel' of things when pole-bridging: 'Now I'm going to pick up the red carton – it feels cold and hard and slippery.'

K Help children remember the organization of information by explicit teaching of structured note-taking using shapes, space and colour; encourage them to move their finger around and notice the spaces, shapes and colours.

K Use memory maps and ask children to 'walk' you through their ideas.

K Role-play whenever possible; ask children to act out erosion or a volcano erupting.

K Encourage children to use their bodies to represent ideas, such as 2D and 3D shapes in maths.

K Ask children to pretend to be the people you are learning about, to walk like them, talk like them, mime their actions and imagine their feelings.

Plus engagement

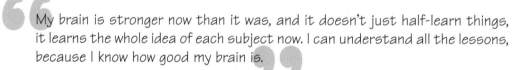

My brain is stronger now than it was, and it doesn't just half-learn things, it learns the whole idea of each subject now. I can understand all the lessons, because I know how good my brain is.

Laura age 10

✓ Encourage descriptive, reflective and speculative thinking.

✓ List, select, predict.

✓ Encourage the best guess: 'What makes it the best guess?' 'What things do you reject in favour of the best guess?'

✓ Encourage outcomes thinking and personal performance targets and do so in relation to the accelerated learning cycle.

✓ Use peripheral posters with positive messages in your classroom and around the school and ask children to make up their own personal logo or motto or positive message.

✓ Ask children to devise their own above-eye-level learning posters to take home and put above their bed.

✓ Encourage them to practise at home by covering up the learning posters and testing on the content.

✓ Ask children to shut their eyes and visualize their memory map on the affirmation wall; talk their way through it; how does it make them feel?

✓ Remind the children, 'Imagine the teacher showing you the answer, or telling you the answer, or try to remember your pole-bridging; if you are really stuck, trust your intuition.'

✓ Use lots of open-ended questions with processing time.

✓ Encourage pupils to struggle with complexity and stay with it.

✓ Model the new three Rs in your classroom.

Seven ways to VAK

VAK suffuses our thinking throughout this book. Our learning model places the VAK approach at its core and uses it for engaging different levels of sustainable cognitive challenge. In this section we look at how VAK can help with classroom display and with English, maths and science, and so be at the core of your practice too!

Visual display

Visual display is an important part of the ALPS package. Who established the convention in primary schools that children's work has to fill the display space? An opportunity for enhancing learning could be lost in a wall covered by twenty-eight facsimile copies of the Magna Carta, or supposed book covers, or pseudo Second World War posters, or cross-sections of Hadrian's Wall. We do not argue against these activities, but against the culture of using visual display mainly to show off what work has been done, rather than to accelerate learning.

Visual display will improve recall in dramatic ways, some argue by as much as 70 per cent! Many primary schools have rewritten their policies on display once they have begun to develop the ALPS method™. Display is then used for the purpose of:

▲ reinforcing learning and aiding recall;

▲ stimulating further thinking;

▲ making connections between concepts;

▲ reminding of rules and targets;

▲ celebrating and affirming success.

The rationale about valuing pupils' achievement through displaying their work has been questioned by many ALPS teachers, who limit the amount of work that they display in this traditional manner. This is particularly true of the later years. In the early years the display of pictures and work is an important part of classroom life and an essential tool for creating a feeling of belonging and security. However, experienced ALPS children already feel valued through RAP, affirmations, meeting targets and celebrating success. We asked a group of children in a Year 5 ALPS classroom if they missed having their work displayed in the traditional way, and received a unanimous 'No!' This was what Carolyn said:

Grown ups do not have their work put up on the wall like that, so neither do we. I know if my work is good, so I do not need it to look pretty – it's just a waste of time. Our classroom is interesting to be in because it has tons of stuff up about what we are studying. I'd much rather read about that, than look at my work up there.

The ALPS classroom uses every available space for display of key facts, memory maps, rules, targets, celebrations and affirmations. Windows, doors and all areas of walls are used. In many classrooms a network of ropes and lines are permanently fixed across the ceiling from which posters are attached just above eye level using brightly coloured pegs. Open-ended questions are pinned up before and after lessons, and answers are added. Some teachers prefer to create areas for display for each curriculum area, while others are more flexible; this is a matter of personal choice. Throughout every ALPS classroom are affirming and positive messages that reinforce the message that every pupil in that room is intelligent and successful.

When children move around as they are grouped for collaborative and creative work, they see all these posters at some time. It may sometimes be necessary to make two copies of some posters. It is also useful to bear in mind the positioning of children in base camp. Many teachers position key posters where particular children will have maximum exposure to certain information. Desk surfaces can be used in a variety of ways. Some teachers attach permanent plastic wallets, into which can be slipped memory maps or target cards. Others use blu-tac or sticky tape for desk labels or flashcards. Any important fact from a lesson is transferred onto a visual poster and displayed. Children who have been taught in this way tell us that they can recall information and connections often by visualizing where a poster was once displayed, although it may have long since been removed.

Colour and symbols are used to represent information clearly and succinctly. Some teachers use key colours to aid recall. For example, one teacher used key colours for her science teaching. The liver was always represented in a vivid pink, the kidneys in paler pink, the heart in a bright red, oxygen in pale blue, hydrogen in yellow and so on. Whether oxygen was being represented in connection with respiration or in learning about the water cycle, it was represented in the same colour. A visual diagram showing the effect of smoking therefore needed no labels, as the children knew that pale blue circles represented oxygen, while black represented tar and brown nicotine.

Memory maps are displayed clearly in classrooms. These are working, ongoing documents that provide a record of what is being learned and a visual picture of the connections between concepts. Some teachers create large mind maps that cover whole areas of the curriculum, while others create smaller ones that are removed as others replace them. It is important to follow the rules about memory mapping and keep the words to a minimum, using symbols, keywords and pictures instead. Memory aids that have been used to learn key facts, such as the word 'has' to recall the hammer, anvil and stirrup in the ear, can be used on memory maps once every child can remember the vocabulary. Until then, a bold poster showing the words should be displayed until the information is absorbed.

Teaching spelling through VAK

Teaching spellings using VAK should be carried out in addition to the essential work on spelling rules and phonics, which should never be neglected. Two or three spellings can be actively taught using this method to the whole class in two very short sessions per day. It is most effective if children working on the same spellings learn the same way, as any 'dead time' can be used to reinforce these spellings; for example, at beginnings and endings of assemblies and gatherings, or when lining up or waiting for lunch. Spellings learned through VAK are excellent material for brain breaks at any time, and in our experience are rarely forgotten once learned.

Display the words to be learned clearly to the class. Spend a few moments looking at them and reading them aloud. Ensure that children's pronunciation is correct. It is little wonder that many children have difficulty spelling words such as 'normally' or 'probably', if they pronounce them 'normly' and 'probly'. Notice anything distinctive or quirky in the words that can be used as memory aids. For example, a Year 2 class noticed that carrot was spelled car–rot and made a poster of a carrot with wheels to help them to remember that carrot has two 'r's! A simple way to learn many words is to chunk them into two, three or four letter sections by using coloured pens.

Develop a way to identify words or parts of words that are phonic. For example, hands on hips, with a long, drawn out 'e–a–s–y!' followed by the sounds of the letters, such as 'p–a–t' can be used for the word 'pat'. It could also be used for the first part of the word 'pattern'. Teach children to become aware of the parts of words that they are likely to get wrong. They will soon become adept at pinpointing the letters that they will miss out, or the part of the word that breaks a spelling rule. This is the part that they need to focus on as they learn. This is what eight year old Amy had to say about learning spellings at home before and after VAK:

> I hated learning my spellings. Mummy used to get fed up and my sister would tell me it was easy, because she goes to secondary school, then Daddy would get stressy. I spent ages and ages on Sunday. I used to get about twelve right out of twenty. Then I learned just to say 'easy' if it was just the sounds, then I didn't need to spend time learning those ones. Out of twenty I need to learn about ten. I learn the tricky bits and now I usually get nineteen or twenty out of twenty!

Children should then look at the word as they trace the spelling in the air, with left hand, right hand and both hands, until its form is familiar to them. Songs and actions can be used to help recall. We watched a Year 1 class learning to spell 'happy' by singing 'I am H–A–P–P–Y'. Later they learned other words such as 'proud', 'smart' and 'quick' to the same tune, reinforcing positive feelings about themselves in addition to learning the spellings. All this work should be visually reinforced through posters on the walls, in the corridor and on the walls of the hall. When the children sit in assembly or do PE in the hall, they are visually absorbing the spellings that they have learned in class. Dead time can then be used to practise words that have been learned.

Once words have been 'chunked', find creative ways to learn the more difficult spellings. For example, this is how Sandeep learned to spell the word 'injection'. Sandeep was in Year 2, but her sister in Year 4 had practised this spelling at home. Sandeep had learned it too, leading her teacher to reassess the level of spellings that she was teaching to her class.

Say spelling aloud	Say aloud	Action
in	'put it in'	Pretends to inject arm
ject	'easy, j-e-c-t'	Traces letters in the air
i	'cos you cry'	Points to eye
on	'put a patch on'	Pretends to put a patch on

With a creative VAK approach to teaching spelling, children become enthusiastic and keen to meet fresh challenges. Once they have developed the skills in learning using VAK, they will begin to find ways to learn words that they personally misspell and to suggest methods in your spelling sessions. When this is linked to clear target-setting and RAP systems, the results are outstanding.

Teaching children to use exclamation marks

You will already have drawn children's attention to exclamation marks when reading with them. In this activity you teach children to use exclamation marks in their story writing. Give the Big Picture, telling the class that they will all learn how to include exclamation marks in their writing. Connect the learning by explaining that they have learned to recognize exclamation marks in books, but today they are going to learn to use them. Set the target for the lesson and display it visually. For example: 'Today, everybody is to use at least three exclamation marks in their writing.' Write on the board or on a bold coloured poster a keyword with an exclamation mark, such as:

Bang! Pop! or Crash!

This word will become your central focus for your writing session and should have been taught as a part of your spelling programme that week. Sit all the children cross-legged, where they can look at the word and the exclamation mark. Remind them that an exclamation mark means that something is loud or exciting, and it means that you emphasize that word. When you use that word in the story that you are going to tell, you want them to join in by saying the word, pointing to it on the board and then drawing an exclamation mark in the air, saying 'line ... dot ... jump!' An exclamation mark makes you jump out of your seat, so when they say 'jump!' you want them to jump their bottoms off the carpet!

I am sitting down with my legs crossed and I'm doing 'line dot jump'. That means an exclamation mark. It means you shout it.

Tell a story where the word that you have chosen features strongly and is used in a predictable fashion. There are many such stories in children's books, or you can create one for yourself. This has the advantage of freeing you to look at the class and really engage with them as you tell the story. For example, tell a story of a little girl who climbed her mummy's cabinet to look at her favourite ornament. Each time the little girl almost reached the top, something fell onto the floor and went 'Crash!' Create anticipation in the children as the chosen word approaches, pause, point to it on the display, then say together:

'Crash ... line ... dot ... jump!'

By the end of the story, the whole class should be anticipating the word and joining in the actions. Follow with a short discussion of the children's ideas for loud, exciting words to use in their writing. As they begin to write their own stories, remind them that they must meet your target and draw their attention to posters of words that will give visual aids throughout the session. During the session monitor that each child is following the format for a story with predictable language and use of exclamation marks. Whenever the children need a brain break, sit them on the floor near their seats and practise being exclamation marks, with 'line ... dot ... jump!'

Repeat this exercise in a later lesson with a different word, where the exclamation mark is used to indicate humour. In this session, ask the children to 'wriggle as they giggle' when they have drawn their exclamation mark. We have seen Year 1 children using exclamation marks correctly and consistently following this activity. They have seen the exclamation mark, felt it as they have drawn it, heard a description of it and experienced the emotion that it creates through their wriggle, giggle or jump. This class later used this knowledge within a VAK lesson on using speech marks. By the end of this programme, most of the class could punctuate direct speech correctly in their writing, using question marks and exclamation marks correctly.

The 'Said Tree'

This is a simple activity that can quickly help children to develop their writing skills and can be adapted for use in a variety of contexts. When linked to effective systems of target-setting and RAP, children's progress will be very rapid. Many children do not naturally develop a range of writing styles and vocabulary. It is often necessary to teach this variety and to help them to see ways to improve, in addition to hearing and reading a wide variety of literature and formal exercises to teach grammatical structures. In creative writing activities children can tend to use repetitive, 'safe' language rather than draw upon the wide range that they hear in stories; for example, writing lengthy pieces of dialogue repeatedly using the phrases 'he said' and 'she said'.

Write the word 'said' in the middle of the board. Give each group of children a pile of cards and coloured pens, and encourage them to work together to think of as many words that could be substituted for the word 'said'. You may need to start with some examples and continue to suggest more, or give groups books to look in for further examples. The idea is to pool everybody's ideas to come up with a large number of alternatives. Here is a list of examples, although it is essential that children do this activity themselves and are not simply given a list to learn!

beseeched	argued	debated	muttered	whispered
encouraged	insisted	disputed	murmured	groaned
bragged	demanded	pleaded	mumbled	laughed
boasted	persisted	begged	declared	lisped
agreed	yelled	asked	reasoned	hissed
disagreed	shouted	implored	appealed	spat
chortled	chuckled	moaned	whined	screeched

Once every group of children has several examples, children should start to stick them on the board with blu-tac, discarding duplicates and creating new cards as new words occur to them. As they put a card on the board, they should call out the word in a tone that describes the meaning, muttering 'muttered' or whining 'whined'.

Later, these words should be written or typed clearly on individual labels and displayed in a prominent place in the classroom around the word 'said'. One teacher did this in a huge speech bubble, while another made a large poster of a tree and displayed the words on branches around it. The children in this class categorized the words along each branch; for example, putting all the words that are spoken loudly along one branch and all the boastful words along another. A lot of discussion took place as the children did this activity, as many words fit into several categories. The words were put on with blu-tac so that they could be recategorized at a later date. Any word was said in the right tone, so that the meanings were conveyed as the class worked.

When your words for 'said' are displayed, games can be played using them and targets set for their use in writing; for example, by organizing hierarchies of words, such as the literacy strategy of 'Premier League' words where Premier League words are the best ones to use. The list is never finished, and words can be added as they arise through story-telling, reading or general conversation. Children can be challenged to think of more at home and can add to the ever-growing display over time. Soon they will start to use a wider vocabulary in their conversation and writing. This activity can then be used to teach connective phrases, adjectives, adverbs and so on.

As wonderful, creative language is used in your classroom, highlight it, write it up, pin it on the wall and draw it to the attention of your class. In this way enrichment of language will not simply be left to chance, it will happen in a climate of enthusiastic learning. Try displaying posters of proverbs with pictures that explain the meanings and children will soon start to experiment in their spoken and written language. We have heard very young children relating this to their everyday life; for example, overhearing an infant-aged child saying to a friend in a playground dispute: 'Do not just give a dog a bad name!' If variety of language is reinforced visually in the classroom and all around the school, the progress of pupils will swiftly accelerate.

Full stops and VAK

Some children take a long time to learn to punctuate the beginnings and endings of sentences. Many children learn to punctuate in formal exercises, yet, when they undertake a lengthy piece of writing, they completely forget to use any capital letters and full stops. Hayley was one such pupil. She knew how to punctuate correctly, but once her ideas began to flow, she would completely forget. She found it frustrating and it affected her levels of attainment in all areas of the curriculum. This is how Hayley describes her ALPS teacher's technique for using a strong visual cue to teach her to be aware of her punctuation as she wrote:

I remember the time you talked to me about 'ands' because I never put a full stop in my work. I knew how to do it, but somehow I just forgot every time. My writing just went on and on with 'and then and then and then'. It drove me mad. That night at home I did two sheets full of 'ands'. I did it in all different colours. It took me ages and ages. I put it on the wall and I looked and looked and looked at it. It was funny, because usually you look at something because you want to remember it. I sort of wanted to remember the word 'and' because I wanted to get rid of it!

Now I hate the word 'and'. So when I almost write it, instead I think: 'Uh-oh, maybe I should use a full stop!' Then I decide if I need 'and' or if I could use another word instead.

The next day you came running up the stairs and kissed me because I had punctuated all the way through my story for the first time!

Enhancing scientific understanding through VAK

Role play is one of the most enjoyable ways for children to demonstrate understanding in science, to link concepts and to develop their thinking. Science lessons have endless possibilities for learning through VAK. The ALPS teacher creates opportunities for enquiry, uses open-ended questioning and assesses continually through the use of mind maps. She displays key facts and concepts visually around the classroom and looks for every opportunity to aid memory and recall. Role play can be used in any area of the science curriculum and helps children to recall facts, learn key vocabulary and link new concepts into their overall scientific understanding.

All too often, scientific concepts are learned in isolation. Through this role-play activity, children can make connections between concepts as they create a sequence of actions that represents the complexity of the human body. This activity requires whole-class participation. The class creates an imaginary human body within a set space. Together, the children role-play the various functions of the body through groups or individuals representing various organs, blood cells, gases, nutrients and so on. Eventually the whole human body can be put together and concepts such as smoking and alcohol can be included. Connections between a variety of concepts can be made. Once a class reaches this stage it can be exciting to work in larger groups of two or three classes to create more complex role plays. It is important that children swap roles frequently, so that they experience the scenario from all perspectives.

The shape of the human body is always outlined for body science by two cardboard hands and feet. This activity requires space for children to move around, such as a part of a hall, library or large classroom. You need a large supply of props such as various coloured cardboard circles and coloured crêpe paper to represent the various organs. Beginning with just one simple aspect of the human body, which you have already taught in class, for example, the heart and circulation, organize four children to role-play the heart, draped with red crêpe paper. They should stand in position, wearing labels 'right auricle', 'right ventricle', 'left auricle' and 'left ventricle'. Four other children should role play the lungs, draped in blue crêpe paper. The rest of the class should hold red cardboard circles to role play being blood cells.

As the blood cells progress around the body, they should swap their red cards for blue as oxygen passes through the cell walls into the tissues. When they approach the heart, they should call out 'Right Auricle' then 'Right Ventricle' before entering the lungs, who use the terms 'inhale' and 'exhale' as they breathe. Each blood cell collects a red card from the lungs, calling out 'Oxygenated!' as he takes the card and progresses to the 'Left Auricle' and 'Left Ventricle' before continuing around the body. Once the basic role play is practised, you can add the other organs, the gases in respiration and the digestive system, with children role playing nutrients, urine, oxygen and so on. Health education issues such as a lesson on smoking can be included. Children with black labels can represent tar in the lungs, while the whole class chant 'NICOTINE, NICOTINE, NICOTINE' to create an image of addiction. As the science curriculum is extended, the concepts learned should be added to the role play and all the connections explored.

Children who use role play regularly become extremely creative. One class put together a role play of photosynthesis with human respiration, showing the relationship between the two. They added a role play of the water cycle and the destruction of the ozone layer, developing an understanding of the various states of oxygen as O, O^2 and O^3. The levels of understanding and the connections shown in complex role play were reflected in the complexity of their mind maps. Through role play, concepts that were previously learned in isolation are linked and become meaningful.

Some examples of VAK and maths

Many aspects of maths are learned through practical experience and purposeful investigation. The ALPS teacher also frequently reinforces maths concepts through visual aids and physical activities, core language, pole-bridging, generating questions and research. Maths brain breaks are also part of the approach and are fun and easy to create. For example, in the Introduction we described a class jumping backwards and forwards as they role-played decimal points and multiplied and divided by ten and one hundred. This activity was later used as a maths brain break that reinforced the work that had been covered that week in class. Clear visual posters reinforced the concept until it was absorbed. In another class the children demonstrated turning through 90, 180 and 270 degrees by turning their arms in large circles as a regular brain break. Again, the concept was visually displayed in clear, bold posters on the walls.

Visual posters are a vital aspect of the ALPS method™ of teaching. Whenever a new concept is introduced, a poster is made either by the children or the teacher to represent the concept.

In ALPS classrooms large, bold and clear visual posters reinforce learning and connect concepts. For example, the concept of fractions is linked to that of decimals and then to percentages. Visual aids help remove the mystery that children sometimes feel about maths and create an environment where numbers and shapes are familiar and fun. Every time a child gazes at the percentage poster, he is subconsciously absorbing the fact that 50 per cent is a half, which is the same as 0.5.

In one Year 6 classroom we saw a display in bold colours showing many aspects of the number 100. The teacher explained that although the class had worked their way through a maths scheme, few of them confidently recalled or used any significant facts about the number 100. Her posters made it a friendly number, and the children now knew without calculation that 100 is ten tens, twenty fives, four twenty-fives and a tenth of a thousand. They could multiply and divide by 10, 100 and 1000, and they talked enthusiastically about the number 100's special qualities.

This class often worked in percentages as an everyday activity. For example, being told: '50 per cent of us are going to play football in PE, 25 per cent will practise shooting, and 25 per cent will practise throwing skills, then we will all change around.' The teacher spoke mathematically and the children all understood, because they had covered the work through meaningful activities while their posters had reinforced the concepts. Continual seizing of mathematical opportunities by this teacher was reflected in the confident approach of the children and enthusiasm for maths.

We watched this teacher demonstrate on the board the difficulties of dividing 100 by three. The children puzzled about the 1 left over after 99 was accounted for. They had no difficulty with fractions, as ⅓ works well, but what about representing it in decimals? The teacher led the class through an explanation of recurring numbers. Every child sat absorbed in the concept and went home to investigate recurring numbers on calculators. 'Just six months ago, they couldn't tell me that 100 was four 25s without using their fingers!' commented the teacher.

The ALPS teacher often asks children to make posters as a part of their investigative work or to demonstrate understanding. Making mathematical posters can be a great opportunity for collaborative work. Similarly, grouping children to create role plays to represent maths concepts often frees them from the feeling of maths having answers that are simply right or wrong. We watched groups of six children create a short sequence that represented the word 'perimeter' and show how to calculate the perimeter of a rectangle. The children then demonstrated their work to the other groups. One role play involved four children as corners, with their hands held in 90 degree positions, while the two others marched the perimeter, counting paces. They paused to ask each 'corner' who they were. 'Corner, ninety degrees, a right angle, Sir!' shouted each 'corner'. At the end of the sequence the children altered their shape to become a square. 'Multiply one side by four, Sir!' shouted the 'corners'. They had incorporated work on angles into this activity, while other groups had included the concepts of parallelograms, area and triangles.

Grouping can be organized to foster teamwork among differentiated groups, with higher ability children being asked to represent more difficult concepts, or in mixed groups where explanations between children can reinforce learning. These activities can also aid in assessing children's understanding and depth of thought. Asking children to talk through their posters and role-play sequences can be a useful exercise in both the assessment and the process of pole-bridging. These activities demand that children communicate their thoughts and co-operate. Once simple role plays have been mastered, challenges can be set to create role-plays that link a wider variety of mathematical concepts. Parts of these role plays can subsequently be used as reinforcing brain breaks.

❸ Structuring time on task

The optimal time on task

A HEADLINE FROM the *Times Educational Supplement* from May 1998 read, 'Literacy Hour is Too Long'. This caught our eye. How long is an hour? Leaving aside questions posed by philosophers and students of quantum mechanics, we could probably reach agreement that it is, more or less, sixty minutes. That is of course four times fifteen minutes, or three times twenty minutes, or even five times twelve minutes. With our Literacy Hour or indeed any other lesson teachers can, and ought to, chunk it down, giving attention to the transition between activities, ensuring that the Big Picture is given and providing opportunities for physical reprieve. To just move from one activity to the next without refocusing, connecting the learning and giving the Big Picture is to immediately set limits on learning.

Our model for optimizing time on task involves chunking in a structured way, with the 'chunks' linked by activities that accelerate learning. It looks like this:

> **Connect – preview – focus on task – diffuse – focus on task – diffuse – focus on task – diffuse – review**

The 'optimal time on task' is complex to define. 'Optimal' for what? What sort of task? What sort of learner? Our model for optimizing time on task derives from research into the human's ability to give sustained attention. We offer it for you to take, adapt and use. It is not a prescriptive formula. The underlying principle and the related strategies are what matter.

Our model begins with activities that connect to prior learning. Each child has some sort of prior understanding that she brings to an experience. Every starting point therefore differs. Connecting activities are designed to share understanding and to make connections with the child's world. The teacher seeks examples from the child's world and makes links with what the class has learned before.

Preview provides the Big Picture and orientates the learner, locking into pre-processing. The teacher does three things: says what the class are about to do and how, embeds open-ended questions and assigns significance to the key vocabulary. Wherever possible, she registers each through a visual prompt.

Rather than attempt to maximize the duration of engagement with any one task, the teacher structures it down, using the crude formula of 'the younger the learner the shorter the task'. In other words, an ALPS teacher would break up Eddie's geography lesson with short, practical activities that energize in addition to helping children to refocus. She would deliberately limit the duration of each chunk and would string the chunks together with meaningful learning interventions called 'diffusions'. Each chunk of the lesson is carefully timed and each diffusion is deliberately planned. The overall result is that more time is spent purposefully on task and engaged with meaningful learning.

Examining the nature of focus and diffusion within our model we see that:

■ optimal focus on task time will vary by task and by learner but, as a general rule, the younger the learner, the shorter the focus time;

■ it is essential for the teacher to explain the model and why she is using it;

■ diffusions are shifts of focus accompanied by opportunities for physical reprieve;

■ diffusions enhance the learning by structured re-engagement with the task;

■ learners come back to the original task, not to new tasks.

Research done by Karl Pribram (1975; see also Jensen, 1998b) on arousal, activation and effort in the control of attention, pointed to physical limits in the duration of certain types of attention. We recommend a model of optimizing time on task based on using different modes of engagement with that task. We suggest that the optimal time on task for learners in the age range 7 to 16 will be chronological age plus one. For a ten year old this means focused attention for eleven or so minutes before some sort of change. For younger children the limit for focused attention will be even shorter, and teachers need to be aware of the attention spans within their class. We acknowledge the weaknesses implicit in such a formulaic response but believe that the underlying principle of 'maxima' is worth working to.

When a teacher explains to the pupils how and why she structures variety in learning, she helps them break free of a trap that assumes that learning occurs only when the teacher talks or when children engage in a some sort of written follow-up activity. Explain why you choose to structure the learning the way you do. Use language such as 'focus', 'brain break' and 'concentration' and encourage the pupils to do so also.

Diffusions are necessary for two reasons. First, they encourage the pupil to re-engage with his own learning. Second, they offer the chance of a physical break. Attention studies show that there are physical limits to focused, external, vigilant attention. Writers such as Eric Jensen (1996) posit that we tune in and out naturally, and that eight or nine minutes of focused external vigilant attention might be as much as could be hoped for in a classroom. Diffusions can exploit this pattern by re-engaging learners at this drop-out point. With each diffusion activity, the teacher asks for a different sort of learning. Some examples of diffusion activities include:

▲ In pairs and using the core vocabulary, take turns to describe what you have just learned.

▲ Individually think of three things that you think are important, then swap them with someone nearby, then, with your partner, agree on five.

▲ Write out three new things you have learned in your book.

▲ What three good questions should someone ask to learn about this topic?

▲ Add three new items of vocabulary to your key vocabulary list, then get someone to test your spelling and your use of the word in a sentence.

▲ What will happen next? Write your prediction and at least three clues that make you believe it. Compare with someone else.

In each case the effort goes in to making sense of the focused learning experience. A different mode of engagement is encouraged. In some classes diffusions are also used for stretching exercises or brain break activity before going back to focus on work.

Pole-bridging to increase intelligent response

> Thinking is when your mouth stays shut and your head keeps talking to itself.

Clint, Year 5

Neuroscientists, such as Professor Colin Blakemore of the University of Oxford, inform us that 'there is one firm fact – our brains pass through a particular window for language by the age of ten' (1998). They assure us that learning how to learn is more important at that stage. He and his team argue that:

> all babies from all over the world classify sounds and notice changes in sounds in the same ways and at 3–4 months babies are taking in most language. At 18 months there is an explosive improvement in speech and full language and if a child is not exposed to speech by 8 years then they will never develop speech. It is the same for a second language.

Colin Blakemore, 1998

Professor Janet Huttenlocher, a psychologist at the University of Chicago, claims that 'infants whose parents talk to them more frequently and use bigger, "adult" words will develop better language skills' (quoted in Kotulak, 1996). In a pioneering study looking at language acquisition and children (Diamond, 1998), researchers at the University of Chicago showed that when socio-economic factors were equal, babies whose mothers talked to them more had a bigger vocabulary. At twenty months, babies of talkative mothers knew 131 more words than infants of less talkative mums, and at twenty-four months the difference was 295 words.

Dr Sally Ward of the Speech, Language and Hearing Centre in London gained the headlines in 1998 when the popular press caught hold of her research. The headline in the *Daily Express*, 18 October 1998 read:

'How to Boost Your Child's IQ: Shock research says babies denied one-to-one talk are less intelligent'

Dr Ward studied 140 children over a seven-year period and made clear the link between talk with the babies from a very early age and language acquisition. She described the findings after an intervention group of parents were coached in how to talk to their children, while another control group were left to their own devices:

> The language skills of the intervention group were significantly higher than the others but even more remarkable, there were enormous differences in the general intelligence of the children in the intervention group compared to the other children. The average intelligence of the intervention group was a year and three months ahead of the other group.

Sally Ward, 1998

In the ALPS classroom the teacher creates opportunities for pupils to utilize language in a wide variety of contexts. The more children use language in a structured, on-task way, the better. One of the best and most accelerative methods is called pole-bridging. The University of the First Age in Birmingham describes pole-bridging as 'muttering your understanding'. Driving instructors might describe it as 'talking yourself through it'. Some children – and even some adults – cannot stop themselves from doing it!

Pole-bridging is a deliberate attempt to connect-up internally one's own understanding using the appropriate language. The purpose is to use the vocabulary that relates to the real experience within the experience. Not afterwards, when you write it up, nor afterwards when the teacher asks, 'Put your hand up if', but there and then, during the real experience. Pole-bridging requires the child to notice what he is doing. It requires him to pay attention to phenomena and comment aloud on that process. It encourages observation of detail, classification, reflection and speculation. All are powerful tools for developing an intelligent response. When a child does this at a very early age, he is laying down discreet neural pathways: connecting language sites with other 'poles' within the brain.

This is how Jamie pole-bridges as he engages in water play:

> Now I am going to take the red bucket which is on the table by the window and fill it with water. I am filling it with water and I look that the water is skooshing into the bucket and making bubbles – oops, cloudy bubbles, oops, that's the play dough making the water dirty – Sam put it in the water, not me. That's naughty! Oh! My hands got wet. When it's nearly at the top I'm going to stop. Then I'm supposed to put it into the big bucket and not spill it. Jo spilled it on the floor last time.

The purpose of helping children pole-bridge their way through an activity is to help them develop the capacity to order, label and articulate an experience. In our example of Jamie filling his bucket, he is at once manoeuvring himself and an object, while engaged in describing, observing, selecting, predicting, speculating and then reflecting and giving a language to his thinking. When he does this he accelerates his learning.

> **"** It is important to give learners the time and opportunity to talk about thinking processes, to make their own thought processes more explicit, to reflect on their strategies and thus gain more self-control. Acquiring and using metacognitive skills has emerged as a powerful idea for promoting a thinking skills curriculum. **"**

Carol McGuinness, April 1999

The ALPS teacher creates an educational atmosphere where talking about one's own thinking is actively pursued. In this environment children question, predict and reflect, as they engage with the experience of the classroom. You can help the process of pole-bridging in two ways. First, draw attention to the vocabulary related to an experience. There is a vocabulary related to art and the generation of an artistic product that a child may never encounter. She can create a painting in a given genre or in the style of a nominated artist and do so from beginning to end without ever having to use the key vocabulary. Why not provide it for her by placing it on laminates around the room above eye level, or on laminated cue cards, or on both? Encourage pole-bridging using the words – depth, dimension, shape, colour, contrast, perspective, tone, hue, tint, pigment – and model the process yourself when you demonstrate what has to be done.

Pole-bridging

As you work alongside each child ask them to explain why they have made the decisions they have made and what the end product will look like. You are encouraging them to reflect and predict: look back, use language to describe what happened; look forward, use language to describe what will happen. This is the second thing you can do to enhance the process of pole-bridging: provide the questions.

Pole-bridging at higher levels

Analysis	Application
Compared to ...	The reason I did ...
The best part ...	A way to ...
On the positive scale ...	I want to ...
An interesting part is ...	A connecting idea is ...
Take a small part like ...	A film this reminds me of is ... because
A logical sequence seems to be ...	If this were a book I'd title it ...
By contrast	I think this applies to ...
Similarly ...	Does this mean ...

Problem Solving
I wonder
Suppose
Combine
Possibly
Imagine
How about
What if
I predict

Synthesis
I'm stuck on ...
The best way to think about this ...
I conclude ...
I'm lost with ...
I understand, but ...
I'm concerned about ...
My problem is ...
A question I have is ...

Evaluation
How
Why
It seems important to note
If then
It seems irrelevant that
One point of view is
The worst
The best

Decision Making
I disagree with ... because ...
I believe ...
I prefer ... because ...
If I had to choose ...
My goal is ...
I hate ...
One criticism is ...
I can't decide if ...

Pole-bridging through different representational systems

Visual Representations
Try to visualize
My picture of this
A diagram of this idea looks like
This looks like
Let me show you how

Verbal Presentations
Another way of saying this is ...
I learned
I discovered
This sounds like
Let me explain to you how

In a powerful book entitled *Inside the Brain*, journalist Ronald Kotulak (1996) described the significance of language-rich environments in the home. In a section entitled 'How the brain learns to talk', he describes the work of Hart and Risley:

> One of the simplest ways to raise intelligence is talk. Parents or other caregivers who talk a lot to infants during the first three years of life not only help them build better vocabularies, they also help them do something far more significant – raise their IQ level. In a long-term study of 43 Kansas City families, Betty Hart of the University of Kansas and Todd Risley of the University of Alaska, Anchorage, found that children who were talked to the most had strikingly higher IQ's than children whose parents didn't talk to them very much.

The highest IQ of children who were talked to most doing the first years of life reached 150, while the lowest IQ of children of non-talkative parents fell to 75. The correlation between exposure to language and IQ achievement is staggering:

● Children in white collar families hear 2,100 words per hour on an average day, compared to 1,200 words per hour in the average working-class family, and 600 per hour in the average welfare family.

● By age four, children in welfare families have 13 million fewer words of cumulative language experience than the average child in a working-class family.

● White-collar parents give children positive feedback more than 13 times per hour, twice as often as working-class parents and five times as often as welfare parents.

● Children in welfare families hear negative remarks twice as often as positive ones.

● Overall, white-collar parents spend twice as much time interacting with the children as welfare parents.

Further analysis reveals that parents' education, social status, race, or wealth are not as important to IQ levels as how much they talked to their children and interacted with them in other ways. Parents who talk to their children the most tend to praise the children's accomplishments, respond to their questions, provide guidance rather than commands, and use many different words in a variety of combinations. This type of interaction can accurately predict the vocabulary growth, vocabulary use, and IQ scores of children.

Kotulak goes on to point out that the researchers found the higher IQ levels attained by the age of three remained stable when the children were tested again six years later: 'the intellectual advantage linked to talking persisted'. The sample was small and the definitions of different classes of family questionable, but the underlying message persists: talk to children and start early!

Craig Ramey of the University of Alabama proved that an early intervention programme for children who had been born into impoverished backgrounds and who had not had early exposure to a stimulating language-rich environment could, nevertheless, restore IQ levels. In a longitudinal project involving thousands of youngsters, some as young as six weeks and with most younger than four months, Ramey and his team (1996) used play and stimulating learning environments as part of a compensation programme.

All this evidence reminds us to make classrooms language rich! Restrict teacher talk. Encourage pole-bridging! Our argument is that pole-bridging gives a child their first learning tool. This mechanism allows children to make their own internal world more language rich. It is lifelong and transferable! It costs nothing!

Managing the moment of impulse

> In the classroom we should teach children how to think for themselves. One way is to group children so that they're talking to one another, they're asking questions of one another, they're learning to be teachers. One of the most important concepts for a five year old to know is that he or she can teach because you have to understand something to teach it.

Marian Diamond, Professor of Neuroanatomy, University of California, 1998

According to the Institute of Intelligence, the second intelligent behaviour is 'managing impulsivity'. Among the desirable attributes listed by the Harvard Dispositions of Thinking Project are: 'the drive to set goals, to make and execute plans, to envision outcomes; an alertness to lack of direction'. How often have you outlined a task, given preliminary instructions and before you have

Managing the moment of impulse

finished speaking, several children are off? Before you know it, Jamie is back proudly, with glue dripping, ready for your approval! Managing the moment of impulse – the ability to delay immediate gratification – is a desirable lifelong learning attribute and should be modelled in the classroom and taught explicitly. This can be done through the following classroom practices:

! Personal targets described aloud before and during a task.

! Pole-bridging during a task.

! Reflective and predictive thinking during the process of pole-bridging.

! Outcomes thinking before embarking on a task. For example, 'I will know I will have successfully completed my work when ...', 'Someone looking at my work when it is finished will know it is successful because they will see ...'

! Mental rehearsal before the lesson, such as 'The Private Cinema' exercise.

! Brainstorming, prediction exercises, speculation activities in pairs or small groups before beginning an activity.

! Templates or writing frames, such as those developed by the Exeter Extended Literacy Project, to help structure written responses.

! Mapping plans and talking through them in advance of writing.

Each of these tools is described in detail in different sections within this book. Each one successfully builds the ability to manage the moment of impulse and works particularly well because it requires the pupil to talk through her thinking in advance of action.

❹ Demonstrating understanding

What is intelligence?

> Habits of thinking need not be forever. One of the most significant findings in psychology in the last twenty years is that individuals can choose the way they think.

Martin Seligman, 1991

> While there is a significant element of inheritance in what we call intelligence, it is also now clear, beyond dispute that much of what we might call applied intelligence can be learnt from experience and explicitly through being taught.

Michael Barber, Times Educational Supplement, May 1999

THE PRINCIPAL OF THE COLLEGE WAS WORRIED. This particular year had a group of students whom he thought would not graduate at the end of the academic year. Their performance was awful. Their young teacher had resigned in tears. The Principal saw that his reputation as the troubleshooting figurehead of the College was on the line. He had never had a failure. What was he to do? He mulled it over for a day or two and decided to send for Mrs Hubbard.

Mrs Hubbard had just retired. She had been one of the best he had ever seen at motivating diffident adolescents. He needed her help. He called her. She agreed, reluctantly, to teach for what remained of the year and help out. He went to meet her and passed on the previous teacher's register. Mrs Hubbard took up the reins. Quietly, efficiently, she began to take over. Very soon the group grew to like her and her ways. She fired them up with enthusiasm and got them working again and believing in themselves. At the end of the year they all matriculated and took their place on the roll of honour.

215

The Principal was mightily relieved and sat aglow at the matriculation ceremony. His reputation was saved. He was effusive in his thanks to Mrs Hubbard. She did not see why the fuss was necessary. She thought they were winners from the outset. 'I do not know what the problem was,' she said. 'Look at these intelligence scores.' She held out the register with the numbers alongside the students' names. The Principal looked down and across. He did not recognize the figures. 'How could I fail with these IQ scores?' Mrs Hubbard added. Suddenly, the Principal recognized the numbers. 'They are not their IQ scores,' he said. 'They are their locker numbers!'

Theories of intelligence abound. If the hundreds of different tests that claim to both define and measure intelligence were to be eaten by a computer virus and disappear overnight, would we be able to tell who was 'intelligent' and who was not? Would it make a difference? We would probably have a sort of idea of who 'had it' or did not in our classrooms. We may also be able to make crude judgements about who in our family, or local community, or society in general, 'had it' and who did not. We share a sense of what intelligence is, but perhaps that is derived from outdated notions that assert themselves in a Western culture. Strip out all these influences and how confident are we about what intelligence is, how it can be measured, and how it can be applied?

Is intelligence a given commodity? Is it predetermined by circumstances of birth or might it be capable of development thereafter? Is it capable of development and, if so, to what extent? Are there pre-ordained limits? Is intelligence learnable? Is intelligence an operant that is independent of the nature of a task? Or do the circumstances play a part in shaping the response? Could intelligence be interpreted as a set of performances in different realms? Is intelligence a general, all-purpose, unitary phenomenon? Is it possible that intelligent behaviours are separate from intelligence itself? Is it measurable? If it is measurable, can this be done through timed paper and pencil tests? Is there an intelligence of the emotions? What about moral intelligence?

In an attempt to direct you to answers to some of the above questions, here is an outline of what some contemporary theorists have said about intelligence.

General intelligence (G). The general intelligence theory posits that there 'is indeed a general mental ability we commonly call intelligence and that no matter their form, or content, tests of mental skills invariably point to the existence of a global factor that permeates all aspects of cognition' (Gottfredson, 1998). For such theorists, intelligence is best described as the ability to deal with cognitive complexity. The G factor, or 'general intelligence' factor, is associated with the sorts of behaviour generally considered 'smart': problem solving, abstract thinking, reasoning and adeptness in learning. IQ (intelligence quotient) tests work on the assumption that G can be measured. A person's mental age, as recorded via the test, is divided by the chronological age and then multiplied by 100.

Modifiable intelligence. Reuven Feuerstein worked with children who were considered profoundly learning disabled. They had endured trauma or suffered physical limitation that affected their learning. Feuerstein identified stages in the thinking process and then designed interventions called 'instruments' for each stage. The purpose was to teach thinking skills and modify the cognitive skills brought to an experience. His work challenged the notion that intelligence was a given commodity and was not susceptible to development beyond pre-ordained limits. Feuerstein's work has been profoundly influential all around the world and is the basis for some of the thinking skills programmes running in the UK.

Proximal intelligence. Leo Vygotsky died in 1934 but his influence persists. Although not directly concerned with 'intelligence', he was concerned with intelligence of response. His model suggested that in assessing a child's cognitive development, not only the chronological and 'mental' age of the child need to be considered, but also the child's potential capacities – 'the zone of proximal development'. This, he argued, can be done by comparing how the child solves certain problems by himself, along with a second indicator – how the child solves similar tasks with the help of a teacher. The difference is the measure of the zone and a guide to the child's potential.

Learnable intelligence. David Perkins of Harvard is the academic behind the theory of learnable intelligence. Realm theory suggests that intelligence does not operate outside of context and that an intelligent behaviour is to know your way around. Realms are topics or situations that people encounter. They contain an action system with actions or behaviours appropriate to that realm; a belief system with beliefs, values and feelings related to the realm; and a concept system with concepts that are critical to the acquisition and expression of beliefs and actions. Individuals operate with different degrees of success across the realms. Our brain systems, our useful experience and our capacity for reflective self-regulation influence how we operate with intelligence.

Intelligent behaviours. Professor Arthur Costa of the Institute of Intelligence at Berkeley researched intelligence as a set of dispositions or acquired behaviours. Included in the list are: persistence, managing impulsivity, empathy, flexibility in thinking, metacognition, checking for accuracy and precision, questioning and problem-posing, applying past knowledge, precision of language and thought, gathering data via the senses, ingenuity and insightfulness, curiosity and transference.

Practical and creative intelligence. Professor Robert Sternberg holds the view that successful individuals balance creative, analytical and practical intelligences. Creative intelligence includes those cognitive processes that individuals use to identify and formulate good ideas and solutions to problems in different areas of life. Analytical intelligence is used when they consciously recognize and resolve problems; formulate strategies; structure and accurately present information; allocate resources and monitor outcomes. Practical intelligence is the intelligence of everyday survival that involves successful negotiation of changing situations and the accumulation of experience to resolve challenges.

Moral intelligence. Robert Coles's theory is based on how values are born and shaped through the 'moral archaeology of childhood'. We become what we live and what we live is guided by the living example of influencers and through explicit dialogue about the big issues, moral questions and philosophical interrogation. Coles holds the view that children can become smarter in their inner characters and can learn empathy, respect, and how to live to a personal set of values and principles. Coles would argue that a moral intelligence is a valid theory of intelligence.

Emotional intelligence. Daniel Goleman's work (1996) on emotional intelligence suggests that there are five elements and that the combination of these elements is more valuable than a high IQ. The elements are: self-awareness, mood management, self-motivation, empathy and managing relationships.

Multiple intelligence. Howard Gardner's model of multiple intelligence suggests that intelligence is not a unitary phenomenon nor is it necessarily fixed. Gardner's intuition, later substantiated in his 1984 book, *Frames of Mind*, was that human beings are better thought of as possessing a number of relatively independent faculties. He defined such faculties as 'a psychobiological potential to solve problems or to fashion products that are valued in at least one cultural context'. Gardner identified seven separate intelligences and later an eighth. They are: linguistic, logical-mathematical, musical, spatial, bodily-kinesthetic, intrapersonal, interpersonal and naturalist. As we write he is pondering a ninth – existential. For Gardner, all humans possess all his intelligences but no two individuals have exactly the same profile. He has the view that: 'these intelligences, which do not reveal themselves in paper and pencil tests, can serve as a basis for more effective educational methods' (Gardner, 1998). Gardner differs from all the other theorists in that he attempts to trace his intelligences back to particular neural structures within the human brain, relating this to a distinct evolutionary history.

The differences of view outlined above provide a caution against the presuppositions that underlie much of our everyday thinking about intelligence. Our presuppositions about intelligence tend to shape our perception of what a child in our class is, or is not, capable of. If the teacher were to assume that a child was blessed with intelligence, just as she was blessed with brown eyes or blue eyes and that it was an inherited commodity, then she would also be making the implicit assumption that there were limits to what she could do with this.

CLAP CLAP CLAP

We all try to encourage each other. If someone makes an improvement, we clap. It makes you determined to get a good mark. It feels so good to be clapped.

Think about Annie and her ability in art. Is she really 'useless at art'? Or think of Eddie. Is he weak in geography, or was that geography lesson simply not designed in a way that was accessible for him? Was Annie born 'useless at art' and Eddie born 'bad at geography'? Or is there potential to develop their abilities in art and geography by developing key intelligences? Of course, some of us have a talent in some areas that others do not. Nisha will be an artist when she grows up, whereas Eddie will learn, eventually, to concentrate for longer periods, and will be a great engineer. He will learn to read accurately and with concentration: he will develop greater emotional intelligence. Amrit is already developing his musical intelligence, whereas Annie may go to adult education classes, and decide that she is, in fact, quite good at art.

The debate over intelligence, what it is and how it is defined, will continue around us. For the purpose of the ALPS model, we operate under the guiding belief that teachers can intervene in meaningful ways to develop intelligent responses. They can do so in every classroom. Our recurring message is that the teacher should extend the horizons of possibility of each and very child in her care. This is done by the exercise of professional judgement about classroom teaching and about the skills and strategies applied there. To have too narrow or too prescriptive a view of what intelligence is, and who does or does not have it, disables our professionalism.

These models of intelligence allow us to act with professionalism and teach for intelligence, through intelligence, about intelligence and with intelligence.

At the core of the ALPS model is a structured variety. VAKplus provides a basic model for structured variety; the theory of multiple intelligence is more refined.

Developing different types of intelligence

> **“** We know people truly understand something when they can represent the knowledge in more than one way. We have to put understanding up front in school. Once we have that goal, multiple intelligences can be a terrific handmaiden because understandings involve a mix of mental representations, entailing different intelligences. **”**

Howard Gardner, 1998

Many ALPS teachers use the model of multiple intelligence to structure opportunities to activate understanding. In a classroom this means that the teacher plans ahead against the more expansive guiding framework multiple intelligence theory has to offer. Howard Gardner himself warns against trivializing the use of the intelligences. His wish is that the multiple intelligences be used for more effective pedagogy and assessment. The educational power of multiple intelligences is 'exhibited when they are drawn on to help students master consequential disciplinary materials'. For example, a topic such as the main stages in the human life cycle can be accessed and understood in different ways. It is like using seven or eight different doors into the same house. Each door is a different access point. Each door better suited to different children. So access could be via a story, a logical step-by-step theory, modelling, artwork, a mathematical diagram, a series of visual images, a dramatic realization involving dialogue and movement, or a series of debates and discussions. Here is an outline of each of the intelligences and how to draw upon them.

Interpersonal

The interpersonal intelligence includes the ability to form, build and maintain a variety of relationships. Children who show an ability from an early age to play collaboratively, to empathize, to see things from someone else's point of view, to take turns, to enjoy being in a team and want to help others in the team, show an interpersonal intelligence.

Goleman talks of the significance of this intelligence when describing the consequences of what he calls 'emotional illiteracy'. He quotes research that suggests that the school drop-out rate is between two and eight times greater for children who are rejected by their peers than for those who have friends. Many children who become 'rejects' socially are those who have not learned the skills of being able to read the emotional cues of others. Goleman demonstrates connections between the popularity with peers of children at the age of seven and the incidence of mental health problems in adult life. Popular children who can interact positively with others, fare better throughout life. Gardner argues that the ability to form, build and sustain a variety of relationships is a highly desirable lifelong learning attribute.

A child with a well-developed interpersonal intelligence will:

- ☞ identify the emotions of others;

- ☞ see others' points of view;

- ☞ form, build and maintain a variety of social relationships with others;

- ☞ play with others;

- ☞ position along the collaboration-to-competition spectrum comfortably.

In your classroom:

- ☞ use circle time or some other mechanism for developing social co-operation;

- ☞ vary groupings;

- ☞ share protocols about groupings and about the variety of learning methods used;

- ☞ teach children how to play with others;

- ☞ agree class rules;

- ☞ set and work towards group goals.

Intrapersonal

'Intra' means 'within'. Children with an intrapersonal intelligence will show an understanding of their own feelings and emotions. They may be curious about those feelings and begin to isolate and make sense of them. They may prove stubborn if they are asked to act in conflict with their feelings. They may talk more openly about how they are feeling than their peers. They may talk to an imaginary friend about how they feel. They may ask questions about the larger, philosophical issues.

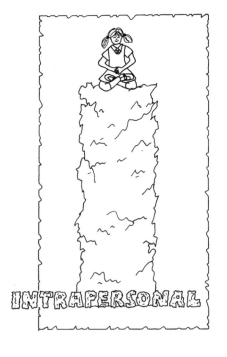

A child with a well-developed intrapersonal intelligence will:

- ✎ be aware of their own thoughts, feelings and emotions;

- ✎ find appropriate outlets for expressing those thoughts, feelings and emotions;

the alps approach – Accelerated Learning in Primary Schools

✎ engage in self-talk;

✎ be curious about the motivations and behaviours of others;

✎ be self-contained and well motivated;

✎ be curious about philosophical issues.

In your classroom:

✎ allow lots of processing time for reflective thinking;

✎ be patient and answer all the open-ended and philosophical questions;

✎ use the aspirational wall;

✎ use memory mapping;

✎ find out about philosophy for children and begin to use it as an adjunct to Literacy Hour;

✎ explore feelings and motivations as part of circle time;

✎ use desk labels.

Linguistic

Children who enjoy words and can find pleasure in using the written and spoken word show a linguistic intelligence. It includes sensitivity to the meaning of words, to their order, to sounds, to the rhythm and inflection of words and to the capacity of language to change mood, persuade or convey information.

A child with a well-developed linguistic intelligence will:

❝ learn through listening, writing, reading and discussion;

❝ imitate or mimic the voices of friends and family;

❝ experiment with words;

❝ be better than average for their age with both written and spoken language;

❝ speak early.

In your classroom:

❝ minimize your talk and maximize children's talk;

❝ maximize purposeful, structured on-task language exchange;

- 66 pole-bridge;

- 66 use keyword and themed vocabulary techniques;

- 66 use writing frames;

- 66 explore different uses of language for different purposes and audiences and via different media.

Mathematical and logical

Children with a mathematical and logical intelligence are problem solvers who can construct solutions non-verbally. They delight in sequence, logic and order and can readily discern patterns and relationships in the world around them. They sort the toys in the box. They work out cause and effect. They grasp opportunities to see patterns, to classify, to speculate and predict, and to detect the rules of maths and logic that underlie everyday events.

A child with a well-developed mathematical and logical intelligence will:

- λ be familiar at an early age with concepts such as time, space, quantity, number, cause and effect;

- λ know what symbols mean and be able to construct their own;

- λ be fascinated by the patterns in everyday experience;

- λ enjoy sequencing activities;

- λ be collectors and classifiers;

- λ try to organize and order objects around them.

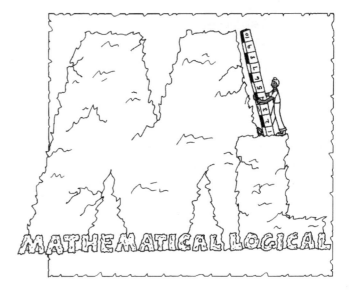

In your classroom:

- λ draw attention to the protocols and routines that you use in the classroom and explain why you use them;

- λ do lots of number work across different disciplines and make numbers exciting;

- λ explore the connections between maths and everyday life;

- λ teach categorization, classifying, prioritizing and prediction skills;

- λ provide problem-solving templates for use in different disciplines;

- λ promote interest in logic, for example by starting a puzzle club.

the alps approach – Accelerated Learning in Primary Schools

Visual and spatial

Children with a well-developed visual and spatial intelligence will be readily able to create or re-create images of scenes or objects. They will remember how things looked and where they first saw things. They may be able to imagine themselves or an object displaced into a very different context. They will be able to give and follow directions or envisage themselves following a particular journey. They will remember where they put things. They will be able to visualize objects manipulated through three dimensions and through space and time.

A child with a well-developed visual and spatial intelligence will:

- learn through seeing and observing;

- remember the look of things and how they were positioned;

- be able to visualize imagined scenes easily;

- remember the look of words or pictures on a page;

- be able to imagine how shapes would look unfolded or rotated;

- spell by remembering the look of the word.

In your classroom:

- use learning posters and memory maps up around the room and make regular reference to them;

- change the visual display regularly;

- complement written and oral work with visual realization techniques such as mapping, flow charts, annotated graphs and poster displays;

- bring in props and artefacts and integrate their use into lessons;

- use yourself and your movements as a visual and spatial prop to enhance learning, to exaggerate for effect, to make extravagant gestures.

Kinesthetic

Children with a kinesthetic intelligence will show physical dexterity at an early age. They may be able to manipulate themselves or objects through complex routines. They will walk early and show dexterity with play objects. They will be comfortable with laterality, for example, co-ordination of left and right movements. They may be restless in class. They may be highly physical and robust – runners, tree-climbers, kickers, swingers. For them, movement aids memory.

A child with a well-developed kinesthetic intelligence will:

 learn by doing;

 show dexterity in fine and gross motor movement;

 remember most clearly what was done rather than what was said or seen;

 be concerned over improvement in physical performance;

 demonstrate creativity through construction, physical movement and expression;

🚲 show co-ordination, sense of movement, timing, balance, dexterity.

In your classroom:

🚲 structure practical activities into each day;

🚲 rehearse learning through movement, role play, simulation and practical activities;

🚲 practise skills which require physical dexterity such as handwriting by brain break activities;

🚲 build in frequent physical breaks to your classwork;

🚲 teach and practise playground games.

Musical

Children with a musical intelligence notice patterns of sound and will be able to discriminate between sounds at an early age. Tones, rhythms and larger musical patterns may constantly be in their consciousness. They will enjoy all aspects of music and may show skill with an instrument at an early age. They will be interested in and curious about music in and around their everyday environment.

A child with a well-developed musical intelligence will:

♪ enjoy improvising and experimenting with sounds of different sorts;

♪ notice and respond to mood changes in music;

♪ have a sense of rhythm and be able to respond to music artistically;

♪ be curious about music and seek to develop categories and preferences;

♪ remember tunes and songs.

In your classroom:

♪ use music to demarcate time on task, for beginnings and endings, authentication of a theme, to change mood and to energize or relax;

♪ use music to recall content;

♪ use patterns of sound to learn to discriminate changes in pitch and improve awareness of variety and modulation of sounds;

♪ encourage individual interest in the various ways of making and enjoying music;

♪ create regular opportunities to experience music as a whole-class participative activity.

Naturalist

Children who enjoy being outdoors and who delight in finding patterns and relationships there show a naturalist intelligence. This intelligence is evident in children who show a sense of wonder in, and an affinity with, the natural environment. This could be in their immediate surroundings – the local park, the canal bank, and the school playground – or in larger and more open spaces. Children demonstrate this intelligence when they notice detail, are curious about the species they observe, and speculate about the existence of different species. Gardner suggests that there is an evolutionary purpose and a designated site within the brain for this.

A child with a well-developed naturalist intelligence will:

♣ be sensitive to harmony and disharmony in the natural world;

♣ be able to see patterns of relationships within and between species;

♣ show awareness of the inter-related nature of environment, change and time;

♣ be comfortable in different types of natural environment;

♣ be fond of and curious about different sorts of creatures;

♣ demonstrate concern about the impact of human intervention on the natural environment.

In your classroom:

♣ find time to visit local environmental sites;

♣ be responsible, with your class, for the upkeep of a designated area in or around the school;

♣ explore the impact of humans on the environment alongside thinking about cause and effect;

♣ conduct species counts and observations;

♣ model responsibility for both natural and man-made environments in and around the school.

When a teacher is able to utilize multiple intelligence theory and the models of classroom practice it offers, she replaces the question 'How intelligent are you?' with a much better one – 'In what ways are you intelligent? Show me!'

❺ Using review for recall

How we remember and why we forget

> *Success at GCSE is dependent on having a good memory, not a high IQ, according to new research into exam performance by cognitive psychologists.*

Times Educational Supplement, front page, June 1999

PROFESSOR LYNN NADEL IS ONE OF THE WORLD'S LEADING RESEARCHERS into memory and the brain. If you listened to him talk about human memory you would hear him use terms like: 'multiple modules of memory', 'internal cognitive maps', 'procedural' and 'contextual' memory, and 'implicit and explicit' memory. Talking about human memory and the brain, he would refer to sites within the brain: 'the neo-cortex', 'the hippocampus', 'the amygdala', 'the thalamus', 'the cerebellum'. Can this mix of technical terminology and jargon carry any significance for classroom teaching?

We believe a better-informed understanding of human memory and the working of the brain should guide some of our thinking about classroom practice. We also believe that the findings of some of the world's leading researchers affirm the techniques we espouse throughout this book.

Whenever, as part of staff development activities, we conduct memory tests on teachers, predictable patterns of response emerge. Try it out for yourselves and see if your staff reacts the way that we describe below. At the beginning of a meeting, tell everyone that you are going to conduct a test. Listen to the gasps as they worry about your motives! Are you going to publish their scores, they wonder, or use them for some sinister purpose?

Tell everyone to get a pen and paper, and then read aloud the words on the list below. Pause for ten seconds, then tell them to write as many as they can remember in any order they choose. Tell them that you will give them two minutes for this activity. Look at your watch as they begin.

hotel	taxi	cloth	apple
window-cleaner	train	castle	verb
peach	motorcycle	bicycle	envy
plant	noun	thought	bus
orange	adjective	train	pear
memory	piano	house	farm

This is likely to be the response: twenty to twenty-five seconds into the activity there will be a nervous giggle from somewhere in the room. This will coincide with a colleague, who has a temperament more susceptible to anxiety, stopping after writing five or six items. Then someone's little voice will be heard saying: 'I can't think of any more!' The nervous giggles are a reminder that tests, however modest, cause anxiety. As you watch people write things down, they will tend to do so in short bursts, with two or three words coming at a time. Some individuals will look up and around the room. They will try not to look as if they are copying. What they actually want to know is how many words other people are remembering. As long as someone else is going to have as low a score as they are, they feel comfortable.

Others will have their heads down and will be lisping sounds. A few faces will be red and if the telephone rings, for once there will be a rush to answer it! Other people will have categorized their list on the page. Some will have written in the first three or four words and then will have left a space and written in the last two or three, before attempting to remember all those in the middle. Others add up their total, write it in and, in doing so, give up. There will be some sighing, a comment such as, 'I have a terrible memory!' and a sense of depression and finality at this point. Of course, one or two smug people will be totalling frantically and looking pleased.

Pause. Distract everyone by talking about or doing something else very briefly. This will be difficult, as they will all want to add up scores and compare with the person next to them. After a few moments, do exactly the same activity again. Ask them to put their original attempt out of sight. Tell them in advance this time that there are twenty-four words, but not to bother adding

227

up the scores. Your interest is simply in the methods that they use to remember the list. You are not interested in how good they are at remembering, but about the processes that they use in the test.

The second attempt will feel calmer and more purposeful. There will be a sense of determination to improve. In fact, everyone will improve the second time around, unless they have attempted a new strategy with which they are not comfortable. There will be a great sense of achievement as everyone realizes that they have improved. People worry about tests, and want to do well, no matter how immaterial the task actually is!

The overall improvement is due to a sense of familiarity with both the words themselves and the parameters of the test. Listen to colleagues as they describe the different ways in which they remembered the words. Which words were remembered and how? Which were overlooked? Are there patterns? What do the emerging patterns tell us?

Some people will have remembered the words using a visual strategy where images are either sequenced or built up around a connecting image. So they 'see' a *hotel*. A *taxi* pulls up outside, on the bonnet of the taxi is a *cloth* and on top of the cloth an *apple* that is about to be eaten by a *window-cleaner*. This method of recalling the words through associated visual images is common with this sort of test and works well, except for with words like *verb* that do not render themselves into a ready visual image.

Some people make associations through patterns of sound. So *peach, pear, piano* and *plant* are often listed together. So are *motorcycle* and *bicycle*.

Classification is easier the second time around when the participants have had the Big Picture. When people classify they usually create separate columns of words on the paper. Many people remember the first four or five words and the last two or three. Almost everyone recalls the last word from the list. Words that have an immediate personal association are remembered; for example, if someone has a piano they remember this word readily and often report that they 'see' their own piano.

Words that are difficult to remember in this test are those such as *envy* and *thought*. This is, in part, due to their more abstract quality. If words such as *noun* or *verb* had been in the list on their own so that they could not be locked into an easy category of recognition, then a similar difficulty occurs.

The word *train* is repeated in the list, yet most people do not write it down twice. This is an example of a mindset impacting on our performance. No other word is repeated so why should this one have been? Participants hear the word but do not trust their immediate judgement and so discount it.

Finally, words that are so different such as *window-cleaner* are either immediately given attention and remembered, or are so disruptive to thought patterns that they inhibit recall of the next two or three words read from the list. So often *window-cleaner* will be remembered, but not *castle* or *peach*.

The purpose of this type of activity is three-fold. Nobody is truly interested in whether Angela has a better memory than Sue or the headteacher! But the test does highlight the fact that when you know what is expected of you and have practised, your performance improves. It also shows that everyone has a physical and emotional response to test situations. You all did, even though, as teachers, you will have taken hundreds of tests in the past! Finally, the activity initiates discussions about the workings of memory. With your colleagues, consider the information below about the workings of memory, and our suggestions for maximizing the performance of students in test situations. If the reality is that children have to take tests, your responsibility is to ensure that they are assessed for what they know, not for how they handle test situations.

To make sense of some of the above responses, we need a model for the working of memory. Nadel and others agree that some memories are stored in highly specific structures within the brain while others are spread across it. This makes sense given that different parts of the brain are involved in acquiring and engaging with different types of sensory information. The model of immediate, short- and long-term memory is becoming out of date.

Nadel describes memory systems that operate at different levels. Humans have systems for sensory perceptions, systems for procedures and meanings, and systems that relate to contexts and values. Each system engages different areas of the brain but in highly specialized ways. Some of the systems are in place at birth. Those, for example, related to implicit memory – imitation, mimicry, habits, response to certain stimuli associated with warmth, food or safety – can be seen in babies. The other systems develop as a result of interaction with the environment after birth and are more sophisticated. Both Nisha and Annie would have had the same instincts regarding their mothers feeding them as newborn babies, but their other memory systems are now individualized.

In all of this, Nadel points to the fact that the differing levels are affected by stress in different ways. Some memories are encoded as being significant as a result of associated emotional arousal, and are thus easier to access. Sometimes you remember how you felt not what you were supposed to learn. Remember Annie and the word 'thermometer'? Even in her secondary school years, if she meets the concept of temperature in class she will recall that word thermometer and fear that she will look foolish in front of the class. Nadel also shows that two sites deep within the brain's limbic system – the amygdala and the hippocampus – are fundamental to learning and memory. Another eminent neuroscientist, Joseph LeDoux, points to this dual system and to the significance of emotional arousal in memory:

> The brain has at least two systems for assessing the value of events. One system leads to a conscious recall, through memory, of options for action and of representations of future outcomes. Then we use logical reasoning and knowledge to decide that we will do X instead of Y. Another system, probably evolutionarily far older, acts even before the first one. It activates biases related to our previous emotional experience in comparable situations. These non-conscious biases affect the options and reasoning strategies that we present to our conscious selves. We do ourselves a disservice when we think of human beings as exclusively

229

logic- or knowledge-driven, and fail to pay attention to the role of the emotions. The two systems are enmeshed because that is the way our brain and our organism have been put together by evolution. **"**

Joseph LeDoux, 1998

The amygdala is sometimes described as 'the emotional sentinel' of the brain. It is involved in attention and arousal. Attention, which is an encoding system, is partly governed by a sense of danger, perceived novelty and a need to discern relationships. Once danger has been eliminated, novelty leads to curiosity, arousal and thus attention. Damage to the amygdala can mean that an individual is unable to measure the emotional consequences of an action or feel the emotional temperature of a situation.

The hippocampus is involved in laying down memories. It does not fully function until two or three years of age. Damage to the hippocampus can lead to lack of curiosity and lack of spatial understanding and difficulties in discerning patterns of relationship. Scientists speculate that the hippocampus is central to the storage of memory but is not where memories are stored. Rather it acts like a relay service initiating electrical and chemical responses in specific sites and across regions of the brain and so helps connections be established.

A brain consists of multiple systems with some highly specialized sites and some distributed functions. It is capable of different levels of engagement and arousal and this is, in part, governed by curiosity. So what can we glean from the mixed results of our memory test and our knowledge of the brain?

I can learn my spellings by writing them in the air. I can remember hard spellings like 'ambulance'.

The ten principles that underlie our strategies for improving memory and recall are listed as follows.

the alps approach – Accelerated Learning in Primary Schools

Principle one. Minimize performance-related stress by practising in realistic test conditions and mentally rehearsing test techniques

When an individual is told that he will have to take a test, nagging doubts emerge. Because the test puts him into a situation where he perceives himself to be out of control of his immediate environment, stress occurs. Stress can, in the short term, heighten arousal and improve reactions, but it also comes with certain learned responses and associated limiting beliefs. Test participants mentally rehearse images of failure and dispose themselves to a weaker performance. They focus mentally on what they maybe cannot do, not on what they can do. The idea that children only perform at their best if the test situation has an element of fear is not a useful hypothesis. Children know that a test is a test, and they will wish to do well. Fear only inhibits performance – it is certainly not a performance enhancer! In the ALPS, teachers work to alleviate stress by providing the parameters and familiarizing children with test conditions well in advance. A test should assess what children know and can do, not their nerve.

Principle two. Teach through themes and teach students to see patterns of connection related to those themes

In the teachers' memory test you will have watched people write things in short bursts, with two or three words coming at a time. This reminds us that people remember information in clusters of connectivity, seeking to generate patterns on everyday experience and imposing patterns on everyday experience. The list you read to your colleagues was to them an arbitrary undifferentiated list until they began to impose meanings on it. Teach students to look for patterns of connectivity. Draw attention to connections as you teach. Even if your curriculum is divided up into specific subject areas, work continually to connect the learning in one subject to another.

Principle three. Utilize visual, auditory and kinesthetic learning to enhance the original learning experience

As you listened to the teachers describing the methods that they used in the memory test, you will have realized that some were visual and involved constructing related images, while some used rehearsal of patterns of sound. The list was read aloud to your colleagues. If it had been shown to them or they had been asked to teach someone else the list, then the outcomes would have differed. As it was, elements that were easily rendered into visual and aural cues seem to have been easier to recall. The ALPS teacher utilizes VAK in every subject that she teaches, and encourages children to draw upon the memory of VAK learning when taking tests.

Principle four. Use the beginnings and endings of any learning experience as opportunities to consolidate learning

Some of your colleagues probably wrote in the first three or four words and then left a space and wrote in the last two or three, before attempting to remember all those in the middle. This can be represented as a curve known as the primacy and recency curve (Badelly, 1993, p. 37). Attention is paid to what is perceived of as the beginning and the ending of an experience. This is true across cultures. Students of an Islamic village school in Morocco whose education consisted of learning sections of the Koran by rote also showed this sort of curve. Lots of mini-beginnings and endings where the content is actively reviewed will help both recall and learning. The beginning and end of

your chat to students before a test will also have the most significant effect on them, so make your introduction positive, short and inspirational!

Principle five. Break down the challenge into smaller parts

Many adults, like children, view their performance in terms of the raw score. In the memory test, even if you stressed to your colleagues that the test scores were not what mattered, you can be sure that they all added up their marks! For some people this leads to a sense of defeat. For others it confirms their own view that: 'I'm no good at this sort of thing anyway'. Motivation drops at the point when they write in that score. Yet our purpose in taking the test was to learn about memory. What would have been the outcome with regard to motivation if you had divided the list into four tests with six words in each? Everyone would have scored twenty-four and motivation would have remained high.

If you have an option of taking a break during a test, do so. When you assess children you need to know what they have learned in your class, not how long their ability to stay focused will last. In the ALPS the teacher builds in brain breaks to refocus her class, even during tests. If teacher-directed brain breaks are not allowed during a test, she encourages children to stop, breathe and stretch if at any point they feel that their concentration is slipping.

Principle six. Outline the parameters by giving an overview first

Performance in the teachers' memory test improves second time around. This is in part due to the fact that participants are more relaxed after having heard the complete list of words. They also have a sense of what the test entails and so can begin to discern patterns more readily. The first attempt provides an orientation or Big Picture, making what follows easier. Explaining that there will be twenty-four words provides the other orientation. If you had said, 'There's a list of words, I'm not sure how many', this would have been disorientating. In classroom teaching say, 'List the three causes of ...' rather than 'List the causes of ...' Again, it focuses and so improves performance. Practise the format of the test several times so that nothing comes unexpectedly. If children are unfamiliar with the format, you are testing their ability to adapt to test formats rather than what they know or can do.

Principle seven. Connect new information to what is already known by giving examples to which children can relate

Where participants in the test can make personal associations or can render the new information into a familiar pattern, then recall is easier. For example, if a participant had been a taxi driver, then that word and others with which it could be associated would be more readily remembered. If you are able to associate the new and unfamiliar with something familiar, then it is easier to remember things in sequence. This is the basis of the 'pegging' system used by many memory professionals. Teach children to look for a link to their own lives, in order to remember a new word or fact.

Principle eight. We remember experiences in context and also those that are perceived to be 'different' or carry a high emotional association

People remember things in context. For example, you may walk from one room to another to get something. It takes four seconds. The distance is ten feet. You arrive. You forget! It has happened to us all. Your immediate response is to go back to the original room, which helps because it contains embedded cues. These are cues, or memory prompts, of which you are perhaps not consciously aware. You glance at the vase of flowers that your husband gave you yesterday, and return to the kitchen remembering what you went to get. (It was actually a pen to write the card to your aunt to thank her for the birthday gift that she sent your two year old daughter. You remember that you had to thank her through the associated idea of gifts, after glancing at the flowers.) You can help students in this respect by varying the learning contexts to make them more vivid, distinctive and memorable. Draw their attention to the cues that you create, and ask them how they will remember each fact.

Principle nine. Provide distributed practice and build in assimilation time

Some researchers talk of the importance of 'incubation' or 'downtime' for learning. When the brain is not asked to select from competing stimuli, you have 'downtime'. Under stress the brain's capacity to index new memories is inhibited. Create spaces for active reflection. Go back and rehearse tests. Ask children to surface their understanding after due processing space. After a test, go back and do it again, after asking children to reflect on their performance. ALPS teachers who do this find that children's scores increase substantially after being allowed opportunities to practise how to be successful.

Principle ten. We remember when we have to dismantle and then reorganize against our own criteria

How many times have you read to the bottom of a page and realized you have taken none of it in, because you were thinking of something else at the same time? When we wrote this book we included devices such as the four children, Annie, Amrit, Nisha and Eddie, to help you to connect what you read to your own criteria – probably through linking our anecdotes to the Eddies or the Annies in your class! You can take notes from a staff meeting, write those notes down and then one week later not recognize what you have written! Likewise, children need help sometimes to make connections, and the ALPS teacher purposely teaches children to look

233

for meaning or significance, relating information to their own experience. You have to set about this process with intent to teach connections.

In research for the NACD (National Association for Child Development) in the USA in 1996, John M. Jaquith tested digit span in an attempt to correlate it to performance in standardized tests:

> Each child's visual digit span was tested in the same way. Each student was presented with a card with a sequence of three numbers for a total of three seconds. The student was then asked to repeat the sequence back to the examiner. If the sequence was repeated accurately and in the same order, the examiner marked it correct, and moved on to a longer sequence of numbers that was one digit longer than the previous. The procedure was then repeated (same exposure time) until the student responded incorrectly. For an incorrect response, the examiner gave a sequence that was one digit shorter than the first. If two responses were incorrect for any given sequence length, the test was stopped and the digit span was recorded as the highest sequence length responded to correctly.
>
> Auditory digit spans were tested by the examiner dictating a sequence of numbers to the student. Each digit was dictated monotone with an interval of one second. The student was then asked to repeat the sequence back to the examiner. Procedures for accepting correct answers and determining digit span was the same as with the visual digit span.
>
> In general, the data shows a correlation between digit spans and standardized test scores. The higher the digit span, the higher the test score. As demonstrated earlier, digit spans reflect processing. The correlation that the better one's auditory or visual processing, the better one's standardized tests scores should be. The data also suggests that there are points at which a one digit increase with digit spans represents a significant increase in one's auditory or visual processing.

Jaquith, 1996

The implication of this data is that as an individual improves his auditory and visual digit span, and thus auditory and visual processing, his academic function relative to grade level will improve. It can be implied from that data that the more information one can process at one time, the higher one's level of academic work.

So, how can you increase digit span? Our argument is that this will not necessarily happen without intervention, and it is therefore the responsibility of the teacher. In the ALPS classroom the teacher develops resilience, resourcefulness and responsibility by paying attention to all the variables that impact on a child's learning. She teaches for the new three Rs. Just as the skills associated with the new three Rs can be taught, so too can the skills of memory. You can teach memory techniques through deliberate interventions.

Guaranteed memory techniques

Practice does not make perfect. Perfect practice makes perfect. What is perfect practice? It is practice that helps find imperfections and allows opportunities to learn from those imperfections. Professor Lawrence Lowery of the University of California talks about the importance of rehearsal. Rehearsal, for him, is perfect practice and it takes place when pupils do something again in a similar but not identical way, to reinforce what they have learned while adding something new. Rehearsals 'strengthen the connections among the storage areas within brain systems. If connections are not strengthened, they will disengage and fade away. Thus the adage, use it or lose it' (Lowery, 1998).

Frequent informal and varied testing is a form of rehearsal: the ALPS teacher provides frequent opportunities for children to test themselves, test each other, test the teacher, and test the class. She uses different sorts of testing to provide educative feedback. This helps children to focus consciously on what they can remember and what they need still to learn or consolidate. Testing is done in safety and in a manner that is honest and reflective.

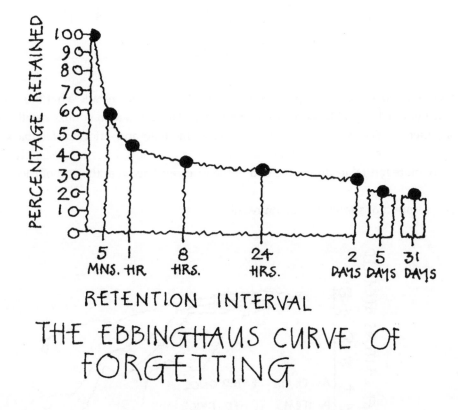

RETENTION INTERVAL

THE EBBINGHAUS CURVE OF FORGETTING

The German researcher Ebbinghaus (quoted in Baddeley, 1993) researched the ability to recall information over time. His early work showed that you 'get what you pay for' and that the relationship between the amount learned and the time devoted to learning is fairly simple. The more time put in, the easier subsequent recall became. However, subsequent work by Baddeley and others (1993) pointed out the significance of the 'distribution of practice effect'. They found that it was better to distribute your learning across a period of time rather than try to mass the learning together in a single block of time. A little and often is better, which reminds us that regular brain breaks are a fundamental aspect of working in the ALPS.

235

Here is the impact of little and often on recall

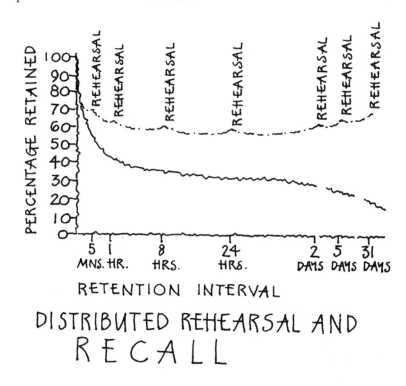

Here is the impact of little and often on recall

DISTRIBUTED REHEARSAL AND
RECALL

They went on to discover that 'spaced presentation' is better for recall. What this means for the ALPS teacher is to be flexible with rehearsal routines. The aim is to maximize recall at the longest possible interval. The ALPS teacher uses short, immediate and informal feedback within the learning experience, then at the end of the day she gives short, informal tests. This is followed by slightly more formal testing at the end of the week and again at the end of each half-term.

Here is the impact of spaced testing on recall

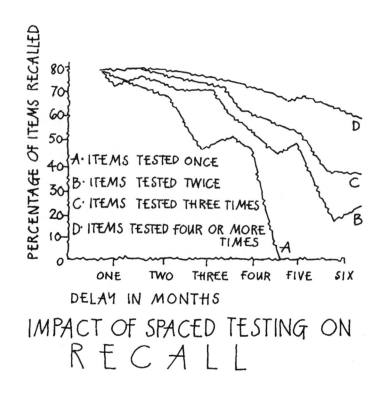

IMPACT OF SPACED TESTING ON
RECALL

Further research conducted by Gates on fifteen year olds and recall of nonsense syllables (Gates, quoted in Rose and Goll, 1992) demonstrated that what mattered most in recall was not the time spent on the task, but what was done in that time.

Percentage of time reading	Percentage of time on review	Average no. of syllables recalled
100	0	65
80	20	92
60	40	98
40	60	105
20	80	137

We know from published research already cited on homework that it is what you do in the learning that impacts most on performance. Rote repetition of additions, subtractions, multiplications or divisions will not necessarily provide a positive yield for the amount of time put in. If you are a bad golfer, practising your bad golf swing again and again will leave you with nothing other than being better at having a bad swing! Forcing Annie to speak up in class will only help her to practise being nervous of speaking up in class. If her teacher helps her to practise with familiar topics in small groups, she will practise how to speak confidently, not how to be nervous.

You can practise and develop memory techniques with children. Research shows that memory tools used in combination work best. Start in the classroom. It is in the classroom where you can safely experiment with and model the techniques listed below. This will take you and your class into a steep learning curve. For this reason we use the mnemonic PRECIPITOUS to summarize our techniques.

P personalize it   Make it personal to the children.
It is easier for a child to remember if he makes a strong personal connection with the information. Say things like: 'How will you explain this to your mum or dad when you get home tonight?' Check next day that children have done it.

R relate it   Relate it to other things.
Encourage thematic and connective thinking by the use of topic webs, spider diagrams and memory maps. Encourage 'compare and contrast' activities and promote awareness of similarity and difference through lots of examples. Use metaphors.

E exaggerate it   Exaggerate it so that it is unusual.
Experiencing or rehearsing learning in ways that are unusual helps children to recall facts. Deliberately practise spellings in loud or soft voices, use dramatise gestures, and unusual props.

C chunk it   Chunk it down – rehearse it in smaller units.
Break things up and rehearse a little at a time. Encourage learners to chunk by teaching them how to make 'family trees' of information using keywords. Whole units of work can be remembered this way.

I imagine it   Imagine you are using the skill or information.
Ask children to imagine aspects of lessons. For example, ask them to describe a journey from the source of a river to the sea; imagine that they are walking around different geometrical shapes, or imagine that they are being evacuated during the Blitz. What do they see?

P parcel it   Parcel it up into recognizable units.
Practise learning things in little parcels, then sequence the parcels, give them names. Mix the parcelled information up, then restore it to the original order. Add numbers to provide parameters: 'Three things you need to know about ...', 'List the five steps involved in ...'.

I imitate it   Use VAKplus to imitate.
Learn through seeing, hearing and doing

T talk about it   Tell yourself the story.
Talking through an experience and then attempting to explain it to an imaginary audience will help children to remember all the details. Teach children to pole-bridge.

O organize it   Organize your thinking in a different dimension.
Ask children to learn and rehearse by writing information in order, or by using a flow chart, a series of prompt postcards or by making a poster.

U use it   Use what you have learned.
Think of ways in which the information can be used. By thinking of applications for knowledge and generating lots of questions, you will make it easier for children to remember.

S share it   Share it, test it, teach it to someone else.
Provide lots of opportunities to test understanding as a powerful aid to recall. Use strategies such as 'Each one teach one', preparing a lesson plan for teaching a group of peers or explaining a memory map to the class and answering key questions.

❻ Success in public examinations

Improving performance in tests

> When people who are prone to anxiety are asked to perform a cognitive task, such as sorting ambiguous objects into categories, and narrate what is going through their minds as they do so, it is the negative thoughts, the nagging little voice of doubt – 'I'm no good', 'I'll never be able to do this' – and so on that inhibits performance.

Daniel Goleman, 1996

RESEARCH CITED BY GOLEMAN (1996) demonstrated that control groups who were asked to worry on purpose for fifteen minutes before trying a task, struggled with the task. The same groups had no problem with the task if they were given fifteen-minute relaxation activities beforehand. Conclusion? Anxiety will paralyse performance.

Adults and children alike have anxieties about tests and testing. Leaving aside the question of whether we should be formally testing young children at all, we can see ways in which tests and testing can be used positively to give teachers and children useful information, to motivate and to rehearse performance improvement under challenging conditions. This is not an endorsement of the current testing regime in England and Wales, but is recognition that it is statutory and could offer some positive learning. We advocate using the testing regime to test understanding and not purely to test nerve.

Children express anxieties about tests and testing and describe the physiological manifestation of such anxieties. Here is how one 11-year-old boy in his first year of secondary school put it:

> When I have tests I feel nervous and very sick. I feel cold and my pen stops writing and I can't think straight. I do not like it when the results are read out. I get embarrassed especially if the class is so big.

239

Some of these physiological responses can be overcome. The following can help:

❑ guided visualizations;

❑ mental rehearsal of exam technique;

❑ frequent informal testing – test the teacher, test each other, test ourselves;

❑ practising exams and tests in circumstances close to those of the statutory tests;

❑ using data to target-set for improvement;

❑ making tests and test results an integral part of the everyday learning experience.

Here are some further, very specific, suggestions for enhancing exam performance:

▲ Have a rehearsal week where you get as authentic an approximation of the test week as possible: different timings; different playtimes; different structure to the day.

▲ Rehearse the tests in the environment where the children will sit the real test. Ideally this should be a familiar and friendly place. If this is not possible, attempt to make it so by practising there.

▲ Use the visual display posters as part of your learning strategy but reassure the pupils that they will not need to see the posters to remember the facts. In the week before, cover the posters and test informally: 'Who can tell about magnetism with the poster covered? Turn to your partner and describe what the poster says. Now your partner will do the next one.' The day before the exam take the posters down altogether: 'Now look at the space and who can tell me what the poster said?'

▲ Do not put children being read to by an adult in the same room as those reading to themselves, as those children start going back over their papers to check that they read the question properly and become distracted.

▲ Practise regularly how much you can write in the allotted time. For example, use forty-five minutes for a timed slot on creative writing including a plan. Do so on the sort of paper you will use on the day.

▲ Practise using the correct equipment.

▲ Teach pupils to note how many marks are allotted for questions so that they do not waste time expanding an answer for one mark.

▲ Teach pupils to look through the test at the start to see how much they have to do.

▲ Where appropriate, teach children to map out a memory map plan – in an essay for example – and work from the plan.

▲ When you practise, do so with the adults present who will be there on the day. Keep the number of adults as low as possible.

▲ Practise how you will remind children of the amount of time left.

▲ Teach children to move on if unsure, but to mark the page and return later.

▲ Use 'entering music' for the time before formally starting the exam.

Mental rehearsal for success

ALPS teachers do what they can to alleviate anxiety around performance. The skill of mental rehearsal can be taught. A research project conducted in the USA by Shelley Taylor looked at exam performance and mental rehearsal. The control group, who were taught exam techniques and allowed time for mental rehearsal of the application of those techniques on several occasions beforehand, outperformed groups who were simply taught exam technique or given no exam technique teaching. The improvement was 10 per cent.

Mental rehearsal of an activity in advance of the activity offers a number of benefits. It allows the individual to begin to apprehend what a positive and successful outcome may be like. It begins the process of clarifying the characteristics of a successful performance and allows the mind to sort and order the stages involved. It aligns a physiological response with the mental stages. When someone conceptualizes a positive and successful outcome,

I learn my spellings on my mind map then I shut my eyes and think of them. I am good at spelling tricky words.

they begin to experience the associated physical sense of well-being and elation. This is part of a positive and resourceful loop rather than one that is negative. For children this is of critical significance. It plays a part in shifting the negative associations with specific types of public performance – exams and tests – towards something positive and safe.

If Annie is prepared for the fact that she will need to answer a question in public, and she has mentally rehearsed for the good feeling that she will have when her teacher maintains eye contact with her and gives her an encouraging nod and a big smile, she will speak up! She can visualize success. Guided visualizations involve the teacher directing the class through a positive experience of mental rehearsal. It requires practice. Eventually, the children can do it by themselves.

Children can be taught how to practise relaxation techniques. In an article in the *Times Educational Supplement* (21 May 1999) a secondary school teacher describes how she began every lesson with relaxation techniques and GCSE passes 'rocketed to 98 per cent A–C'. The headteacher commented: 'We're preparing them for their own version of the Olympics and I wanted them to find some way of being able to relax and lessen the stress.' The teacher concerned, Monica Troughton, said of the exam performance improvement: 'I'm sure it was because they were calm and focused.' In any class you can help children learn to relax. For some it may be something that they have not yet encountered anywhere else in their lives. Relaxation techniques help children to develop listening skills, through increased focus of attention. They help children to become more independent and resistant to distractions.

Begin with this simple exercise to familiarize the pupils in your class with relaxation methods. Make sure that the children are sitting comfortably with their feet on the floor or tucked under the chair. They can fold their arms or place them on the desk and put their heads down. Select some music from the lists in Part Two, and speak in a gentle tone above the music. You could develop a script of your own or use the following script:

> As we begin I would like you to relax. Breathe slowly and deeply. Breathe in, breathe out. Continue to breathe slowly. Now we will relax even more. Let's start with your eyes. Close your eyes and feel your eyelids becoming heavy. Continue to relax and breathe slowly. Now relax your mouth. Notice how slack it's become. And your neck too. As you continue to breathe deeply, relax your neck and shoulders. Let your shoulders sag and then let your arms. Breathe deeply. Feel your breath going in and out, slowly, slowly. Your legs are relaxed too. Finally, your feet are relaxed. You can feel the soles of your feet. Continue to breathe deeply and notice how every part of your body is feeling calm and relaxed. As you breathe listen to the sounds of your breath slowly and quietly going in and out, in and out.

This is a basic relaxation activity that has not yet been concluded. You could allow time to listen to the music, then conclude by slowly 're-animating' each body part in turn in the following way:

> As you continue to breathe ever so gently, feel your toes begin to wriggle. Lift your heels up gently off the floor. Keep breathing regularly. Your legs are moving gently up and down. Now begin to take deeper breaths. Count in: one, two, three. Count out: one, two, three. Feel your chest expanding out then going in as you breathe. Push your shoulders back slowly and gently. Now stretch your arms out a little and roll your shoulders up and down easily and gently. Once, twice, three times. With your eyes closed, open your mouth. Stretch your mouth wide. And now your eyes, look up, look down, then to the side. Notice how better you now feel. And now that we are all back and paying attention let's give ourselves a clap.

Alternatively, you can go on to do a guided visualization activity with the pupils in a more relaxed and receptive state, before returning to this closing sequence. Always use the closing sequence and gradually move from alertness to relaxation to alertness. Guided visualizations are intended to help pupils become more resourceful. They experience a strong sense of self-control and begin to learn better mood management and how to control and direct their own thoughts.

Guided visualizations vary by purpose and intended outcome. The first two are variants on a theme to help pupils feel more relaxed and positive.

The next visualization is useful for improving story writing. It can be preceded by a short discussion about what makes a good story, about beginnings and endings and about atmosphere and mood.

Now we are going to visit your own private cinema. Settle in the best seat. Feel the chair and how comfortable it is. As you look at the screen notice the colour of the curtains and how nice they are. Everyone else in the cinema is quiet too. They are waiting to see and hear your story on the screen. The curtains swish as they slowly pull back and there is the title of your story on the screen. Read it to yourself quietly. Next is your name and it says 'a story by …' and it's your name up on the screen. Make yourself comfortable and ready to enjoy it.

We are now seeing the first scene. Notice what's happening there. Pay attention to what's happening. What do you notice first? Describe what you see to yourself. Take your time to do this. Are you watching the people on the screen? What are they doing? Can you hear them talking to each other? In what sort of voices? What do you think is happening? Before you go to the next scene remember what it looks like; the colours and the places. Remember other things too; smells and sounds in the background.

Now the pictures are changing and we are in the next scene. What sorts of things are happening in your story now? Pay attention to what you can see and what you can hear and what you can smell. Is it a good feeling to watch your story?

Now let your story carry on. As my voice goes quiet, you can watch your story and listen to it more carefully.

Take time to let your story finish. What is happening as it finishes? How are the audience watching it with you feeling? Notice all the things that are happening as the story finishes.

The curtains are closing now and the story has come to an end. It's time to come away from the cinema so let's open our eyes again and look around and if we have enjoyed watching our story we can give ourselves a clap!

After this exercise each child could tell the others in a trio what he experienced in his story, with as much sensory detail as possible. In effect, children have then mentally rehearsed what they are going to write beforehand, added words (twice) by describing it to others and rehearsed a mental script to make writing easier. Many children may wish to memory map their plan immediately, then organize it by discussing it with a friend. Should they get 'stuck' in their story they can re-visit the cinema.

The next visualization is useful for reviewing the content of a lesson or connecting with previous learning. In classic accelerated learning, music is used alongside voice to evoke mood, to relax and to engage a deeper mode of thinking. Your voice should be just under the volume of the music and your phrasing should match as near as possible that of the music. Suggestions for music were given in the previous section. Use music with a steady repetitive rhythm and without words. With or without music here is a suggested format:

> This morning we learned all about ... Let's remember together all the things we learned about ... The first thing we found out was that we already knew lots of things about ... isn't it amazing how much we already knew about things we have to learn in class? We already knew that ... and that ... and that ... then we began to find out a little more. We learned that ... and that ... So now we know that in the future when we are asked a question about ... we will give a good answer. We will say ... We know how good our brains are at remembering things when we need to. We help our brains by being relaxed and calm and breathing nice and slowly. When we had learned for the first time about ... we made sure we would remember by telling each other what we had found out. Just to help us remember what we found out listen to yourself telling someone else about the important things we learned. Listen to how clever you are as you tell someone else all you have learned ...
>
> And now just to make sure we will remember it we will practise it one more time ... then we open our eyes, look around and to finish we give ourselves a clap.

Music can be used with powerful effect to connect learning experiences. Using the same music for each experience can be a powerful tool. Accelerated learning traditionalists may disagree with this, but our practical experience suggests that the connective power of the music ensures deeper engagement with the content.

Our final example of a guided visualization can help improve exam performance. Practise the visualization in the room where children will sit the test. Explain that the children are like actors who must learn their script before performing it for the public. The better they know the script and rehearse it, the better the performance. To get the best performance they must be relaxed.

> Now that we are properly relaxed and feeling comfortable we will rehearse our exam script. The exam script reminds us what to do and in what order. We practise it in our heads so that when we do the exam our brains work at their best!
>
> It is the morning of your first exam and you are excited about being given a chance to show how good you are. You have been to bed early the night before and had

something to eat before you left for school. You can feel your pencil case in your hand as you make sure it is already in your bag for school. See yourself with a smile on your face as you walk through the school gates. How are you feeling? You see your friends and you all talk about how well you are going to do. You are breathing deeply and are feeling relaxed. You know how to feel relaxed. You have practised it many times. After registration you go to your seat. Because you have sat in this seat before you know where to go and sit down quietly. As you sit down you look around. You feel good. Listen to your breathing. Nice and slow. Feel the palms of your hands. Dry. In front of you is a little booklet. It is the booklet in which you will write all your answers. Next to it is the question paper. Do not open it yet. Continue to make yourself feel comfortable ... I am at the front and I am reminding you to (continue with the details of how your pupils will respond positively to the testing arrangement).

At Hutton Rudby County Primary School in North Yorkshire, Dale Robinson uses guided visualization successfully in a number of ways. He practises relaxation techniques via 'children's own private clouds'.

The cloud 'picks the child up' and the child sits within it and guides it over specific landscapes. The cloud has a window in it and the child guides it to his own special place. Dale says of his method: 'I say some things and leave the rest to them and I try to feed in suggestions using VAK – "notice the temperature against your skin", "feel the sun shining down on you".' He then uses the method to let children imagine all their worries dropping out of the cloud like rain and all the bright, positive things shining in to make them feel good.

For Year 3, he mentally rehearsed the school pantomime so that the children were not overawed by public performance. With the Year 6 football team he taught them to visualize working successfully as a team. With one child with aggressive behaviour he managed to get him to visualize a red traffic light with 'stop' written on it, wait for it to change through amber to green and then walk away without lashing out with his fists. The boy's mother came into school and thanked Dale personally for all that he had done. Dale's inspiration came from a 1955 book by Richard de Mille called *Put Your Mother on the Ceiling*, which provides lots of practical examples of visualization exercises.

We have seen impressive examples of children being taught relaxation techniques in the schools that we visit. We frequently hear that teachers are accused of 'teaching to the test' when they prepare children for assessments. We would argue that to assess children without showing them how to respond to assessments is to neglect your duty as a teacher. If we would not test someone on calculus before teaching her calculus, it stands to reason that we should not test a child before teaching her how to tackle a test. These techniques mean that children are prepared. Relaxation and visualization of success are important components of the ALPS method™ towards learning and are vital skills that will stay with children for life.

When you reach the end of your first year in the ALPS your class will have achieved higher standards than you believed possible, and you will not need test results to prove this to you! You will look back down the mountain and marvel at how far you and your class have journeyed. Take time to celebrate your success and to map your future. In the next section, our postscript, a headteacher tells how he and his staff used accelerated learning for radical improvement of standards. After that, in Part Four, we give some useful resources and practical information to aid you in your journey into the ALPS.

ALPS is a lifelong journey and we wish you every success along the way.

Review of Part Three

What is the significance of primacy and recency to classroom learning? What three things should you focus on at the beginnings of classroom lessons?

VAKplus is at the core of the ALPS method™. Consider ways with your colleagues of integrating VAKplus more into your classroom teaching.

We described a model for optimizing time on task based on research into attention. How can this be used for the National Literacy and Numeracy Strategies? What sorts of activities are appropriate for diffusions?

What is pole-bridging? How might it increase the intelligent response of each child in your class? What would a visitor observe in a successful lesson where pole-bridging was taking place?

Is there such a thing as an 'able' child? In what different ways do children demonstrate intelligent response? In what specific ways do you identify and develop such intelligent responses in your classroom?

According to some researchers 'memory is more important to success in public examinations than IQ'. How can you model memory techniques in your classroom practice? Which techniques would you start with? How would children be given a chance to practise them?

To what extent do you practise mental rehearsal? What specific techniques will you now use to help children improve exam performance? Which of these techniques can be practised through mental rehearsal?

the alps approach – Accelerated Learning in Primary Schools

Postscript: Does it work? The headteacher's perspective

DOES IT WORK? THAT IS A CLEVER QUESTION TO ASK. Why disperse energy, time and resources into a fad? Why embark on a demanding journey without conviction that the effort is worth it?

As part of our case for beginning the journey, we looked for solid examples of managed improvement. At a school in outer London we interviewed children and their teachers who had spent two years using the ALPS approach. The comments of the children are provided in full alongside our interview with a headteacher.

Howard Kennedy is headteacher of Holy Family RC Primary, Langley, Berkshire and is currently seconded to the London Leadership Centre, where he is Deputy Director. He described the development of aspects of the ALPS approach in his school during a talk given on 22 September 1998.[18] Some of the approaches are familiar, others less so. Here is a summary of what he said.

The Holy Family School journey began when, as Howard Kennedy describes it, he arrived at the school as headteacher in 1984. The school, described by some as 'the worst school in Berkshire', was an underachieving primary school of 128 pupils situated in a disadvantaged area of Slough. It now has 450 children on roll. In 1992 the school became grant-maintained, a decision which at the time had caused much heart-searching, but had since proved to give an amount of freedom that enabled him to develop his ideas and put them into practice. Howard Kennedy attempted to utilize some of the thinking of US management guru Peter Senge in order to begin creating a school that was an organization in which

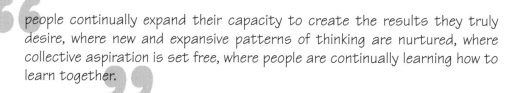

people continually expand their capacity to create the results they truly desire, where new and expansive patterns of thinking are nurtured, where collective aspiration is set free, where people are continually learning how to learn together.

Peter Senge, 1990

Howard had learned the importance of Peter Senge's five disciplines in the development of a learning school: team learning, shared visions, mental models, personal mastery and systems thinking. Also he had been able to make good use of the seven tips also given by Senge:

★ Thrive on change.

★ Encourage experimentation.

★ Clarify and communicate successes and failures.

★ Facilitate learning from the external environment.

★ Facilitate learning from employees. (Here Howard Kennedy dwelt upon 'The Iceberg of Ignorance'. This suggests that the leader had knowledge of only 4 per cent of the problems in the organization; senior management had knowledge of 9 per cent; middle managers, 74 per cent; whereas the 'chalk-face' employees had knowledge of 100 per cent of the problems!)

★ Reward learning.

★ Intentionally retain and retrieve organizational memory.

What does accelerated learning mean for you?

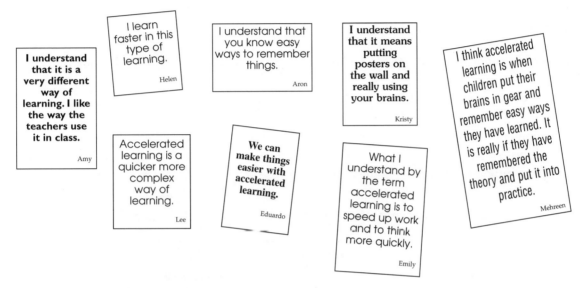

Of particular significance was his decision to engage an external consultant from whom he learned a great deal, including the techniques of 360-degree appraisal. First, Howard Kennedy himself underwent the process of 360-degree appraisal conducted by the external consultant. In accordance with a pre-arranged timetable, the appraiser gathered information from representatives of every class in the school, all staff (teaching and non- teaching), governors and parents. Then the consultant held a conversation with Howard Kennedy and the staff to discuss the issues raised during the information gathering exercise and later produced a report, subsequently made public.

Howard then took the staff away for a weekend to determine an agreed policy on how decisions were going to be made. The analysis of decision-making was based on 'tell, sell, negotiate, consult and consent': in other words the group decided the way forward.

The weekend led to implementation of key policies, including the following:

A flat organization. The traditional hierarchical structure was changed to enable everyone to join in and contribute to decision-making processes.

Rights of access. The deputy heads were given access to all information. All staff had a right to be involved in decisions that affected them. Executive meetings were introduced as the decision-making forum, and all staff had access to decisions; everyone – regardless of seniority – was given a chance to take the chair.

249

Core values. The staff worked together to produce agreed aims, values and beliefs for the school. As they did so, they held in mind the words of Archbishop Murphy in 1958:

> You cannot educate the mind and neglect the heart. When they leave the school they will forget quite a number of subjects, but there is one subject they will never forget and that is you. Your person is going to have a greater influence on their future life than all the blackboards in the country.

Corporate headship. This meant that three people (the headteacher and two deputies) were leading the school. It also involved sharing offices, which had turned out to provide a brilliant opportunity for succession training.

Roles and responsibilities. These were 'up for grabs' and were to be negotiated annually.

Task forces. These were established as the result of data analyses.

Development planning. This had three areas of focus: the curriculum, with the aim of achieving overall success; parents, with a view to improving the flow of information; and teachers, with a particular emphasis on improving their lifestyle.

How has accelerated learning helped you this year?

> This has helped me a lot because I can do things this year that I couldn't dream about doing last year.
>
> Liam

> One thing that has helped this year is when we learn with actions e.g. have people acting out the different parts of a flower.
>
> Amy

> It has made learning more interesting, fun and enjoyable. It helped me remember everything I had to.
>
> Rebecca

Future thinking. This was important in developing a vision for the school in the future. A document, entitled 'Our Vision for the Future' described, in detail how:

● *External support* would be used in every aspect of the school's development.

● *Teachers and teaching* were to provide the most important focus for development. The manifestation of this focus included:

  - adapting the school building to suit teachers and the learning process;

  - teachers working and planning with colleagues;

  - review and modification of teaching methods on a frequent and regular basis;

  - enabling colleagues to report and discuss the effectiveness of their methods;

  - class reorganization;

- support visits by the head, experienced staff and external experts;

- the involvement of pupils ('the most under-used and undervalued resource in a school') through pupil surveys and interviews – which proved to be a powerful tool in changing teacher behaviour;

- a focus on data through the implementation of baseline assessment through the use of PIPS (Performance Indicators for Primary School, Durham University);

- the use of 360-degree appraisal for all teachers;

- the use of pupils in training and INSET days (this needed courage, but the remarkable maturity and perception of pupils demonstrated its value).

● *Learning* was to become a focus for school growth. 'I've never met an average pupil' was adopted as a slogan to challenge the idea that schools need to avoid institutionalizing failure. The school's target became 100 per cent success, as no school could afford to say that any single child would fail. This in turn challenged the whole way in which the school was organized. Every moment and every square inch in school was to be regarded as an opportunity for learning. Consequently much effort was put into the application of cognitive science through *accelerated learning* and the creation of the *optimal conditions for learning*.

In establishing the latter, a number of practical ideas were put into practice. These included: carpeting throughout the school; air-conditioning in the school's mobile classrooms; superb murals painted by a professional artist; redecorated toilets; availability of drinking water for the children; use of background music throughout the school; signs and quotations, found or designed by the staff. The latter, particularly, gave very powerful messages in helping the school to aspire towards becoming a learning community, which:

> embodies an attitude, an atmosphere. The desire to learn can be found in individuals, teams, processes, systems and structures. Learning is the central cultural value of the organization. In this environment, innovation isn't just encouraged, it's celebrated. Change is avidly sought rather than avoided.

And where:

> the spirit is one of experimentation and enquiry where everyone participates in surfacing and testing each other's mental models.

At Holy Family School, Howard and his colleagues were having an exciting time learning, as adults, about many new discoveries related to learning and applying them in the classroom and the whole school. They were beginning to understand their relevance and possible impact, not only on individual learning and whole-school attainment levels, but also on the quality of life.

251

At Holy Family, many of the principles of accelerated learning were being used, with the most visible being the application of visual, auditory and kinesthetic (VAK) learning. The basis of VAK was the understanding that all learning took place in these three ways and that individuals had a dominant learning mode. Howard Kennedy was of the opinion that in British schools the predominant mode of learning had been auditory, and this had been successful with about a third of the population, but had obviously failed a greater proportion. Accelerated learning, however, showed that individuals could access education more successfully if information was presented in a combination of the visual, auditory and kinesthetic means.

What things have helped you achieve this year?

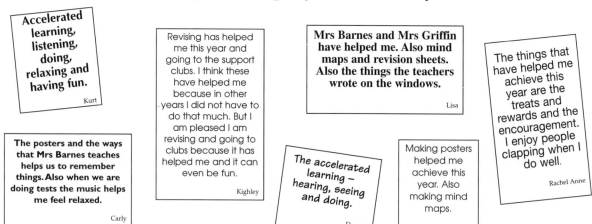

The challenge for teachers was to design into their programmes of study practical ways in which lessons could be delivered using a variety of media and to incorporate different ways for children to participate in learning.

For example, in Holy Family a lesson on decimals in a traditional sense (auditory) would have been presented by the class teacher talking to the children, possibly engaging them (or some) in dialogue and then setting them examples to complete. Presenting this lesson visually might include: peripheral messages around the room, containing all the information to be learned; pictorial representations of the concept through diagrams shown by means of overhead projectors, chalkboards or whiteboards; the use of children, for example, demonstrating place value through their representing the various numbers and the decimal point.

For the school, VAK had been immensely powerful, and Howard and his colleagues were surprised with regard to the potential of 'physical' learning and the impact it had on some children. The school had discovered that children do have dominant learning styles and that information presented in different ways was much more successful. However, it became clear that it was very demanding to incorporate into every lesson and needed an investment of time, energy and thinking to explore new programmes of delivery. But there was no doubt that it carried a powerful message for all teachers as to how to engage all pupils in their own learning: children enjoyed finding out about their dominant style.

Music was used in a variety of ways at Holy Family School: it was played throughout the school because it was enjoyable, enhanced the atmosphere and educated the whole-school community.

How do you prepare for homework and for SATs?

When I get home I get organized for my homework. I get a drink and sit at my table. When I am revising I work for half an hour and then get my mum to test me for half an hour. The night before a test I do not worry or do any work, I sit down and relax by listening to calm music.

Hayley

I organize my homework with my mum, first I do a bit then show my mum and then I repeat that.

Andrew

I work hard on my homework because when I go to secondary school I will have to bring it in every day. When I do my homework I sit in a place where I cannot get disturbed.

Kighley

I prepared for the SATs because I wanted to get the best results that I could get and show myself that I am clever. I also promised my mum that I would get a good mark for her.

Sam

I did not used to do my homework because I hated it. So I thought to myself 'I'm going to start doing my homework because I want to be brainy and clever when I'm older'. Also I do not want to waste my life at school.

Kelly

I sit in my room and listen to my music quietly so I do not get stressed out.

Claire

I get organized for my homework by getting a sharp pencil, a rubber and a ruler so that I do not have to find them in the middle. I prepared for SATs by having a long play and then coming to revise for a couple of hours.

Shaun

When you do your homework you should get everything you need then read the questions carefully. When you have finished you should show your mum or dad.

Jo'Anne

Many children and staff arrived in school in a 'stressed' state, so Howard and his colleagues used music in the school to relax and encourage all to move into a state of relaxed awareness. The music had to be contemplative, and science suggested the most successful was baroque.

A series of high-frequency tapes were purchased. These had been devised by Andreas Tomatis and were aimed at repairing and restoring the performance of the inner ear. He had produced outstanding results with autistic children, with stammerers, and with opera and theatrical stars and performers. The tapes provided a quite remarkable experience: after the initial shock, they were found to be therapeutic and relaxing.

To be effective, the tapes had to be used regularly over at least six weeks. At Holy Family School the tapes were introduced for a child who was slightly autistic and who exhibited a range of intense and disturbing behaviour. Psychologists were doubtful about his chances of attending a normal school. The boy concerned was now in the third year at the school and could not be picked out in a normal classroom. His learning curve had been 'supersonic', and the staff were confident that he would be able to live an independent life at some time in the future. The school had had no interest in claiming life-enhancing properties for the innovation, but individual colleagues had become convinced it was a prime mover of advance in the boy's life.

The advent of music in the school had been really exciting and had convinced Howard Kennedy and his colleagues that it had great potential in improving children's learning. It had been used to good effect in some classes and had provided teachers with a sense of relaxation, for them as well as the children. The school was also experimenting with different types of music, including many of the 'natural' tapes currently being published; for example, waterfalls, rain, sea, dolphins and whales. Children took to the music quite naturally; they did not make the anticipated constant requests for 'pop' music, but they did make comments about the particular music used. Certainly the type of music used was crucial to its impact.

Brain Gym® exercises began to be used at the school. The physical exercises – which crossed the 'mid-line' and joined both sides of the brain – were designed to enhance learning and, in many cases, to make learning more accessible. The staff at Holy Family started by introducing them to a small group of strugglers, but their effect was so great that they had been extended to whole classes.

Brain Gym® was seen as simple and great fun, but it was also very powerful. Some exercises were designed for specific parts of the curriculum, but for a number of children the exercises provided a 'gateway to learning'. Similar claims were made by another school where children had been taught to juggle – also a 'crossing the mid-line' exercise. Howard Kennedy said that Western civilization was probably sceptical about such claims but just as large tracts of Eastern civilization believed and practised daily routines of mental and physical exercise, he believed that Brain Gym® had much to offer both children and adults. The staff at Holy Family had developed variants, and practised 'brain breaks' across the school that were simple 'energizers' and a healthy break from too much passive learning.

Has your attitude to work changed this year? If so, how and why?

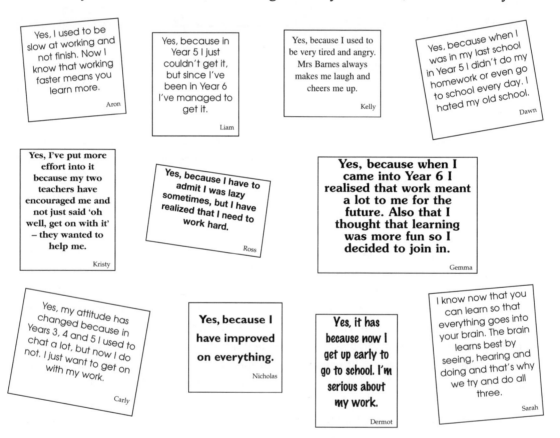

> Yes, I used to be slow at working and not finish. Now I know that working faster means you learn more.
> Aron

> Yes, because in Year 5 I just couldn't get it, but since I've been in Year 6 I've managed to get it.
> Liam

> Yes, because I used to be very tired and angry. Mrs Barnes always makes me laugh and cheers me up.
> Kelly

> Yes, because when I was in my last school in Year 5 I didn't do my homework or even go to school every day. I hated my old school.
> Dawn

> Yes, I've put more effort into it because my two teachers have encouraged me and not just said 'oh well, get on with it' – they wanted to help me.
> Kristy

> Yes, because I have to admit I was lazy sometimes, but I have realized that I need to work hard.
> Ross

> Yes, because when I came into Year 6 I realised that work meant a lot to me for the future. Also that I thought that learning was more fun so I decided to join in.
> Gemma

> Yes, my attitude has changed because in Years 3, 4 and 5 I used to chat a lot, but now I do not. I just want to get on with my work.
> Carly

> Yes, because I have improved on everything.
> Nicholas

> Yes, it has because now I get up early to go to school. I'm serious about my work.
> Dermot

> I know now that you can learn so that everything goes into your brain. The brain learns best by seeing, hearing and doing and that's why we try and do all three.
> Sarah

Many children who failed to learn successfully in school exhibited poor co-ordination skills, often accompanied by poor handwriting. Howard and his colleagues had become convinced that Brain Gym® helped them to advance; they had had some outstanding results with individual children.

An approach to Neuro-Linguistic Programming (NLP) had also been developed at Holy Family, and some remarkable results had been achieved with individual children. Background music was used for relaxation; children were taught to breathe with the stomach rather than the upper diaphragm; suggestive techniques like 'changing heads' were used and then children were encouraged to 'plug into' the visual memory.

How do your teachers help you remember things from class?

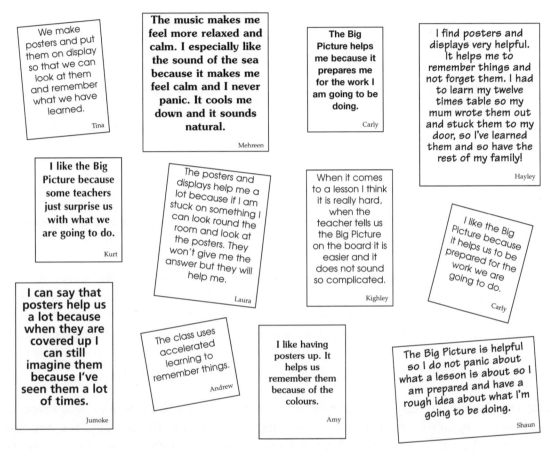

NLP was a technique that needed to be learned and one in which the practitioner needed to be confident. The technique was simple, but teachers need to have an above average competence in dealing with children if they were to apply it successfully with individuals, as it required the child to have total confidence in the adult to enable thorough relaxation in order to 'allow it to happen'. Through the process, Howard Kennedy had discovered the enormous power of the visual memory. He cited an example of a child's quite remarkable improvement in handwriting that had resulted from only half an hour's NLP.

The school was pursuing the concept of developing the optimal learning environments for both adults and children with the aim of getting children's education 'right first time' through an environment that enabled children and adults to perform to the best of their ability. This meant analysing and improving every aspect of the workplace.

the alps approach – Accelerated Learning in Primary Schools

Ionizers were used to clean the air and produce negative ions to negate the effect of fluorescent lighting. Opening windows also helped although this was not always possible.

Atomizers were used to promote aromas around the building. Aromas had a role in learning and their power to relax and stimulate was becoming more commonly understood. Indeed, the school had learned that aromas had a more powerful impact on learning than had been anticipated, especially in helping information to 'stick'.

Attempts were made to control the temperature in a more stable way, especially in external buildings that suffered from extremes of temperature.

The staff were encouraged to have water available in every classroom, and children were allowed to drink as much and as frequently as they wished: water can have a significant impact on enhancing the performance of the brain.

Howard and the staff of Holy Family School had worked for a long time to produce an environment more like a living room or lounge than a school, but they now also appreciated the scientific value in getting this right.

Howard Kennedy found that remembering was simple and easy to do if only teachers spent a little time finding out about it and applying what they had learned. Staff were now using visual mind maps with great effect to add to the peripheral vision environment that had been created. An increasing use of mnemonics was being made as the technique could be applied successfully to the learning of all children regardless of ability. Such techniques could have an enormous impact on attainment in a system that demanded learning and regurgitation.

Howard Gardner, Professor of Education at Harvard University had identified seven types of intelligence: linguistic, mathematical and logical, visual and spatial, physical, musical, interpersonal, and intrapersonal. Schools have traditionally been predisposed to the first two but, if all children were to be successful, a lot more value had to be placed on other areas. As the pressure to teach an obligatory curriculum had relaxed, Howard Kennedy and his colleagues moved into exploring how these concepts could be put into operation. A growing number of schools in the United States were already doing so, and there was an increasing worldwide interest in the concept of multiple intelligences.

Many in the school had argued that thinking skills should be part of every lesson, and there was a powerful academic lobby who believed that there were generic thinking skills that should be taught explicitly and applied throughout anyone's education. The Holy Family School's experience with the Somerset Thinking Skills and Year 6 had demonstrated that much could be gained from such an approach.

Howard had been interested to read that in the book *Emotional Intelligence,* Daniel Goleman (1996) had commented that stress stopped the working of the frontal lobe of the brain. This meant that stress activated hormonal release, which in turn stopped the short-term memory operation of the brain and was the physiological explanation of something most teachers had always known: many 'failing' children had very short concentration spans and were in a constantly agitated state. This 'state' was not always externally created, and the process of education if badly delivered could be a main cause of such an emotional state in the classroom. Another crucial element of Goleman's findings was that the most critical indicator of children's future adult success was their ability to form, build and sustain positive relationships with others. This emphasized the need for schools to incorporate this development as a significant element of the education process and in reporting to parents.

Much of the learning of the staff in Holy Family had been in the area of emotional intelligence. Staff had been involved for two years in 'TRIADS' – confidential meetings in groups of three focusing on important issues in their lives.

What are your wishes for the future?

I want my future to be exciting and I would like good jobs to be available. I'd like to be a pilot, or work at the airport in a good job.

Sam

I want to get a good education. I want to use my brain and achieve well. I want to be able to choose the job that I do, not just do any job I can get. I want to pass all my exams and get good grades.

Laura

I would like to be a cartoonist. I would like to have a family and get married. I would send my children to this school.

Dermot

My wishes are to pass my SATs and to get a good reputation in Secondary School. I want to be known as an intelligent, bright girl who can solve anything. When I'm older I want to get a good job and be a good wife and maybe a mother. I want to get paid a lot of money. I also hope that the genes I have of being intelligent will be passed onto my children and maybe to my grandchildren.

Jumoke

For the future I wish that I get a good job as a pilot and have a growing family. My next wish is that I will see my teachers when I am in High School.

Rashvir

I want to have a family. I want a good job to pay all my bills without worrying. I want to be able to afford to live in a nice neighbourhood. I want to keep in touch with friends, and in the future I'd like to go into primary schools to help out. I'd like to go in and teach the kids some of the stuff that I have learned.

Dermot

My wishes for the future are to get good grades for my GCSEs, leave school, go to college, go to university and get a good job with computers.

Hayley

I want to stay on at school and study and do well. I want to get married, and I want to get a well paid job so that I do not have to worry about money.

Andrew

My wishes for the future are to have a wife and family and a large portion of money in my wallet.

Shaun

My wishes for the future are to have a good job so that I can feed our children.

Andrew

These meetings took place regularly and were designed by a member of staff within a set format of listening in silence to a piece of reflective music, reading a selected (often inspirational) text and working through some large issues. Issues that were covered included the significance of work, getting old, change, school successes and failures, personal relationships. The meetings were confidential and not reported to others.

The TRIADS had had an interesting effect on participants, by providing a special period when people could spend time in peaceful surroundings with each other discussing the important things in life. They had had a profound effect on the operation of the school, and it had become clear that, in schools, emotional intelligence was critical for adults and children equally.

The pace of change at Holy Family was both rapid and exciting. Some of the benefits were measurable, such as the numbers on roll increasing from 128 to 450. Other results were less easily measurable but equally significant, as the staff and children grew in confidence and emotional intelligence. In answer to our question 'Does it work?', staff, pupils and parents would undoubtedly answer with a resounding 'Yes!'

Part Four

Resources

❶ Sample timetables

THESE ARE SAMPLE TIMETABLES FROM an ALPS infant and a junior classroom. It is not important whether you work an integrated day or a formal, subject-oriented timetable, as ALPS is a teaching method, not a curriculum. This is by no means an exhaustive list of the valuable activities that happen in the ALPS, nor is it meant to be an entire model for working. It is more an overview to help the reader to see how the method can be translated into any timetable. For the sake of clarity, we have used subject-based timetables, from which we hope you will find ideas that can be adapted to suit your individual classroom.

Infant timetable

Entry music
On days when assessments will be the first task, serene music is used along with relaxation exercises to enhance performance. At other times, more upbeat music may be used to energize. In the early years, parents are often asked to enter with their children to read the daily or weekly To Do list so that they can discuss events with their children at home.

Spellings
Once children have a basic phonetic knowledge, spellings are taught in two short daily sessions using VAK. This often involves physical movement, rhythm or music. The words are displayed on a memory map in the classroom and are connected to the main writing task that week. Copies are taken home for children to practise with parents in addition to practise of phonics work.

Spelling and maths tests
In preparation for their spelling, phonics and maths tests, children listen to relaxing music as they take a look at the spellings, letters or maths concepts that are about to be assessed. The aim is to help every child to attain 100 per cent in the assessment, reinforcing the idea that they are all highly intelligent. If a child makes more than a few errors, their targets are reviewed and an action plan is drawn up.

Spelling and maths certificates and results
Children who attain 100 per cent marks are given recognition through applause in the class or in assembly. Results of assessments are taken home on certificates at the end of the day.

Infant timetable

	Mon	Tues	Wed	Thu	Fri
8.50	Registration Entry music Spelling tests	Registration Entry music Brain Gym®	Registration Entry music Brain Gym®	Registration Entry music Brain Gym®	Registration Entry music Maths tests
	School Assembly: Spelling certificates	Infant Assembly	Infant Assembly	Class Assembly	School Assembly: Maths certificates
9.10 10.15	**Literacy** Connect/Preview Alphabet or phrases Phonics Scheme or VAK spellings Shared Text Word work Group-work Review	**Literacy** Connect/Preview Alphabet or phrases Phonics Scheme or VAK spellings Shared Text Word work Group-work Review	**Literacy** Connect/Preview Alphabet or phrases Phonics Scheme or VAK spellings Shared Text Word work Group-work Review	**Literacy** Connect/Preview Alphabet or phrases Phonics Scheme or VAK spellings Shared Text Word work Group-work Review	**Literacy** Connect/Preview Alphabet or phrases Phonics Scheme or VAK spellings Shared Text Word work in preparation for: Writing task
	Break				
10.30 11.20 12.00	**Mathematics** Connect/Preview Times tables Maths to music Mental/Oral Maths Teaching activity Review **Foundation subject**	**Mathematics** Connect/Preview Times tables Favourite numbers Mental/Oral Maths Teaching activity Review **Foundation subject**	**Mathematics** Connect/Preview Times tables Maths to music Mental/Oral Maths Teaching activity Review **Foundation subject**	**Mathematics** Connect/Preview Times tables Favourite numbers Mental/Oral Maths Teaching activity Review **Foundation subject**	**Literacy continued** Writing task ctd Weekly review **Mathematics** Times tables Body maths Mental/Oral Maths Teaching activity Review
	Lunchtime				
1.00	Registration Brain Gym®	Registration Brain Gym®	Registration Brain Gym®	Registration Brain Gym®	Registration Brain Gym®
   1.45	**Science** Review	**PE**–Apparatus Listening games Locational geometry Review **Foundation subject**	**Science** Review	**PE** – Hall. Eurythmics Body maths Gym/small apparatus Review **Foundation subject**	**Science** Review
2.00 2.30	**RE**		**RE**		**PHSE/Circle Time**
2.35	Phonics Scheme or VAK spellings	Phonics Scheme or VAK spellings	Phonics Scheme or VAK spellings	Phonics Scheme or VAK spellings	Phonics Scheme or VAK spellings
	Afternoon Break				
2.45	**Music**	**Story**	**Music**	**Story**	Review of week Class celebrations
3.15	Recall of day To Do list	Recall of day To Do list	Recall of day To Do list	Recall of day To Do list	Week's To Do list
	Spelling results				Maths results
	After school clubs				

260

the alps approach – Accelerated Learning in Primary Schools

Alphabet and phrases

Daily practice of the alphabet, involving use of large visual aids, props and music, takes place in the Nursery and Reception classes. Phrases are taught verbally in the early years. These may be proverbs or rhymes connected to the writing topic of the week. A richness and variety of language is used continually in each classroom and teachers seize every opportunity to highlight new phrases and vocabulary.

Brain Gym®

Brain Gym® activities are specifically timetabled for the Nursery and Infant classes twice a day. Each session takes just three or four minutes. Brain Gym® involves cross-lateral movement and aids the development of gross and fine motor control along with hand–eye co-ordination. Often the exercises are linked to the phonic or number work that is being taught.

Phonics scheme

There are some schemes for teaching phonics that actively engage children through VAK and complement the ALPS method™ of working.

Listening games

The rules for 'good listening' and 'good sitting' are taught explicitly from the early years. They are displayed in every classroom. Nothing is taken for granted in the ALPS classroom and the rules are reinforced through games and daily practice in lessons.

Music

Music is an essential element of the ALPS process. Specific music lessons are in addition to music being used continually to aid learning across the curriculum.

Favourite numbers

It is essential that children perceive maths as a fun subject, yet it is amazing how many adults tell stories of being discouraged about maths at an early age. Activities to develop agility and confidence with number help to dispel the feeling that anyone is weak at maths. Many ALPS teachers take the time to explore and have fun with favourite numbers as a set activity in the early years.

Body maths

This is a VAK activity that in the early years is often timetabled for a specific session. Alongside oral instructions, visual cues are often used, such as cards with numerals, symbols or words. Young children are asked to represent a number or concept with their bodies, either individually or in groups, such as making a square, a triangle, a group of six, an odd number, a wide, narrow or long shape, and so on.

Maths to music

In the younger classrooms, specific times are set aside for the singing of number songs, rhymes and maths songs. Simple, well-known tunes are used for songs, in addition to published tapes and CDs.

Eurythmics

These are activities that teach young children to sense musical concepts such as pitch, rhythm and beat. Children are asked to respond to musical stimuli through activities such as 'Lay down if I play a low note', or 'Walk if a beat based on crotchets is played'.

Locational geometry

Through work on large apparatus in the younger age ranges the teacher reinforces body awareness and maths concepts through questioning and asking children to use pole-bridging as they climb, using mathematical language to describe their movements. Language use is encouraged during these sessions.

To Do lists

In the early years, the To Do list is simple and follows a familiar pattern. Children are encouraged to share the list with their parents and links with home-life are forged. The ALPS teacher strongly encourages home participation and creates systems whereby all parents are aware of the current topics and interests in the classroom.

Story

The richness of children's literature and story-telling is a vital component in language development. ALPS classrooms are stocked with good-quality books, and anything worn or tatty is discarded. Books are treasured items that children learn to care for. When interesting, imaginative and unusual language is used at story time, it is drawn to the children's attention and subsequently reinforced aurally and with visual posters.

Use of 'dead time'

All opportunities for learning are seized. The times that could otherwise be wasted, such as lining up, or waiting for lunch or a lesson to begin, are utilized in the ALPS classroom for short activities such as songs, rhymes, Brain Gym® or spellings. This leads not only to increased achievement and motivation, but also to a more positive behavioural response from children.

Playtime

Playtimes in the ALPS provide opportunities for learning through a wide variety of activities. ALPS schools consider their playgrounds as a part of the learning environment and are creative in their use of resources and space. Adults interact with children and use RAP to reinforce desirable social behaviour.

Junior timetable

Entry music
By the time children reach junior age, they have been exposed to a wide variety of music and have developed the knowledge and emotional intelligence to make decisions about the selection of music to enhance mood and learning.

Spellings
In addition to formal work on spelling rules, words that are connected to writing tasks or other curriculum areas are taught twice each day using VAK. Common words are taught systematically and linked to targets. Spellings are displayed in the classroom and around the school.

Spelling and maths tests
Children will have been taught the content of the tests systematically during the week before and will have practised at home. Testing is a part of classroom routines and children are taught techniques for relaxation and success. Results are used to affirm success, build self-esteem and target-set for future success. If a child makes more than a few errors, her progress is assessed, any obstacles removed and an action plan is drawn up with the child.

Spelling and maths certificates
Children who attain 100 per cent marks are given recognition through applause in assembly, or in other ways in the classroom. Those who do not gain 100 per cent reflect on their performance and agree with their teacher how to improve. The language of success means that the phrase 'not yet' is used in place of 'not'.

Spelling and maths results
Results of assessments are taken home on certificates at the end of the day. Targets are shared with parents, and children are taught techniques for home-study.

Phrases
Proverbs, sayings and new vocabulary are taught verbally and then displayed on posters to reinforce meanings visually. A richness and variety of language is used continually in each classroom and teachers work using VAK to teach phrases and their meanings aurally, through visual posters and through role play.

Brain breaks
Brain breaks are used to break lessons into shorter chunks and refocus attention. They are short activities that are usually connected to the lesson and are frequently used to reinforce key concepts or vocabulary. Sometimes there are also Brain Gym® activities, but their main purpose is to create the best mental and physiological state for learning.

Foundation subjects
For the sake of ease, we have generalized the foundation subjects on this timetable, except for music and PE, which have a specific relevance to the ALPS method™ of teaching. Information technology also plays an important role in the ALPS. Teachers find many ways of utilizing computers in the classroom, and the internet is invaluable for accessing information. VAK activities in science complement practical work and do not replace it.

Junior timetable

	Mon	Tues	Wed	Thu	Fri
8.50	Registration Relaxation music Spelling tests	Registration Entry music Tasks on board	Registration Entry music Tasks on board	Registration Entry music Tasks on board	Registration Relaxation music Maths tests
	School Assembly: Spelling certificates	**Junior Assembly**	**Junior Assembly**	**Class Assembly**	**School Assembly:** Maths certificates
9.10	**Literacy** Connect/Preview VAK spellings & phrases	**Literacy** Connect/Preview VAK spellings & phrases	**Literacy** Connect/Preview VAK spellings & phrases	**Literacy** Connect/Preview VAK spellings & phrases	**Literacy** Connect/Preview VAK spellings & phrases
9.20	Shared Text Word/sentence work Group/indep work	Shared Text Word/sentence work Group/indep work	Shared Text Word/sentence work Group/indep work	Shared Text Word/sentence work Group/indep work	Shared Text Word/sentence work in preparation for: Writing task
10.20	Review	Review	Review	Review	
	Break				
10.30	**Maths** Connect/Preview Times tables	**Maths** Connect/Preview Favourite numbers	**Maths** Connect/Preview Times tables	**Maths** Connect/Preview Favourite numbers	**Literacy ctd** Writing task ctd Weekly Review Target-setting
11.00	Mental/oral Maths Teaching activity Review	Mental/oral Maths Teaching activity Review	Mental/oral Maths Teaching activity Review	Mental/oral Maths Teaching activity Review	**Maths** Times tables
11.35	**Foundation subject**	**Foundation subject**	**Foundation subject**	**Foundation subject**	Mental/oral Maths Teaching activity Weekly review Target-setting
12.05					
Use of Dead Time	**Lunchtime**				
1.00	Registration Tasks on board VAK spellings/phrases **PE**	Registration Tasks on board VAK spellings/phrases **Science**	Registration Tasks on board VAK spellings/phrases **Science**	Registration Tasks on board VAK spellings/phrases **PE**	Registration Tasks on board VAK spellings/phrases **Science**
1.50	**Foundation subject**				
2.00		**Foundation subject**	**RE**	**Foundation subject**	**RE**
2.40					
	Music Recall of day	**French** Recall of day	**Music** Recall of day	**PHSE/Circle Time** Recall of day	Review of week Class celebrations Life maps
3.15	To Do list	To Do list	To Do list	To Do list	Week's To Do list
	Spelling results				Maths results
	Homework clubs **After school clubs**				

the alps approach – Accelerated Learning in Primary Schools

Review

Review is a vital part of the accelerated learning lesson cycle. In the ALPS teachers allow time for review at the end of all lessons and for overall learning review at the end of each week. Review aids recall and connects learning, and it is also a vital component of assessment and the target-setting process.

Times tables

Learning of vital facts such as times tables can be accelerated through use of VAK.

Favourite numbers

In the junior classroom, activities with favourite numbers can generally be incorporated into maths teaching. For example, once every child's favourite number is displayed in the classroom, team points can be given for anyone spotting the square or a factor of their own or someone else's favourite number.

We offer suggestions for teaching maths through VAK on pages 278–281

Clubs

Clubs can give invaluable learning experience in the ALPS. They can be held during lesson time or out-of-school hours. In the ALPS children become motivated learners who welcome opportunities for home study. Many children, however, do not have ideal facilities at home for study, and so many ALPS schools offer clubs after school for children to work.

Circle time

Many schools use circle time as an effective way to raise self-esteem and teach communication skills, both of which are essential parts of the ALPS philosophy.

To Do lists

Just as the ALPS teacher gives the Big Picture at the start of every lesson, so she gives children the Big Picture for the day ahead – the day before! Once children become accustomed to this process and understand that it is linked with assessment and target-setting, they begin to contribute confidently. The removal of the mystery and of consequent anxiety, the time to pre-prepare at home, the ownership of personal targets, the feeling of being valued as a partner in one's own education, and the opportunity to voice concerns or personal preference, all help to increase motivation and raise achievement.

Review of week

At the end of the week the class reflects upon their learning and upon targets that have been met. Additional posters may be made at this point to reinforce the lessons of the week, and homework tasks and challenges may be set.

Class celebrations

Celebration when targets are met is a powerful aspect of the ALPS method™. During these times of celebration and reflection upon success, attention is drawn to children's aspirational life maps, which become increasingly important as children mature. By the top of the junior school, reference is made to life maps and aspirations on a daily basis.

Next week's To Do list

Like the daily To Do list, this is an agreed plan of action, but on a Friday it is drawn up for the following week. It can be mind mapped on the board, typed on the computer, or written on individual pieces of paper. The important principle is that this is a shared process, with the teacher leading and all children contributing. This information is shared with parents. Some schools send copies home, while others invite parents in to see the list in the classroom.

Writing task

Many ALPS teachers arrange their timetable to allow for one longer writing session per week, where children can complete a lengthier piece of writing. This would seem logical, particularly as children are often expected to write for approximately an hour for their statutory assessment.

We discussed life maps on pages 100–103

Target-setting

After reviews for any subject, progress is measured against targets and new targets are set.

Playtime

Opportunities are provided for children to read or write during playtimes, often just by providing a sheltered sitting area on the playground. In some schools facilities are created for children to spend time inside, in the library or on computers.

French

All the evidence we can gather from neuroscientists points to the dramatic difference that early exposure to a foreign language can make. After about the age of ten, when the process of 'trimming' in the brain has begun to decline, learning a new language and replicating novel sounds that are part of that language becomes increasingly difficult.

❷ Teaching Literacy: three reading strategies compared

WITH THE ADVENT OF THE LITERACY HOUR IN THE UK, literacy is now, if it has not been before, firmly on the agenda. It is a source of anxiety for parents. It is a source of concern for government. Opinions on a way forward differ. Is there a timetable for learning to read? If this process has not occurred by a given chronological marker, is the child developmentally delayed? The imperative is to get this right, and the possible trauma for all concerned by getting it wrong means that few, if any, are prepared to volunteer a definitive view. One commentator on the brain and learning suggests that there is no absolute timetable for learning to read, and that differences of three years are normal. Some children will be ready to read at four years, while others, just as normal, will be ready at seven or even ten years.

Early exposure to language interactions impacts on the architecture of the brain. Researcher Patricia Kuhl at the University of Washington suggests that 'infants develop in their first year perceptual neurons in the auditory cortex: the brain dedicates special neural connections to be receptive to particular sounds' (1992). The greater the range of sounds the child is exposed to, the better. We support those who argue that language-rich environments where there are early, positive, extended interactions between an adult and a child create brains that are better wired for manipulating language. Expose the infant to a wide range of sounds – singing, cooing, parentese, poetry – and phonemic awareness is being developed. This helps the brain get ready for learning! Between the ages of four and ten, synaptic connections are being made, reinforced, or perhaps trimmed away through neglect or lack of stimulation. The child's brain is aglow with neural possibility. It is happening at a phenomenal rate that will not be replicated in later life.

The ability to read and write is seen as the essential skill for children to access the curriculum as it is currently structured in schools. For children who have emotional and behavioural difficulties, poor literacy skills can be an underlying source of their poor behaviours. Access to and the use of language is also seen by some as a key player in explaining the differences between girls' achievement and boys' achievement. In this section we compare three sample literacy schemes and look at how they utilize some of the principles recommended in the ALPS approach. All three offer very special things for pupils to pack into their ALPS rucksack ready for the journey. Some children will not learn with a diet confined to one scheme.

In looking at three schemes that are currently very popular in our primary schools, we have tried to identify and extract the reasons behind their success. The three schemes we have chosen – Letterland, Jolly Phonics and THRASS (Teaching Handwriting Reading and Spelling Skills) – all work for the majority of children. All three schemes can demonstrate statistically that they can make positive differences to children. What we are interested in is not the question of whether they work, but why they work.

Let us look at the three schemes in turn and then evaluate them in relation to the ALPS approach.

the alps approach – Accelerated Learning in Primary Schools

THRASS

THRASS stands for Teaching Handwriting Reading and Spelling Skills. It teaches the forty-four phonemes (speech sounds) of spoken English and the graphemes of written English. Each of the forty-four phonemes are illustrated on the THRASSchart, which has forty-four rectangular boxes. Each of the boxes represents one sound. We were unable to obtain permission to print the whole chart but we can illustrate the principles of THRASS by using the 'j' box (see illustration below), which we were given permission to use. On the chart this box is illustrated with pictures of a jam pot, a giant, a cage and a bridge. The 'j' in jam, the 'g' in giant, the 'ge' in cage, and the 'dge' in bridge are all shown separately below the pictures. The THRASSchart draws attention to the fact that different letters and combinations of letters can be associated with the same sound. Children are taught straight away that when one letter makes one sound (as in j and g) this is called a graph, when two letters make one sound this is called a digraph and that when three letters make one sound it is called a trigraph. Collectively, these pictures of sounds are called graphemes. The ALPS teacher is not afraid to use correct vocabulary immediately.

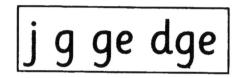

For each of the forty-four phonemes there is a box showing the most common grapheme choices, illustrated by a picture. The THRASSchart therefore enables the pupil to associate the sound to individual words and images. Children can therefore see that the same sound can be made by one letter (graphs), two letters (digraphs) and three letters (trigraphs). THRASS is different from our other two schemes, Jolly Phonics and Letterland, in that it gives the pupils this Big Picture at the start. The THRASSchart is, in a sense, a memory map. Many teachers start teaching the forty-four phonemes by exploring children's names; for example, by pointing out that Jeremy has the same sound at the beginning of his name as Gemma.

To those who may think that infant children are too young to understand that letters can make more than one sound, the ALPS teacher would point out that Jeremy and Gemma already know this. If Gemma did not know it, and had only been taught that 'g' made the sound as in the word 'gate', she would be saying her name very differently. The ALPS teacher can also explain by using the THRASSchart why Charlotte has the same sound at the beginning of her name as Sharon, but a different sound to Christopher. The same principle is used in many accelerated learning language programmes.

The ALPS teacher uses the THRASScharts and associated resources to simultaneously teach reading, writing and spelling skills. She explains to her class that when they are reading they are turning pictures of sounds, 'graphemes', into speech sounds, 'phonemes'. She teaches them that this is called 'decoding' and that when they turn the phonemes into graphemes on the page they are 'encoding'.

The word level work in class can be further explored using the THRASS interactive CD. On the CD pupils can hear the forty-four phonemes being made by different grapheme choices, they can see the word associated with the sound and practise making the shape of the letter. The pupils can explore the THRASSchart by playing games designed to help them to identify individual sounds in words. In one section pupils are asked to demonstrate their understanding of the structure of words by identifying the number of phonemes in a word and the phoneme order within the word.

THRASS, with its growing number of support materials, can be used as a programme to fulfil the word level requirements of the National Literacy Strategy. It can also act as a framework to support sentence and text level work in the classroom. The charts, keywords, graphemes and pictures can be used to help children understand the formation of any word. The resources and materials currently being produced by THRASS UK are designed to help children learn the THRASSchart and the associated keywords. Initially the charts act as a physical resource, a place where children can go to find the graphemes and the sounds in the words. As they become more familiar with the chart, so it becomes more and more internalized. Eventually a stage is reached where pupils know, for example, that the letter 'a' can make six sounds, such as in ant, baby, banana, swan, ball, and zebra, and that letters can combine together as digraphs, trigraphs and quadgraphs to make individual sounds.

The methodology of teaching the forty-four phonemes and the 120 grapheme words is multisensory. Using the charts and support materials, children can see, hear and overwrite the graphemes, keywords and pictures. There are overwriting sheets, lively music and videotapes with the forty-four phonemes and the 120 grapheme words set out in musical raps. The interactive CD-ROM provides the children with aural and visual opportunities to investigate and learn reading, spelling and writing skills.

When you read what some teachers say about aspects of this method, which they find valuable, it is easy to see how some of the principles we advocate in ALPS actually work within the scheme.

> It has provided us with the building blocks of reading and spelling in a very logical and structured way, enabling teachers to empower children to make their own spelling choices (graphemes) and select sounds (phonemes). Teachers' own expectations of children, particularly with word level work, have risen greatly. The children enjoy hearing and repeating various raps; they enjoy making their own spelling choices. Learning English, made so difficult for us all with its multiplicity of idiosyncrasies, can be fun.

S. M. Bradshaw, Primary Head, Glastonbury, Somerset

Overview, structure, self-direction and choice, high expectations and fun! Others point to behavioural gains as children experience success with their learning.

> There have been behavioural gains as well as literacy gains as disturbed children begin to find that reading makes sense for the first time.

Carol Sheehan, Sheffield Literacy Advisor

Letterland

As the name suggests, Letterland is a place where children go to find out about letter behaviour. The thinking behind Letterland is that from the perspective of the child the alphabet is initially seen as a set of signs without significance or meaning. Until meaning, association and understanding of behaviours of letters is grasped, children may as well be looking at random shapes such as ####.

To a young child, letters are random marks on a page and they will continue to be meaningless until the child has been initiated into the workings of the symbols system. In Letterland each letter has a character built around it. For example, the letter 'h' is brought to life as 'Hairy Hat Man', and his body and name become instant clues to the correct shape and sound of 'h'. Each character has a series of stories. Stories are used to introduce children to the letter and the 'initial sound' that it makes. Later on, stories are also used to explain why the same letter can make different sounds and why letters combine to make different sounds. No prior learning has to be undone. So, for example, the 'ch' sound is explained by the story that when Hairy Hat Man meets Clever Cat his hairy hat makes Clever Cat sneeze, making the 'chhhh' sound.

Children are introduced to Letterland by being told that all the letters they see in books really come from a secret place called Letterland. As in any ALPS classroom, the teacher is deliberately creating a playful, stress-free environment that engages natural modes of curiosity and interest. Teachers may sing a song with pupils before they visit Letterland, getting pupils to cover their eyes and open them when they 'arrive'. Alternatively they may mime a bus or train journey in which the children close their eyes for a few moments before they arrive in Letterland. The classroom becomes 'Letterland' with wall friezes, displays and mobiles acting as visual reminders, as well as being an ongoing celebration of achievement. Once in Letterland the children can role-play 'being' a Letterland character. Letterland gives letters an identity that is physical and relevant to a child's age and experience.

Letterland is a comprehensive language programme with a multitude of video, cassette and book resources. Comprehensive teacher guides take teachers step by step through the programme and there is a freedom for teachers to go with the flow and let the class dictate the pace.

Programme 1 introduces children to letters and their characters. It introduces phonemes, blends and some common digraphs. For each letter there is a wide range of resources. For example, picture cards tell stories that explain that Sammy Snake has a sister called Sally Snake who loves making the 'ss' sound with him. Children can be asked to look out for words where Sammy and Sally are together in words, as in 'mess'. Or they can identify words where 's' is on either side of a letter, as in 'sister'. Sammy Snake is sometimes a sleepy snake, which results in his making the noise 'zzzz' in words like 'has', 'was', or 'boys'. When Sammy Snake appears at the beginning of important words he takes a deep breath and gets bigger, becoming a capital letter. He says: 'Now I'm a super sized snake!' The children can sing Sammy Snake's song from the handwriting cassette as they make his shape in the air or on paper. The resources include stories such as 'Sammy Snake and his visit to the Seaside', and 'Sammy Snake and the Snow'.

Stories that introduce each of the Letterland characters are rich in words that use the same sound, reinforcing the letter sound that the teacher is focusing on. For example, when learning about Sammy Snake and the sound that he makes, the story uses language such as 'a sweet little smiling snake, not a scary snake at all'. The story can be used to support the child in the written production of the letter. In the teacher manuals the teacher is given lists of words that have the same grapheme producing the same phoneme, and the most common words are highlighted.

Language Rich

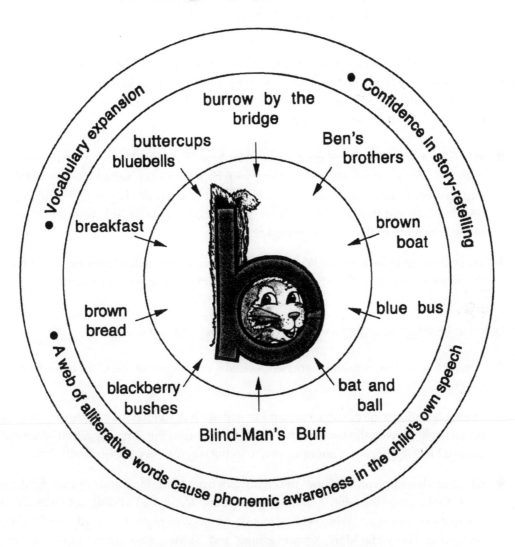

vocabulary expansion
Confidence in story-retelling
A web of alliterative words cause phonemic awareness in the child's own speech

burrow by the bridge
buttercups bluebells
Ben's brothers
breakfast
brown boat
brown bread
blue bus
blackberry bushes
bat and ball
Blind-Man's Buff

Words become like
Iron Filings to a Magnet

Once children have been introduced to all the characters they are then introduced to further letter behaviour such as:

◆ Word endings – 'Naughty Nick and friends come together to make endings such as – 'nt' and 'nd'.

◆ Shared sounds 'ff', 'll', 'ss' in which firemen Fred and Frank, snakes Sammy and Sally, and lamp ladies Lucy and Linda come together as best friends to make a single sound.

◆ Consonant blends such as Lucy the Lamp Lady with Bouncing Ben 'bl', Clever Cat 'cl', Golden Girl 'gl', Fireman Fred 'fl' and Sammy Snake 'sl'.

◆ The vowel men 'aeiou' being the only people in Letterland that ever say their names in words: Mr A is the Apron man, Mr E is the Easy magic man, Mr I is Icecream man, Mr O is the Old man, and Mr U is the Uniform man.

Programme 2 builds on stage one by introducing children to additional phonemes, further blends and more complex word structures. At stage two additional stories are used to illustrate letter behaviour and to explain why certain letters, when placed next to each other, make certain sounds. For example, children are taught that:

◆ When Poor Peter Puppy 'p' meets Hairy Hat Man 'h', Hairy Hat Man, being the happy man he is, tries to cheer Poor Peter Puppy up by taking his photograph. When this happens Poor Peter Puppy smiles and Hairy Hat Man laughs happily, but quietly, with his mouth almost shut and his teeth on his lips. So he makes a 'ffff' sound that we hear at the beginning of the word photograph.

◆ When Annie Apple 'a' meets Wicked Water Witch 'w' the witch turns back and makes the apple taste awful. This story is used to explain the 'aw' sound in awful, paw, saw.

In Letterland teachers and pupils enter a world of imagination and play.

◆ Art. Picture coding is used to 'anchor' a child's experience of the letter behaviour being taught.

◆ Stories are told to introduce letters and to explain letter behaviour, with children dressed up and role-playing the parts of the letters from within the story. Again children are exposed to a significant amount of new vocabulary in a very user-friendly way.

◆ Children dress up and 'become' the characters from Letterland and/or they hold picture cards that explain the letter's character and sound for word-building activities. Teachers ask questions such as: 'Which characters do we need to make the word "hot"?' Children dressed as 'Hairy Hat Man', 'Oscar Orange' and 'Ticking Tess' come to the front and arrange themselves in the correct order. Pupils are asked: 'Who can think of a letter that we could change, add or take away to make a new word such as turning "hat" into "what"?'

◆ Songs. For each of the stories, there is a supporting song on tape.

Sentences giving lots of examples of the letter sounds dealt with in the stories and songs are given in the manuals, along with lists of words that teachers and pupils can use to make more sentences.

Each of the behaviours is illustrated, so that, for example, in the word 'what' the Wicked Water Witch can be seen in the illustrations knocking Hairy Hat Man's hat off with her stick.

The wide range of resources make Letterland more than a word strategy scheme. Children can go to story books, games and other items to reinforce, revisit or extend existing learning. Display materials support the emphasis on physical manipulation and active engagement through art and craft types of activities.

Teachers point to the fun aspect of the programme and to the visual dimension as key motivational features.

The Wicked Witch whacks off Hairy Hat Man's hat

The Wicked Water Witch hates it when the Hairy Hat Man gets in her way so that she can't see ahead in the Reading Direction. Not only is he tall, but he wears a hat as well! So what does she do? She whacks his hat off! This makes the poor Hat Man too startled to speak. That is why we can't hear him at all in words like when.

She whacks most often in the five question words: when, which, what, where and why.

The second story, which is an extension of the first, explains the few exceptions where the Hat Man gets angry and hits back in the words: **who, whose, whom** and **whole**.

The Hat Man gets angry with the Witch

*Every once in a while, the Hat Man shows that he has had enough by shouting at the Witch "**Who** do you think you are?" Then he grabs her broomstick and hits her hat off instead! Now **whose** turn is it to be too startled to speak? Yes, the Witch!*

> "The pictograms give meaning to the sound–symbol relationship and have been the key to unlocking some learning difficulties in my classroom. Parents are also excited about this innovative programme that has brought joy and fun for learning into my classroom."

Barbara Peters, Year 2 teacher, Norfolk

Also, when things are perceived to be fun, different and desirable, younger children often want it too.

> "Although we have a Nursery class we never intended to teach them formally to read or write. To our amazement these young children were absorbing the Letterland skills that older siblings were being taught."

J. A. Dredge, Head of St Faith's at Ash, Canterbury, Kent

Jolly Phonics

In Jolly Phonics the emphasis is on teaching forty-two sounds of English. Children are introduced to the sounds through the use of stories, pictures and words. Body movements and actions represent the sounds. Children are taught what each of the forty-two sounds look like when represented graphically as a letter. Jolly Phonics does recognize that there is more than one way of representing the same sound with different letters or combinations of letters. First, children are introduced to the principal sound of a letter. Later alternative sounds of each letter are covered. For example, the sound 'ai', as in 'rain', is taught before the alternatives such as 'ay', as in 'play' or 'a-e', as in 'plane'.

When children are taught the 's' sound, as in 'sun', the suggested storyline is that of a child taking a dog for a walk in the country. The dog starts to bark. There is a 'sssssssss' sound and a snake slithers away. At the same time children are taught the action to associate with this – weaving their arms like a snake while making the 'sssssssss' sound. The effectiveness of using stories to help retain the information is again emphasized, but Jolly Phonics also puts an emphasis on movement.

> It's a lot more enjoyable for the children but they're still learning the basics about words and word formation, how words are made and how they can recognize them so that they know how to write them ... You tell them a story and it helps them retain the message about the sound you are introducing.

Ms Daly, Primary Teacher

When children articulate the sound, they also make the body movement. In turn this body movement is associated with the story that was used to introduce the sound initially. Thus children can see the sound represented in words and by movement. The story used to introduce the sound has associations with seeing, hearing and doing. This multisensory approach provides the children with a number of different ways of committing the sound and the letter shape to memory.

The teacher's manual states that the forty-two sounds can be introduced in about nine weeks, or about one letter sound per day. The letter sounds are introduced in a particular order, with the forty-two sounds of Jolly Phonics being broken down into seven groups of six. The letters are grouped to allow children to start blending sounds into words after only the first group of six has been taught. This group – 's', 'a', 't', 'i', 'p', 'n' – allows children to start reading words such as 'sat', 'pin, 'tin' immediately. ALPS teachers challenge personal beliefs relating to potential and expectations. Jolly Phonics has challenged traditional beliefs about when teachers should start to teach blending skills. Blending skills are taught simultaneously with the introduction to the first six sounds.

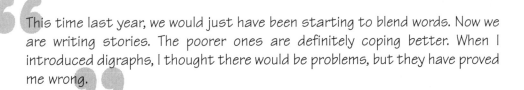

This time last year, we would just have been starting to blend words. Now we are writing stories. The poorer ones are definitely coping better. When I introduced digraphs, I thought there would be problems, but they have proved me wrong.

Year 1 Teacher

In Jolly Phonics, decoding is aided by the fact that the children are helped in identifying the sound that goes with each letter(s). They have both a movement and a story that they can associate with the letter(s) in the word. Each of the sounds is introduced in the same way as the 'ssss' sound described above.

The other groups of six sounds are:

c, k, e, h, r, m, d

g, o, u, l, f, b

ai, j, oa, ie, ee, or

z, w, ng, v, oo, oo

y, x, ch, sh, th, th

qu, ou, oi, ue, er, ar

Jolly Phonics has a wide range of support materials. For each of the groups of six sounds there are Finger Phonic books, workbooks, videos, a phonic wall frieze and stencils.

The Finger Phonics books have cut-out sections that enable the children to feel how the sound is made. They also tell the story behind the movement that goes with the sound. Again fun and active involvement are emphasized.

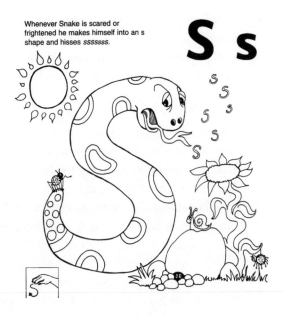

Whenever Snake is scared or frightened he makes himself into an s shape and hisses *sssssss*.

The Finger Phonics have been fun for our children. They have been better at learning the letters, and with the actions it has been easier to keep them involved. They have also been much better at mastering how to form the letters correctly.

P. Toghill, Nursery Teacher

Jolly Grammar

A recent extension to Jolly Phonics is *The Grammar Handbook* by Sara Wernham and Sue Lloyd, published in March 2000 (ISBN 1 870946 85 5). The grammar programme builds upon the work covered in *The Phonics Handbook*, introducing the rudiments of grammar while extending children's phonic knowledge. While the handbook could be used in isolation, there is a range of other materials to support the scheme.

The grammar scheme is designed to be used in two literacy sessions per week, with one lesson devoted to spelling and the second to grammar. Work done in these sessions should be related to the broader language curriculum. There is emphasis given to using the correct terminology with young children while teaching them grammatical structures. Worksheets accompany teachers' notes for each block of work.

Jolly Grammar has the multisensory approach that one would expect from this scheme. Actions accompany the learning; for example, for proper nouns the children are taught to touch their forehead with their index and middle fingers, whereas for common nouns they touch with the whole hand. Actions accompany concepts such as verbs and tenses. The action for a verb in the past tense is to point backwards over the shoulder with a thumb, whereas for the future tense, the child points forwards. Colour is also used to promote visual learning. In many of the accompanying worksheets children are asked to underline in certain colours, such as red for verbs, black for nouns and pink for pronouns. The teacher can use this colour connection when working on the board. Auditory learning is used when children chant and learn spellings by the 'say it as it sounds' method.

Weekly spelling lists are given with the aim of most children gaining full marks and building confidence and self-esteem. There is recognition that there are many 'tricky words' that children need to learn to spell in order to become competent writers. Children are taught the list of words in class in addition to taking the list home, and weekly tests are given. The lists combine words that follow phonic rules, along with a few 'tricky words' and one longer word to build a sense of achievement. Children are encouraged to focus on the sounds in regular words, to say letter names for the tricky words and to chunk down the challenge of longer words – all strategies that we recommend in the ALPS approach.

The emphasis is on active teaching, along with building of achievement and self-esteem. It would seem likely that children who have experienced success with Jolly Phonics will continue that way with Jolly Grammar, and the scheme would seem to be compatible with the ALPS approach and an extremely useful tool for the ALPS teacher.

The three schemes and the ALPS method™

All three schemes utilize accelerated learning principles in their delivery. They all, for example, are multisensory, accessing visual, audio or kinesthetic learning styles. All use a variety of methods to help pupils commit their learning to memory.

In extracting what we could call the 'best' from these schemes, we aim to make available to you practical ways in which you can enhance your own literacy teaching – irrespective of whether or not you use these or any other approaches. All three schemes can be used for individual or whole-class teaching. All three schemes have guidebooks for the teacher and Letterland in particular now has an abundance of support materials. All the schemes are best delivered when they build on children's ideas and enthusiasm.

In all three schemes, children experience success from the beginning. They are able to take hold of what they are learning and establish a sense of ownership or belonging. In Letterland this is made possible by the fact that Letterland is a magical place. Pupils can role-play the characters by dressing up and acting out the part that the character plays in stories. Music and rhyme are used to add poetic and musical illustration to the letters and their sounds.

Jolly Phonics also uses stories to introduce forty-two sounds of English. The story introduces not only the sound but also a body movement, and so kinesthetic learning is exploited to give a sense of involvement. A sense of ownership in THRASS is established immediately by using children's names as a vehicle to start introducing the forty-four phonemes. There is no reason of course why the ALPS teacher could not work with the class to build a story around the pupil's name. THRASS also uses music through the THRASS raps on audiocassette and video.

All three literacy approaches recommend and use a multisensory approach. They all use overwriting of the letters on paper as a means of reinforcing knowledge. Letterland, through its use of 'letter characterization', sets many opportunities for children to 'act out' sounds and letter behaviour utilizing art and craft activities. THRASS has a detailed IT programme that provides 'hands on' activity using the mouse and keyboard. Jolly Phonics' kinesthetic key is its association of each sound with a particular body movement.

All three schemes teach children how to blend letter sounds. Letterland supports this visually through its use of characterization of each letter, Jolly Phonics through its use of the body movements, and THRASS through the association of each grapheme with an illustration on the THRASSchart.

All three schemes are highly engaging and motivating. They all provide a high level of positive emotional arousal and personal involvement. All three schemes provide strong associative connections between the location and circumstances in which the information or experience is accessed. THRASS and Letterland use music, while Jolly Phonics uses movement to help children anchor, contextualize and memorize their learning. In addition, long-term memory is supported by the use of 3D characters and images.

Having witnessed the joy and success that all three schemes can produce, it is clear that to recommend one over another would be counter productive, since they all have their relative strengths. Watching children 'make words' using body movements at play on the playground as they learn to spell and blend is a strong recommendation for incorporating physical movement into the ALPS classroom. The strength of THRASS lies in the fact that it tells pupils from the start that one letter can make more than one sound, and that sometimes more than one letter can combine to make a sound. The THRASSchart makes available to any ALPS classroom the Big Picture that children will need on their journey. Seeing thirty or more children lose themselves in the joy of rapping the forty-four phonemes on their journey is a sight to behold! Letterland's strength lies in its stories and the extent to which it stimulates imaginative play, engagement and fun. If you are going on a journey in the ALPS, you may as well enjoy the ride!

❸ Teaching Numeracy: some ideas from the ALPS

According to the *Times Educational Supplement* of 7 May 1999, schools in Wisconsin that used toy cars, coins and garden gadgets to illustrate mathematical and scientific concepts witnessed startling improvements in their pupils' performance. Some 10 year olds performed as well as 17 year olds, according to researchers from the Wisconsin Centre for Education Research and the National Mathematics and Science Centre.

One of the researchers, Richard Lehrer, said that the new system of teaching had enabled elementary school pupils to visualize and interpret data as skilfully as high-school seniors. 'Historically, mathematics started with geometry, which is very visual, but in the past two centuries, mathematics has increasingly emphasized abstract algebra and related forms of symbolization,' he said. The aim of the research project was to help children invent, test and revise models in maths and science rather than depend on textbooks. The results remind us that teachers need to build plenty of practical experience into maths teaching.

The teaching of multiplication tables often provokes strong debate, but it is undeniable that learning multiplication tables must be supported by practical mathematics and understanding. Children can be taught multiplication tables through rote, bribery and persuasion, rather like bitter pills to be swallowed. The ALPS method™ is based on positive, motivated learning with a clearly understood goal. It is essential that children understand the need for learning to be quick and confident with number. It is also essential that the learning of number facts and the development of skills are made enjoyable and fun. We have seen a variety of methods for teaching children multiplication tables, and here seems to lie the key: variety.

It is normal for very young children to be taught number songs, where the concept of number may be hazy and incomplete at first, but becomes established as mathematical understanding develops. Music can also be used effectively for learning maths in later years. Music is a powerful force, and rhyme strongly aids memory. In one Reception class we heard children sing along to multiplication songs using twos, fives and tens. The teacher used every opportunity to count in these numbers and made regular reference to them; for example, by commenting, 'There are 25 children here today. Let's count to 25 in 5s!' as the children lined up for assembly. As the children went down the corridor, the chant continued, '25, 30, 35, 40'.

It is common in primary classrooms to display multiplication tables, yet very often the print is small and cluttered, and the posters only serve to aid children in finding answers, not in visually absorbing the information. In many ALPS classrooms each multiplication table is displayed on large, bold posters until it is learned. Once it is learned, there is no need to display it. We watched one Year 3 class sing their way through the six times table. Some of the class looked at the poster as they sang, while many chose to turn away. One of the boys told us proudly: 'I can do my six times tables with my eyes shut! Now it's all in my head!'

One of the most innovative ways that we have seen multiplication tables being taught was devised by Mrs Kate Barnes, a senior teacher in a large primary school. Kate wanted to devise a way to help children to learn kinesthetically in addition to visually and aurally, but she also wanted to make it fun. She created packs of cards, which she colour-coded in order to aid memory. On each card she drew outlines of children's hands, and above each finger wrote a number from the multiplication table. For example, for the five times table, above the left hand little finger, was written 5, then above the next finger 10, and so on up to 50. In the middle of the card was written 55 and 60, along with two little cartoon feet. The class then sat with their hands on the cards, and said the times tables, lifting each finger as they said the answer and looked at the digits. The activity ended with them stamping left foot then right foot as they said, in a triumphant tone: '11 x 5 is 55, and 12 x 5 is 60!' What impressed us was the children's enthusiasm for the activity. Again, several children told us that they could do the activity without looking. Kate had noticed that when solving maths problems in practical sessions, many children no longer counted their way through the multiplication tables to arrive at an answer, but wiggled the appropriate finger, shut their eyes, and could visualize the number from the card.

We have also been interested to see children in ALPS classrooms whose practical skills in mathematics have been used to lead into further learning. For example, Christopher, in Year 2, was on the special needs register and was in the lowest groups for both mathematics and English. When his teacher did the life map activity with the class, she discovered that Christopher was a keen gardener. He worked every evening and weekend on his dad's allotment growing gladioli, which he then sold at the market. He was an accomplished little businessman, keeping his own accounts for seeds, fertilizer, boxes and materials. When he brought his teacher a bunch of gladioli for Christmas, he told her: 'There are twelve there,

My brain thinks a lot. It can count in fives, twos, tens, threes and fours. I practise a lot until I can do it. I practise after break and I don't sit and chat when I come in.

that's £3.60 worth!' Not perhaps socially graceful, but it showed that this little boy had a quick mind and an excellent grasp of his multiplication tables. Maths in this classroom was fun, relevant and exciting, and by the end of the year Christopher was well above the national average in SATs results. Similarly, we met a teacher who told us of a boy in her class who had always been perceived by teachers as being one of the poorer pupils in mathematics. In conversation, she discovered that he could work out the odds on horse races and calculate winnings and losses with his uncle at the racetrack. Like Christopher, he had no problem with multiplication when he saw the relevance and was motivated to work out problems. Tales like these are commonplace in schools. The ALPS teacher discovers children's strengths, often

279

through the life mapping activity. She makes learning relevant, describes the outcomes, and uses variety in her teaching methods. Children in her classroom understand why they are learning multiplication tables and imaginative methods are found to make the learning interesting, rapid and fun.

In the ALPS classroom, numbers are friendly and nobody falls into the 'I'm no good at maths' trap. Many teachers need to examine their own attitude towards maths, and if they fall into the 'no good' category, ask themselves: 'When did I decide to be no good at maths?' and 'How can I make myself friendly towards numbers?'

A simple activity is to introduce favourite numbers into maths teaching. Decide what your favourite number is. It may be associated with a birthday, a significant date, a famous event, or you might just like the look of the number when it is written. Share this with the children. Write the number up on the board and tell a number story. Here is Irma's maths story about her favourite number, which is 12:

> I like the number 12 because it is my birthday on 12th May and next birthday I'll be 12.
> I like 12 because it is a 1 and a 2, which are the first two numbers.
> I also like 12 because 1 is 1/2 of 2, but then also 1/2 has a 1 and a 2 in it, which is funny!
> If you add 1 and 2 you get 3, which is the next number from 1, 2, then 3.
> No other numbers do that – if you add 2 and 3 you get 5, or if you add 3 and 4 you get 7.
> I also like 12 because it is an even number. It is in 2 times table.
> It is friendly because 3 and 4 go into it.
> It is also the last number you learn in times tables, so it is a celebrating number.
> I like it because it is a dozen, so you get things like eggs in 12s, or 6s, which is half of 12.
> 6 is half of 12, which is friendly, because if you add 6 and then 1 and 2 twice, you get back to 12.
> These are just some of the reasons that I like the number 12.

Children from the earliest age can make up number stories and apply all the knowledge that they gain in maths lessons to their favourite number, and then to the favourites of the rest of the class. Soon in maths lessons children will spontaneously start to comment on connections between numbers. For example, in a session on squared numbers, a Year 4 child commented: 'Hey, 49 is a square number. That's Sarah's favourite number!' The class never had any difficulty recalling the square of 7, because in their minds they had linked it to Sarah's very friendly number 49. This was the number on Sarah's dad's racing car, a picture of which was displayed in the classroom.

An important message is imparted when a teacher talks of favourite numbers. She is saying that numbers are friendly, can be fun and that mathematics is a favourite activity. Moreover, everybody has a favourite number, and all the favourite numbers feature somewhere in the multiplication tables. Multiplication tables are friendly, and affirming messages in the classroom tell the class that everybody is good at them. Music is used to learn concepts, posters display information and everybody is successful.

4 The homework questionnaire

THIS IS NOT A COMPETITION. Everyone will get different scores for different sections of the quiz. A higher mark does not mean that you are better or worse, it just shows how you are different. We are going to use the information from your scores to decide what sort of learner you are, and help you to improve even more! Everyone will end up with a set of targets when they have finished this exercise.

Read each statement and decide how well it describes you. If you think this is exactly like you, give it a score of 5. If it is not at all like you, give it 0. If it is somewhere in between, give it a score between 0 and 5. The higher the score, the more closely the sentence describes you.

For example read the statement:

'I always choose to do my homework the minute I get home.'

If this is true, you always choose to do your homework the minute you get home, and never leave it until later, give yourself a score of 5. If this is not at all true because you like to do your homework after you have eaten, give yourself a score of 0. If you nearly always do your homework the minute you get home, give yourself 4, or if you rarely do your homework immediately, give yourself 1, and so on. Try to answer quickly and do not spend too long thinking about each one. Just think how well the sentence describes you and give it a mark.

Section one

1   When I do my homework, I always have to look for a different sort of pencil or something.
2   I always lend my pencils and pens to my friends.
3   I keep lots of stuff in my schoolbag and I have to rummage around to find things.
4   I get fed up because when I go to use my pens many of the caps are missing.
5   I often forget where I have put my school things at home.

Section two

> 1 Adults in my family often have to remind me to do my homework.
> 2 I prefer to go to play or watch TV before I do my homework.
> 3 I often ask an adult in my family to write a note to say I didn't have time to do my homework.
> 4 I am often late handing in my homework.
> 5 I am often late to school because I have been doing my homework in the morning.

Section three

> 1 I often do not understand what I am supposed to do when I sit down to do my homework.
> 2 I often ask an adult in my family to write me a note to say that I didn't understand the homework.
> 3 I can only do my homework if someone helps me.
> 4 I often forget what the homework is and have to phone someone.
> 5 I often ask my teacher to explain the homework the next day and do it the next evening.

Section four

> 1 I like to do my homework with the TV or the radio on.
> 2 I often chat to my family while I do my homework.
> 3 I hate to do my homework in a room on my own.
> 4 If the phone rings when I'm doing my homework, I always rush to answer it.
> 5 I like to leave my homework part of the way through and come back to it later.

Now add up your scores for each section and write each total in the box. In which section did you score highest? This is the area that you need most help with, so your teacher will give you a set of targets to help with those. When you have succeeded with all those targets, your teacher will give you a set for the section that you scored your second highest mark in, then the third, then the fourth. This means that the targets are tailor-made for you!

Homework Target Card: Section one

The targets on this card are aimed to help you to become tidier and more organized. It is no good if you are ready to do your homework, but do not have all the pens and pencils that you need. Work your way through the targets and suggestions below, and you will find that you will never have to go searching for your belongings again!

1   Put all the lids on your pens. Throw away any that do not work.

2   Put all your pens and pencils into one pencil case.

3   Never put a blunt pencil or a pen without a lid back into your pencil case.

4   Sort your schoolbag and put things into plastic zip-up wallets.

5   Agree with your teacher or parents a weekly time to tidy your schoolbag and pencil case.

6   Keep one plastic wallet especially for finished homework.

7   Agree with your parents one place at home where you will always keep your schoolbag.

8   Agree with your parents where in your bedroom you will keep your school things.

9   Organize this place with plastic wallets, containers and holders. Label them.

10 Ask your teacher to help you to establish some rules about borrowing and lending equipment.

Homework Target Card: Section two

The targets on this card should help you to manage your time more effectively. Often, you aim to do your work, but the time slips past and you end up in a rush. You need to decide on a plan for how to manage your time, then ask your family and friends to help you to stick to it.

1   Write a list of the times that you do things each evening, such as supper, bath and bedtime.

2   Make a timetable, putting in the activities that you do regularly, such as clubs or sports.

3   Think about the times that you work best, such as before you have eaten, or in the morning.

4   Sit down with an adult in your family and work out the best times each day to do homework.

5   If necessary, tape your favourite TV programmes to watch after you have done homework.

6   If you agree to do homework in the mornings, set your alarm at an earlier time.

7   Draw up your timetable clearly. Display it at home where the whole family can see it.

8   Tell your friends when you plan to work. Ask them not to call for you during this time.

9   Put a copy of this timetable on your desk at school for the first few weeks to remind you.

10 Ask a member of your family to work at the same time as you for the first few weeks.

Homework Target Card: Section three

These targets should help you to understand what homework you need to do so that you do not feel confused or muddled about what to do. You need to become more aware of what is being explained and make sure that you are really listening to instructions.

1   If you do not have a diary for writing down homework tasks, you need to get one.

2   When your teacher explains homework, make sure that you look at her.

3   When your teacher explains homework, think about what she says and make brief notes.

4   Do not look at worksheets unless your teacher tells you to: look at her and listen instead.

5   Never try to do the work as your teacher is explaining – you will miss an instruction.

6   When you have written your notes, check them with another child.

7   Explain the work in your own words to a friend before you leave for home.

8   Ask your friend to explain the work to you in his own words.

9   If you are still unsure, wait until after school, then check your notes with your teacher.

10 As soon as you get home, get out your notes and explain the work to an adult.

Homework Target Card: Section four

This set of targets is aimed to help you to deal with distractions when you are working. You cannot concentrate fully if you are watching TV, playing with pets, or talking while you work.

1   Talk to the adults in your family about the various places that you could do your homework.

2   Agree on a place where you can sit at a table with space to work.

3   Agree that while you work, the television and radio will be turned off.

4   Look up television programmes in a TV guide and tape favourites to watch later.

5   If you like music, agree on suitable classical music, not anything that will tempt you to sing!

6   Agree with the adults in your family that while you do homework, you will not answer the phone or door.

7   Ask your family to tell anyone who calls for you during homework time to call back later.

8   While you work, make a rule that brothers and sisters either work, or leave the room.

9   Make a rule that you always finish your work in one go, and never leave half way through.

10 Ask to co-ordinate the family's homework plan, so that you all do your work at the same time.

❺ Your classroom checklist

✓ Start lessons positively and start on time

✓ Connect to prior knowledge and the previous lesson

✓ Give the Big Picture:
- – describe what you are going to do and how you will do it
- – begin to embed questions
- – assign significance to the keywords

✓ Set personal performance targets

✓ Focus on task – diffuse – focus on task – diffuse – focus on task – diffuse and build in VAK

✓ Demonstrate understanding through different intelligences

✓ Review for recall and for performance targets

❻ Key vocabulary for the staffroom

★ Big Picture

★ Primacy and recency

★ Metacognition

★ The new three Rs

★ Keywords

★ Educative feedback

★ Purposeful language exchange

★ ADDS UP

★ Pole-bridging

★ Desk labels

★ Target motivators

★ Aspirational wall

★ RAP

★ BASIS

★ VAK

★ Multiple intelligence

★ Memory mapping

★ Review for recall

⑦ The most common questions answered

1   Isn't this just another new fad in education?

No. Accelerated learning derives from languages learning and has been established in different forms since the 1970s. We have taken the term because it is well recognized. We explain the theory behind brain-based learning and describe ways in which teachers have developed systems that help children to learn faster, hence the label 'accelerated learning'.

2   Aren't these systems of teaching simply the systems that good teachers have always used?

We have drawn together the theory of brain-based learning with practical ideas that we have used ourselves, witnessed, or heard described in our work in schools. Therefore some of these strategies may be recognized by our readers, but we hope that everybody will find something new that they can adapt and extend in their own situations. All our examples of good practice can be related to our nine principles for brain-based learning, which we consider to be new.

3   Are the suggestions in this book a complete package of accelerated learning?

No. We could not possibly give an exhaustive package for accelerated learning. We do, however, give many suggestions of how to adapt current classroom practices to incorporate accelerated learning methodology and techniques and we do give guidance on where to go for further information. Our websites – http://www.alite.co.uk and http://www.acceleratedlearning.co.uk – are good starting points. As teachers begin on their personal journey into the ALPS method™ of working, they realize that their personal development will be continual.

4   Are there whole schools that have perfected the method of teaching using accelerated learning?

The schools we work with are at different stages of developing accelerated learning strategies. In some schools policies are being developed for the whole school, but in many schools one or two teachers practise aspects of the method. Our book will make it easier for individual teachers or schools to learn about accelerated learning at their own rate and in a manner that suits their own needs.

5   Does this mean major changes of policy within schools?

Not at all. Accelerated learning is not a curriculum or a scheme and does not necessitate any additional paperwork or radical alteration of current policies. It can involve a rethinking of some long-accepted traditions in primary schools, such as the use of display areas, but it need not involve major policy changes. It is simply a more informed process of teaching, because it requires an understanding of how the brain functions. The same lessons can be delivered, just in a more effective manner, enabling schools to maximize learning opportunities for all children.

6   Do all staff have to progress at the same rate?

No. We are all at different stages of learning and have our own individual strengths. We recommend that schools undertake training at their own rate and move towards agreeing a plan for a common framework. Many schools undertake whole-school training in the method, while others first make reading material available for staff. Individual teachers often trial the methods and report to their colleagues. Some make a few simple innovations as whole-school policy in the first instance. One school simply made a whole-school policy of using the traffic light system for checking children's understanding, and left the decisions about how to try out the other ideas to individual teachers. By the end of the first year, accelerated learning ideas had been taken up by most teachers – because they were seen to work! At some point it is important for the whole school to move towards an agreed planned approach.

7   How will I find time to do all of this and the rest?

We have provided sample timetables to prove that this can be done. We have worked with and visited schools which meet all the statutory requirements and do so via the ALPS method™. The methods are not additional and supplementary but require a shift in emphasis and approach. By using these methods you get better results as well as a greater degree of professional satisfaction within the same time constraints.

8   What are the resource implications?

The ALPS method™ requires no extra physical resources other than visual reinforcement materials.

9   Does accelerated learning mean more work for the teachers?

Working in this way may involve different work for teachers, but not more work. The teachers who we speak to all agree that it is a more rewarding and effective way of working, and report a decrease of stress. They feel more effective, more able to be creative and more inspired by their work with children. Many report less stress about behaviour management in their classrooms. The ALPS journey requires that teachers analyse their own practice and re-evaluate some aspects of their work. The positive atmosphere of achievement in ALPS classrooms and the refocus of time and energy means that the same time commitment by teachers can lead to far greater productivity.

10   Are we going to undertake this challenge, then find that some new trend will demand that we take a different course?

We find it impossible to think of any type of learning that is not brain-based! This book explains the current theory about how the human brain functions and gives suggestions about how to maximize the child's learning potential. The curriculum may well alter over time, but effective processes to best deliver such a curriculum will not. The only way to learn is to use one's brain, and so it stands to reason that the only way to teach is to engage children's brains. You are the professional in your classroom so you make all the choices about process. It is best if those choices are informed choices.

❽ Contact list

Accelerated Learning in Training and Education, (ALiTE), Bourne Park, Cores End Road, Bourne End SL8 5AS, UK
tel: 01628 810700 fax: 01628 810310
office@alite.co.uk
www.alite.co.uk
Training in school and classroom approaches described in this book.

Accelerated Learning Systems Ltd, 50 Aylesbury Road, Aston Clinton, Aylesbury, Bucks HP22 5AH
Tel: 01296 631177 www.accelerated-learning-uk.co.uk
Suppliers of excellent accelerated learning publications especially in early years education and in languages.

Anglo-American Books, Crown Buildings, Bancyfelin, Carmarthen SA33 5ND
tel: 01267 211880 www.anglo-american.co.uk
Importers of the most comprehensive selection of books, tapes and videos related to accelerated learning, NLP and self-esteem. Mail order only.

Association for Supervision and Curriculum Development, 1703 N. Beauvegard Street, Alexandria, VA 2231, USA www.ascd.org
The professional development and support organization for US teachers. Organizes excellent training events and circulates useful booklists and regular newsletters. Useful for information on multiple intelligences, thinking skills and brain-based learning.

British Society for Music Therapy, 61 Church Hill Road, East Barnet EN4 8SY
tel: 020 8441 6226 www.bsmt.org

The 21st Century Learning Initiative, Business Centre West, Avenue One, Letchworth, Herts, SG6 2HB
Contact: John Abbott www.21learn.org
An umbrella organization promoting thinking about new trends in education.

Edu-K, contact Kay McCarroll (tel: 0208 202 9747; email: ekukf@mccarroll.dircon.co.uk) *or* email: brain.gymgb@euphony.net or visit www.braingym.org.uk/instruct for list of UK licensed instructors.
Provides training in kinesiology and Brain Gym®.

International Alliance for Learning, 10040 First Street, Encinitas, CA 92024-5059, USA
mail to: info@ialearn.org
www.ialearn.org
The international umbrella organization for promoting accelerated and brain-based learning. Conferences are held each January in the United States.

The Kenedy Leigh Centre, Hadon, London NW4 4HJ
(tel: 0208 457 4745; www.nwrw.org/services)
Trains individuals and groups in thinking skills based on Feuerstein's work and that of Vygotsky.
Offers accredited training in dynamic assessment, instrumental enrichment and mediated learning.

London Leadership Centre, 10 Woburn Square, London WCIH 0NS
http://ioewebserver.ac.uk
University of London Institute of Education centre leading thinking on the management of schools.
Publishes a termly journal.

NASEN, National Association for Special Educational Needs
NASEN Home, 4/5 Amber Business Village, Amber Close, Amington, Tamworth B77 4RP
(tel: 01827 311500; www.nasen.org.uk)
A membership organization for teachers and others involved in teaching children with special
educational needs. Organizes conferences and training events.

National College for School Leadership (NCSL), Triumph Road, Nottingham NG8 1DH
(tel: 0870 0011155; email: ncsl-office@ncsl.org.uk; www.ncsl.org.uk)
Provides career-long learning and development opportunities, professional and practical support for
existing and aspiring school leaders, and is actively involved in research and development and online
learning. Publishes a magazine five times a year.

NLP Education Network, 39 Jennings Road, St Albans, Herts AL1 4NX
mail to: nlpednet@new-oceans.co.uk
tel: 01727 869782
A membership organization for teachers and others wishing to find out more about applications of NLP in
the classroom.

The Nuffield Extended Literacy Project (Excel)
www.warwick.ac.uk/staff/D.J.Wray/exel/info.html
A range of strategies has been developed to extend children's use and control of literature. Includes use of
writing frames, templates, work in a range of genres and linking ten teaching strategies with ten process
strategies.

SAPERE, Society for the Advancement of Philosophical Enquiry and Reflection in Education
Tel: 01278 68347   www.sapere.net
Offers training in the teaching and delivery of a curriculum known as 'Philosophy for Children'.

Society for Effective Affective Learning (SEAL), 37 Park Hall Road, London N2 9PT
Tel: 020 8365 3869   www.seal.org.uk
An organization which exists to promote better understanding about varied kinds of intelligence, right and
left brain learning, valuing the individual and improving learning opportunities for all. Publishes a
regular journal and organizes conferences and training events. Has members world-wide.

Association for Neuro-Linguistic Programming, PO Box 5, Havefordwest, Wales SA63 4YA
info@anlp.org   www.anlp.org
Promotes NLP and related disciplines. NLP training is powerful in work on belief systems and how to
change them, utilizing language with precision and outcomes thinking.

⑨ Some interesting websites

http://www.alite.co.uk	Alistair Smith's website, containing information about accelerated learning and training in these techniques
http://www.acceleratedlearning.co.uk	Nicola Call's website, giving an overview of brain-based learning for the Foundation Stage, KS1 and 2
http://www.ed.gov.uk/databases/ERIC	Educational Research Information Clearinghouse
http://www.brainresearch.com	A good starting point
http://www.newhorizons.org	An American publisher specializing in brain-based learning
http://www.the brainstore.com	Eric Jensen's monthly newsletter
http://www.dana.org	The most recent health-related brain research
http://www.discoveryschool.com	A website listing US education websites
http://www.cainelearning.com	A brain-based learning site with good links
http://www.casel.org	A commercial site on emotional intelligence
http://www.21learn.org	The Twenty-first Century Learning Initiative
http://www.lcweb.loc.gov/loc/brain	The official decade of the brain website
http://www.musica.uci.edu	Music and learning
http://www.scientificlearning.com	Brain-based reading software
http://www.chadd.org	Site on ADD-HD
http://www.canfoundation.org	Site on autism
http://www.thinkingstyles.co.uk	A commercial site on thinking styles
http://www.standards.dfes.gov.uk	DfES site on thinking skills
http://www.braingym.com	Website for Edu-Kinesthetics, publishers of Brain Gym®

the alps approach – Accelerated Learning in Primary Schools

Endnotes

1 Interview on BBC Today programme – BBC News online network 16 April 1999. See http://news.bbc.co.uk/hi/english/education

2 'Evidence suggests that the brain's ability to stay attentive for extended periods of time is not only rare, but also difficult. The normal human brain works in periods of high levels of attention, followed by periods of low levels of attention. The brain needs downtime.' (Jensen, 1998a).

3 Patterns of activity in the brain are reactivated during sleep, as if the brain 'rehearses' the day's learning. The speculation is that the brain sends new learning to the hippocampus for temporary storage and processing until REM states during sleep. There the brain can further process it for long-term memory (McNaughton, 1997).

4 See Harvard web site under http://pzweb.harvard.edu/research/research the official Harvard Project Zero site.

5 Copyright 1999 by Harvard Project Zero and the President and Fellows of Harvard, College. Excerpts reproduced with permission.

6 A schema is 'an encompassing structure of memory, highly organized and containing a great deal of specific and interrelated information' (Marshall, 1995).

7 The final report of the Primary Assessment, Curriculum and Experience project, University of Bristol.

8 See 'Teacher Talk and Pupil Behaviour', a handout to accompany the workshop presented by Barbara Maines and George Robinson, Lame Duck Enterprises, 1991.

9 Author notes on a keynote address given by Arthur Costa at the IAL Conference, San Antonio, Texas, 1998.

10 Author notes from a keynote address given to the International Alliance for Learning Annual Conference, San Antonio, Texas, January 1997.

11 See 'Teacher Talk', a handout to accompany the workshop presented by Barbara Maines and George Robinson, Lame Duck Enterprises, 1991, p. 11.

12 In 1959, Miller published research in a paper entitled 'The magical number seven plus or minus two' claiming that this formula described the chunks of information an adult could readily retain. These 'limits' are often described in texts as though they were universal and real. Dehaene (1997) shows that, although there are limits, it is also a function of the length of the sounds of the words in the language.

13 Author notes from a presentation given to the 4th Annual New Ways of Learning Conference, 'Our Intelligent Brain: How Children Learn, Think and Grow Smarter', Tuscon, Arizona, 15–18 July 1998.

14 King's College London, June 1999 information from BBC News Online, Education, 25 June 1999.

15 Neurological Research, March 1999 cited in BBC News Online, Education, 15 March 1999.

16 'Maths with Mozart', interview with Dr Susan Hallam, BBC News Online, Thursday 20 August 1998.

17 In 1994 Dr Sally Shaywitz of the Center for the Study of Learning and Attention began a study of 200 children to discern what happened in their brains when they processed language. They found that when most of their sample group processed the words phonologically it activated a specific site – the inferior frontal gyrus – within the brain. For the 80 per cent who, when they sounded out the words, had rapid metabolic change in the inferior frontal gyrus, decoding was simple and quick. For the remaining 20 per cent, a defect in their decoding system meant that activity was apparent in other parts of the brain but little or no metabolic change was apparent in the inferior frontal gyrus. They took longer to decode the words. Both boys and girls were as likely to have 'the signature of dyslexia' but girls, because the language centres were more widely diffused in the brain, were more often able to compensate. They went on to find that several different interventions worked in helping the children learn to read more effectively. Some were more like phonics with others more like whole language approaches. Those boys with the 'signature of dyslexia' found rote memorization and rapid word retrieval difficult but did show positive response from direct phonics instruction and could often grasp meaning from context and from the Big Picture.

18 Reprinted with permission of Howard Kennedy.

References

Baddeley, Alan, *Your Memory a User's Guide* (London: Prion, 1993)

Barkley, Russell A., 'Attention-deficit hyperactivity disorder', *Scientific American*, September 1998 (see http://www.sciam.com/1998/0998issue/0998barkley.html)

Benard, B., Fostering Resiliency in Kids: *Protective Factors in the Family, School, and Community* (San Francisco: Far West Laboratory for Educational Research and Development, 1991)

Black, P. and Wiliam, D., *Inside the Black Box* (London: King's College, 1998)

Blagg, N., *Can We Teach Intelligence?* (London: Lawrence Erlbaum, 1991)

Blakemore, C., paper presented at Giving Children a Sure Start Conference, Corby, November 1998

Blood, A. J., Zatorre, R. J., Bermudez P. and Evans, A. C., 'Emotional responses to pleasant and unpleasant music correlate with activity in paralimbic brain regions', *Nature Neuroscience*, 2: 382–7, 1999

Borba, Michelle, *Esteem Builders* (California: Jalmar Press, 1989)

Bornstein and Tamis-LeMonda, *Day Care and Early Education*, Summer, 1994. Also see http://www.nauticom.net/www/cokids.teacher.html

Brainwork, Jan/Feb 1: 9, 1997

Butler, K., *Learning and Teaching Style in Theory and Practice* (Columbia: The Learners Dimension, 1984)

Burningham, John, *Would you Rather?* (Red Fox, 1994)

Buzan, Tony, *Use Your Head* (London: BBC, 1974)

Caine, G., 'The brains behind the brain', *Educational Leadership: How the Brain Learns*, 56(3): 20–5, 1998

Caine, R. N. and Caine, G., *Making Connections: Teaching and the Human Brain* (Virginia: ASCD, 1991)

Campbell, D. G., *Introduction to the Musical Brain* (Texas: Richardson, 1983)

Campbell, D. G., *The Mozart Effect* (New York: Avon Books, 1997)

Campbell, K., *Teaching and Learning Through Multiple Intelligences* (Massachusetts: Allyn and Bacon, 1996)

Carbo, M., Dunn, R. and Dunn, K., *Teaching Pupils to Read Through Their Individual Learning Styles* (New Jersey: Prentice Hall, 1988)

Carlson, Mary, 'Developing self and emotion in extreme social deprivation', paper presented to the Decade of the Brain Symposium Washington, DC, 1998 (sourced from http://www.lcweb.loc.gov/locbrain)

Claxton, Guy, *Hare Brain Tortoise Mind: Why Intelligence Increases When you Think Less* (London: Fourth Estate, 1997)

Coles, Robert, *The Moral Intelligence of Children* (New York: Random House, 1997)

Coopersmith, Stanley, *The Antecedents of Self-Esteem* (San Francisco: W. H. Freeman, 1967)

Costa, Arthur, *School as a Home for the Mind* (Illinois: Skylight, 1991)

Croll, P. and Moses, D., *One in Five: The Assessment and Incidence of Special Educational Needs* (London: David Fulton, 1995)

Csikszentmihalyi, M., Flow: *The Psychology of Optimal Experience* (New York: Harper Collins, 1990)

De Bono, E., CORT *Thinking Programme* (Oxford: Pergamon, 1986)

De Mille, Richard, *Putting Your Mother on the Ceiling* (1955)

Dehaene, S., *The Number Sense: How the Mind Creates Mathematics* (London: Penguin, 1997)

Dennison, P. and Dennison, G. E. *Brain Gym for Teachers* (California: Edu-Kinesthetics, 1989)

Detheridge, T. and Detheridge, M., *Literacy Through Symbols* (London: David Fulton, 1997)

Diamond, M., Enriching *Heredity: The Impact of Environment on the Anatomy of the Brain* (New York: Free Press, 1998)

Diamond, M. and Hopson, J., *Magic Trees of the Mind: How to Nurture Your Child's Intelligence, Creativity and Healthy Emotions from Birth Through Adolescence* (New York: Dutton, 1998)

Dryden, G. and Voss, J., *The Learning Revolution* (Aylesbury: Accelerated Learning Systems, 1994)

Dweck, Carol S. and Leggett, Ellen L., 'A social-cognitive approach to motivation and personality', *Psychological Review*, 95: 256–73, 1988

Elton, R. (Chair), *Discipline in Schools: Report of the Committee of Enquiry chaired by Lord Elton* (London: HMSO, 1989)

Feuerstein, R., Rand, Y., Hoffman, M. and Miller, R., *Instrumental Enrichment* (Baltimore: University Park Press, 1980)

Fisher, Robert, *Teaching Children to Learn* (London: Stanley Thornes, 1995)

Fisher, Robert, *Teaching Children to Think* (London: Blackwell, 1991)

Flavell, J. H., *Cognitive Development* (Englewood Cliffs, NY: Prentice Hall, 1977)

Flood, J. and Lapp, D., 'Reading comprehension instruction', in Flood, J., Jenson, D., Lapp, D. and Squire, J. R. (eds), *Handbook of Research on Teaching the English Langauage Arts* (New York: Macmillan, 1991), pp. 732–42

Fogarty, Robin, *Brain Compatible Classrooms* (Illinois: Skylight, 1997)

Gardner, Howard, *Frames of Mind: The Theory of Multiple Intelligences* (London: Fontana, 1984)

Gardner, Howard, *The Disciplined Mind: What All Students Should Know and Understand* (New York: Simon and Schuster, 1999)

Gardner, Howard, *The Unschooled Mind* (London: Fontana, 1993)

Gardner, Howard, 'A multiplicity of intelligences', *Scientific American*, 9(4): 19–23, 1998

Goleman, Daniel, *Emotional Intelligence – Why it can Matter More than IQ* (London: Bloomsbury, 1996)

Goleman, Daniel, *Working with Emotional Intelligence* (London: Bloomsbury, 1998)

Gottfredson, Linda S., 'The general intelligence factor', *Scientific American*, 9(4): 24–5, 1998

Gregory, Richard (ed.), *The Oxford Companion to the Mind* (Oxford: OUP, 1987)

Greenfield, Susan, *The Human Brain: a guided tour* (Science Masters, 1997)

Hannaford, C., *Smart Moves: Why Learning Is Not All In Your Head*, (Great Ocean Publishers, 1995)

Harris, Judith Rich, *The Nurture Assumption: Why Children Turn out the Way they Do*, (London: Bloomsbury 1998)

Harter, Susan, 'Teacher and classmate influences on scholastic motivation, self-esteem, and level of voice in adolescents', in J. Juvonen and K. R. Wentzel (eds), *Social Motivation, Understanding Children's School Adjustment* (Cambridge: Cambridge University Press, 1996)

Hermann, Ned, *The Hermann Brain Dominance Instrument* (Lake Lure, NC: Hermann International, 1997)

Howard, Pierce J., *The Owner's Manual for the Brain – Everyday Applications from Mind-Brain Research* (Texas: Bard Press, 1994)

Hurwitz, Wolff, Bortnick and Kokas, 'Nonmusical effects of the Kodaly music curriculum in primary grade children', *Journal of Learning Disabilities*, 8, 1975

Huttenlocher, P. R., 'Synapse elimination and plasticity in developing human central cortex', *American Journal of Mental Deficiency*, 88: 488–96, 1984

Idol, I. and Croli, V. J., 'Story mapping training as a means of improving reading comprehension', *Learning Disability Quarterly*, 10: 214–16, 1987

Jaquith, John M., *The Role of Short Term Memory on Academic Achievement* (National Association for Child Development, 1996) (see http://www.nacd.org/stmemory.html)

Jensen, Eric, *The Learning Brain* (California: Turning Point, 1994)

Jensen, Eric, *Brain-Based Learning and Teaching* (California: Turning Point, 1995)

Jensen, Eric, *Completing the Puzzle: A Brain-Based Approach to Learning* (California: Turning Point, 1996)

293

Jensen, Eric, 'How Julie's brain learns', *Educational Leadership: How the Brain Learns*, 56(3): 41–6, 1998a

Jensen, Eric, *Teaching with the Brain in Mind* (Virginia: ASCD, 1998b)

Kidder, T., *Among School Children* (New York: Avon, 1990)

Kotulak, Ronald, *Inside the Brain: Revolutionary Discoveries of How the Mind Works* (Kansas: Andrews and McMeel, 1996)

Kuhl, Patricia, 'Linguistic experience alters phonetic perception in infants by six months of age', Science, 255: 606–8, 1992 (see also http://www.scientificlearning.com)

Lamb, S. J. and Gregory, A. H., 'The relationship between music and reading in beginning readers', *Educational Psychology*, 13: 19–26, 1993

Lazear, D., *Seven Ways of Teaching: The Artistry of Teaching with Multiple Intelligences* (Arizona: Zephyr Press, 1993)

LeDoux, Joseph, *The Emotional Brain* (London: Wiedenfeld and Nicolson 1998)

Loomans, Diane and Kolberg, Karen, *The Laughing Classroom* (Tiburon, CA: H. J. Kramer Inc, 1993)

Lowery, L. F., *The Biological Basis for Thinking and Learning* (Berkeley, CA, 1998)

McCarthy, B., *The 4MAT System* (Arlington: Excel Publishing, 1982)

McGuinness, Carol, *DfEE Research Report: From Thinking Skills to Thinking Classrooms* (London: HMSO, 1999). (See http://www.standards.dfee.gov.uk/guidance/thinking)

Marshall, R. P., *Schemas in Problem Solving* (Cambridge: Cambridge University Press, 1995)

Mathes, P. G., Fuchs, D. and Fuchs, L. S., 'Cooperative story mapping', *Remedial and Special Education*, 18(1), 1997

McNaughton, Bruce, *BrainWork*, 7(1): 9, 1997

Mesibov, G., *TEACCH*, 1985

Miles, Elizabeth, *Tune Your Brain: Using Music to Manage Your Mind, Body and Mood* (New York: Berkley Publishing, 1997)

Mineka, Susan, 'How our emotions affect us – anxiety disorders', paper presented to the Decade of the Brain Symposium, Washington DC, 1998 (sourced from http://www.lcweb.loc.gov/locbrain)

Mirsky, N., *The Unforgettable Memory Book* (London: BBC, 1994)

Moir A. and Jessell, D., *Brain Sex: The Real Difference Between Men and Women* (New York: Carol, 1991)

Moorhead, G. E., *Music of Young Children* (Pillsbury Foundation for the Advancement of Music, 1977)

Newsweek, 10 February 1997, 149(6): 50–9

Ornstein, R., *The Right Mind: Making Sense of the Hemispheres* (New York: Harcourt Brace, 1997)

Perkins, D., *Outsmarting IQ: The Emerging Science of Learnable Intelligence* (New York: The Free Press, 1995)

Pert, Candice, *The Molecules of Emotion* (New York: Touchstone Books, 1997)

Pollard, Andrew and Filer, Ann, *The Social World of Children's Learning* (London: Cassell, 1996)

Pribram, K. H. and McGuiness, D., 'Arousal, activation and effort in the control of attention', *Psychological Review*, 82: 116–49, 1975

Ramey, C. T. and Ramey, S. L., 'At risk does not mean doomed', *American Association of Science*, February (National Health/Education Consortium Occasional paper no. 4, 1996)

Rauscher, F. H., Shaw, G. L. and Ky, K. N., 'Music and spatial task performance', *Nature*, 365: 611, 1993

Rauscher, F. H., Shaw, G. L. and Ky, K. N., 'Listening to Mozart enhances spatial temporal reasoning: towards a neurological basis', *Neuroscience Letters*, 185: 44–7, 1995

Rauscher, F. H., Shaw, G. L., Levine, L. J., Wright, E. L., Dennis, W. R. and Newcomb, R. L., 'Music training causes long-term enhancement of preschool children's spatial temporal reasoning', *Neurological Research*, 19: 208, 1997

the alps approach – Accelerated Learning in Primary Schools

Restak, Ronald, *The Brain: the Last Frontier* (New York: Warner, 1980)

Rose, C. and Goll, L., *Accelerate Your Learning*, (Aylesbury: Accelerated Learning Systems, 1992)

Rose, C. and Nicholl, M. J., *Accelerated Learning for the 21st Century* (New York: Delacorte Press, 1997)

Rosenthal, R. and Jacobsen, L., *Pygmalion in the Classroom* (New York: Holt, Rinehart & Winston, 1968)

Rowe, Mary Budd, 'Science, silence and sanctions', *Science and Children*, 34(1): 35–7, 1996

Rumelhart, D. E., 'Schemata: the building blocks of cognition', in Guthrie, J. (ed.), *Comprehension and Teaching: Research Reviews* (Newark: International Reading Association, 1981)

Rutter, *et al., Fifteen Thousand Hours* (Cambridge, MA: Harvard University Press, 1979)

Schachter, D. L., *Searching the Memory: The Brain, the Mind and the Past* (New York: Basic Books, 1996)

Seligman, M. E. P., *Learned Optimism* (New York: Knopf, 1991)

Senge, Peter, *The Fifth Discipline* (New York: Doubleday, 1990)

Seymour, J. and O'Connor, J., *An Introduction to NLP* (London: Mandala, 1990)

Smith, Alistair, *Accelerated Learning in Practice* (Stafford: Network Educational Press, 1995)

Smith, Alistair, *Accelerated Learning in the Classroom* (Stafford: Network Educational Press, 1998)

Springer, Sally P. and Deutsch, George, *Left Brain, Right Brain: Perspectives from Cognitive Neuroscience* (New York: Freeman, 1998)

Steiner, Claude, *Achieving Emotional Literacy* (New York: Avon Books, 1997)

Sternberg, R. J., *Successful Intelligence: How Practical and Creative Intelligence Determine Success in Life* (New York: Plume, 1996)

Sternberg, R. J., *The Triarchic Mind: A New Theory of Human Intelligence* (New York: Viking, 1988)

Sylwester, Robert, *A Celebration of Neurons: An Educator's Guide to the Human Brain* (Virginia: ASCD, 1995)

Sylwester, Robert, *Educational Leadership: How the Brain Learns*, 56(3): 31–6, 1998

Thayer, R., *The Biopsychology of Mood and Arousal* (New York: Oxford University Press, 1989)

Tomatis, Alfred, *The Conscious Ear: My Life of Transformation through Listening* (New York: Sation Hill Press, 1991)

Vygotsky, L. S., *Mind in Society* (Cambridge: Harvard University Press, 1978)

Watson, J., *Reflection through Interaction: The Classroom Experience of Pupils with Learning Difficulties* (London: Falmer Press, 1996)

Watson, Judith, 'Working in groups: social and cognitive effects in a special class', *British Journal of Special Education*, 26(2): 89, 1999

Wells, G., 1990, 'Talk about text: where literacy is learned and taught', *Curriculum Enquiry*, 20: 369–405

Weinberger, N., 'Music in our minds', *Educational Leadership: How the Brain Learns*, 56(3): 36–40, 1998

Weinberger, N. and McKenna, M. T., 'Sensitivity of single neurons in auditory cortex to contour', *Music Perception*, 5: 355–90, 1998

Weisel, Torstein, see http://www.nauticom.net/www/cokids/teacher.html

Wenger, Win, *The Einstein Factor* (California: Prima, 1996)

Werner, E. and Smith, R., *Vulnerable but Invincible: A Longitudinal Study of Resilient Children and Youth* (New York: Adams, Bannister, and Cox, 1989)

Werner, E. and Smith, R. *Overcoming the Odds: High-Risk Children from Birth to Adulthood* (New York: Cornell University Press, 1992)

Wurman, Richard Saul, *Information Anxiety* (New York: Doubleday, 1989)

Acknowledgements

The publishers wish to thank people and organizations for permission to use extracts from their material in this book. Every effort has been made to contact copyright holders of materials reproduced in this book. The publishers apologize for any omissions and will be pleased to rectify them at the earliest opportunity.

Baddeley, Alan, *Your Memory a User's Guide*, Prion

Barber, Michael, *Times Educational Supplement*

Blood, A. J., Zatorre, R. J., Bermudez, P. and Evans, A. C., 'Emotional responses to pleasant and unpleasant music correlate with activity in paralimbic brain regions', *Nature Neuroscience*

Bornstein and Tamis-LeMonda, http://www.nauticom.net/www/cokids.teacher.html

Brown, Margaret, BBC News Education
Hallam, Susan, BBC News Education
Reproduced from BBC News Education online by permission of BBC, White City, London

Caine, Geoffrey, 'The brains behind the brain', *Educational Leadership*
Sylwester, Robert, 'Art for the brain's sake', *Educational Leadership*
Weinberger, Norman, 'Music in our minds', *Educational Leadership*
Reproduced from *Educational Leadership* by permission of the Association for Supervision and Curriculum Development

Campbell, D. G., *Introduction to the Musical Brain*, Richardson

Carlson, Mary, 'Developing self and emotion in extreme social deprivation', http://www.lcweb. loc.gov/locbrain

Csikszentmihalyi, Mihaly, Flow: *The Psychology of Optimal Experience*, HarperCollins

Diamond, Marian, *Enriching Heredity: The Impact of Environment on the Anatomy of the Brain*, Free Press

Dweck, Carol S. and Leggett, Ellen L., 'A social-cognitive approach to motivation and personality', *Psychological Review*

Elton, R., *Discipline in Schools: Report of the Committee of Enquiry chaired by Lord Elton*, HMSO

Gardner, Howard, *The Unschooled Mind*, Fontana

Gardner, Howard, 'A multiplicity of intelligences', *Scientific American*

Goleman, Daniel, *Emotional Intelligence – Why it can Matter More than IQ*, Bloomsbury

Gregory, Richard,*The Oxford Companion to the Mind*, Oxford University Press

Harter, Susan, in Jovonen and Wentzel *Social Motivation, Understanding Children's School Adjustment*
Reproduced from *Social Motivation, Understanding Children's School Adjustment* by permission of Cambridge University Press, The Edinburgh Building, Shaftesbury Road, Cambridge

Huttenlocher, P. R., 'Synapse elimination and plasticity in developing human central cortex', *American Journal of Mental Deficiency*

Jaquith, John M., *The Role of Short Term Memory on Academic Achievement*, National Association for Child Development

Kotulak, Ronald, *Inside the Brain: Revolutionary Discoveries of How the Mind Works*, Andrews and McMeel

Kuhl, Patricia, 'Linguistic experience alters phonetic perception in infants by six months of age', *Science*

LeDoux, Joseph, *The Emotional Brain*
Reproduced from *The Emotional Brain* by permission of Weidenfeld and Nicolson, The Orion Publishing Group

Lessing, Doris, *The Four Gated City*, Flamingo, imprint of HarperCollins

Letterland
Excerpt and illustrations reproduced from *Letterland* by permission of Letterland International

Lloyd, Sue and Wernham, Sara, *Jolly Phonics Workbook 1*
Illustrations from *Jolly Phonics Workbook 1* produced by permission of Jolly Learning Ltd, Tailours House, High Road, Chigwell, Essex

McGuinness, Carol, *DfEE Research Report: From Thinking Skills to Thinking Classrooms*, HMSO

Mineka, Susan, 'How our emotions affect us – anxiety disorders', from http://www.lcweb.loc.gov/locbrain

Moorhead, G. E., *Music of Young Children*, Pillsbury Foundation for the Advancement of Music

Pert, Candice, *The Molecules of Emotion*, Touchstone Books

Primary Assessment Curriculum and Experience Project, Bristol University, Cassell plc

Restak, Ronald, *The Brain: the Last Frontier*, Warner

Seligman, M. E. P., *Learned Optimism*, Knopf

Sunday Times

THRASS Reading
Excerpt reproduced from *THRASS Reading* by permission of HarperCollins Publishers, London

Times Educational Supplement

Vygotsky, L. S., *Mind in Society*, Harvard University Press, Cambridge, MA

Ward, Sally, *Daily Express*

Weisel, Torstein, http://www.nauticom.net/www/cokids/teacher.html

Wurman, Richard Saul, *Information Anxiety*, Doubleday

297

Index

Bold type indicates major page references; the suffix n denotes an Endnote.

the alps approach – Accelerated Learning in Primary Schools

the alps approach – Accelerated Learning in Primary Schools

the alps approach – Accelerated Learning in Primary Schools

the alps approach – Accelerated Learning in Primary Schools

A selection of titles from Network Educational Press

ACCELERATED LEARNING SERIES General Editor: **Alistair Smith**

Accelerated Learning in Practice by Alistair Smith

The ALPS Approach: Accelerated Learning in Primary Schools
  by Alistair Smith and Nicola Call

MapWise by Oliver Caviglioli and Ian Harris

The ALPS Approach Resource Book by Alistair Smith and Nicola Call

Creating an Accelerated Learning School by Mark Lovatt and Derek Wise

ALPS StoryMaker by Stephen Bowkett

Thinking for Learning by Mel Rockett and Simon Percival

Reaching out to all learners by Cheshire LEA

Leading Learning by Alistair Smith

Bright Sparks by Alistair Smith

More Bright Sparks by Alistair Smith

Move It by Alistair Smith

THE SCHOOL EFFECTIVENESS SERIES

Book 1: *Accelerated Learning in the Classroom* by Alistair Smith

Book 2: *Effective Learning Activities* by Chris Dickinson

Book 3: *Effective Heads of Department* by Phil Jones and Nick Sparks

Book 4: *Lessons are for Learning* by Mike Hughes

Book 5: *Effective Learning in Science* by Paul Denley and Keith Bishop

Book 6: *Raising Boys' Achievement* by Jon Pickering

Book 7: *Effective Provision for Able & Talented Children* by Barry Teare

Book 8: *Effective Careers Education & Guidance* by Andrew Edwards and Anthony Barnes

Book 9: *Best behaviour and Best behaviour FIRST AID* by
         Peter Relf, Rod Hirst, Jan Richardson and Georgina Youdell
         Best behaviour FIRST AID (pack of five booklets)

Book 10: *The Effective School Governor* by David Marriott *(including free audio tape)*

Book 11: *Improving Personal Effectiveness for Managers in Schools* by James Johnson

Book 12: *Making Pupil Data Powerful* by Maggie Pringle and Tony Cobb

Book 13: *Closing the Learning Gap* by Mike Hughes

Book 14: *Getting Started* by Henry Leibling

Book 15: *Leading the Learning School* by Colin Weatherley

Book 16: *Adventures in Learning* by Mike Tilling

Book 17: *Strategies for Closing the Learning Gap* by Mike Hughes and Andy Vass

Book 18: *Classroom Management* by Philip Waterhouse and Chris Dickinson

Book 19: *Effective Teachers* by Tony Swainston

Book 20: *Transforming Teaching and Learning* by Colin Weatherley, Bruce Bonney, John Kerr
         and Jo Morrison

Book 21: *Effective Teachers in Primary Schools* by Tony Swainston

ABLE AND TALENTED CHILDREN COLLECTION

Effective Resources for Able and Talented Children by Barry Teare
More Effective Resources for Able and Talented Children by Barry Teare
Challenging Resources for Able and Talented Children by Barry Teare

MODEL LEARNING

Thinking Skills & Eye Q by Oliver Caviglioli, Ian Harris and Bill Tindall
Think it–Map it! by Oliver Caviglioli and Ian Harris

OTHER TITLES

The Thinking Child by Nicola Call with Sally Featherstone
The Thinking Child Resource Book by Nicola Call with Sally Featherstone
StoryMaker Catch Pack by Stephen Bowkett
Becoming Emotionally Intelligent by Catherine Corrie
That's Science! by Tim Harding
The Brain's Behind It by Alistair Smith
Help Your Child To Succeed by Bill Lucas and Alistair Smith
Tweak to Transform by Mike Hughes
Imagine That... by Stephen Bowkett
Self-Intelligence by Stephen Bowkett
Class Talk by Rosemary Sage
Lend Us Your Ears by Rosemary Sage

**For more information and ordering details, please consult our website
www.networkpress.co.uk**